WHERE NIGHTMARES COME FROM

The Art Of Storytelling In The Horror Genre

EDITED BY JOE MYNHARDT AND EUGENE JOHNSON

Let the world know:
#IGotMyCLPBook!

Crystal Lake Publishing
www.CrystalLakePub.com

OTHER NON-FICTION TITLES BY CRYSTAL LAKE PUBLISHING

Horror 201: The Silver Scream Vol. 1 & Vol.2

Horror 101: The Way Forward

Modern Mythmakers: 35 interviews with Horror and Science Fiction Writers and Filmmakers by Michael McCarty

Writers On Writing: An Author's Guide

COPYRIGHT ACKNOWLEDGEMENTS

This one's for the dreamers

TABLE OF CONTENTS

INTRODUCTION

The Spooky Arts

DIP INTO ANY section of this book and you will learn something.

High praise, but a true statement. There are many pieces one can delve into along the way, as this is not simply another "how-to" effort; the contents within range from inspiration and molding concepts, to the way revision impacts the final draft, to the reasons stories are changed for other media. While not an instruction manual per se, this volume *does* instruct; all one must do is be receptive to different ideas and points-of-view. In fact, any one of these essays or interviews will do the job: teach you how to create or adapt works professionally for print or multimedia, taking you inside the scary business of fashioning memorable tales, with an emphasis on stories of shock and terror. Your guides include, to name just a few of the 30-plus stellar talents in this comprehensive volume, the capable insights of Kevin J. Anderson (as part of a roundtable discussion), Elizabeth Massie ("Playing in Someone Else's Haunted House"), Tim Waggoner ("Horror is a State of Mind"), and Mort Castle ("The Story of a Story").

Here, in these pages, you are made privy to the expert advice that only seasoned veterans can provide.

Open your mind to what they have to tell you as I lay out some of my personal favorites of the treats in store . . .

None other than the King himself—Stephen King, interviewed along with noted publisher/editor/writer Richard Chizmar—discusses the always tricky tightrope act of collaboration. Having personally collaborated with George Clayton Johnson, Ray Bradbury, Richard Matheson, Jason V Brock, Charles Beaumont, and Ray Russell, I found the King/Chizmar exchange particularly fascinating.

The redoubtable Joe R. Lansdale talks about dreaming your way through a story in "It's the Storyteller." As he points out, it is the dreamer, not the dream, who captures the reader. When Joe is telling you a story you *know* you're in Lansdale country. That brash Texas voice is always there, always compelling, often funny (Joe has a great sense of humor). Pure folk art.

And Ramsey Campbell's on board! The always commanding literary lion of Liverpool weighs in with "The Process of a Tale" to offer you a guided tour through one of his moody pieces. From first sentence to last, he takes the reader through several drafts, giving us an inside look at the mechanics of a Campbell story. Here is a man who is at the keys each morning by six a.m., seven days a week. He loves to write, and it shows: A master sharing the secrets of his mastery. Pay attention!

The multi-talented, clear-thinking Jason V

Brock (director of two documentaries, with a third in progress; author of two collections of short fiction, as well as a non-fiction, detailed look at pop culture; editor of several ground-breaking anthologies) has seen his career skyrocket in recent years. There's a reason: His work is always thoughtful, and when he makes a statement or offers an opinion, it is invariably backed up by facts. Here, in this volume, he details the art of filmmaking in relation to horror in "Life Imitating Art Imitating Life." All aspects are covered. A thorough essay from an in-depth writer.

Meanwhile, Richard Thomas in "Storytelling Techniques: The Many Faces of Horror" creates a virtual road map to the craft by the use of headlines prior to each section of his essay: BE SINCERE . . . SPEAK WITH AUTHORITY . . . CONSIDER SIZE AND SCOPE . . . GET US TO CARE ABOUT YOUR CHARACTERS . . . QUIET VS. VIOLENT— CHOOSE YOUR MOMENTS . . . INNOVATE . . . LEAVE ROOM FOR YOUR READER . . . TAP INTO THE PSYCHOLOGICAL . . . LET THE ATMOSPHERE HELP YOU ON YOUR JOURNEY . . . USE THEME AND SYMBOLISM TO PAINT THE BIG PICTURE . . .

I could go on, at much greater length, discussing the many other fine writers who ply their wares in this anthology: the estimable Ray Garton ("Like Curses"), the masterful Clive Barker ("A-Z of Horror"), the thoughtful Lisa Morton ("The Real Creeps, or How to Create Horror Non-Fiction Shorts"), even an interview with the busy and affable Jonathan Maberry, et al. But space limits me. Also, I happen to believe that "less is more." Thus, I have chosen to reveal only the tip of a very large iceberg of talent. Savor these pertinent essays, learn from them, be entertained by them, profit from these wise words.

Forge ahead! Riches await you.

—William F. Nolan
Vancouver, WA
October, 2017

IT'S THE STORYTELLER

JOE R. LANSDALE

STORYTELLING AND PLOTTING are not necessarily the same, though there's no doubt they're kinfolk, and sometimes kinfolk that work at odds with one another. Be it horror, western, science fiction, or any label you wish to put on it, the approach is really the same. Find a story you want to tell, and tell it as well as you can, using atmosphere, the senses, and telling bits of detail.

A story is made believable by development of character and believable dialogue that sucks you in like a whirlpool, carries you to the depths of the pool, then spits you out, exhausted and satisfied.

Plot, in its purest sense is a kind of clockwork mechanism that arranges pieces of a story together to cause it to frequently arrive at an overly contrived solution, where storytelling is more akin to creating a feeling like real life, even if what is being told is as preposterous as a dog airline pilot. A good storyteller, however, can make you believe in a dog pilot, while a pure plotter may lack the panache to pull off that kind of absurdity. I, for one, want to believe in a dog airline pilot.

Plot may be concealed within storytelling, and it

matters, but storytelling in my view is more powerful, and is at its best when it is tied to the inner workings of the individual telling the tale. Stephen King, a writer I deeply respect, once said words to the effect that it's not the teller, it's the tale that matters, but I would disagree with that.

Like telling a joke, some people are good at it, and some are not. You can give the same joke to ten people, and it may sound hysterical when told by one, and utterly banal when told by another. Of course, the listener is part of the effect as well, and not every storyteller will succeed with every reader, but what I have found over the years is that the true storyteller generally has a broader and more successful impact than the pure plotter, though I'm not here to suggest the ability to plot is a pointless craft. A reader needs the satisfaction of feeling like what they are reading is going somewhere, and will arrive without leaving them hanging in mid-air.

So, to point out my disagreement with Mr. King again, I would say it's not the joke, it's the jokester. It's not the story, it's the storyteller, and I might also add Stephen King is one of the best storytellers around. It's his voice, his attitude, his courage that make the story work, where in someone else's hands, *Salem's Lot*, for example, could have been quite the mess and just another story about vampires biting people; he gave it style, character, and thematic depth. Sure, there's a plot, but it's his voice, his passion for storytelling that hooks the reader.

The best of ideas can be as bland as bean curd without the spices of individuality, confidence, and the ability to let a story go where it needs to go, hemming it in gently, not breaking and corralling it like a once magnificent stallion now walking beneath the saddle or hitched to the plow. A story, like character, shouldn't be pushed around like a chess piece. It should feel organic and happening as you read it.

Sam Phillips, Sun Record producer, the man who discovered Elvis, Jerry Lee Lewis and Johnny Cash, Carl Perkins, and others, always tried to have recordings made at Sun sound hot and original. He made sure the recordings came out of a well of passion and excitement, that the source was the performer's own creative hunger, instead of overly preparing and sucking the life out of it before it was recorded. Storytelling is much the same way. It surprises not only the reader, but the writer as well when it comes from that hungry place, that hot as hell creative fire that practically burns the fingertips as the creator writes.

Storytelling lends itself more to character than plotting. Storytelling is the tone and attitude of the storyteller, and a good storyteller is usually releasing their personality into the story, unbound by plot restrictions. The storyteller sees all his or her characters as real people, so even a passing acquaintance in a story can resonate a lot more than it might if the character is only there to grease the cogs of a plot, driven more by solution than by character development.

Another advantage of the storyteller, is that when the story and characters seem organic, it is much easier for the teller of the tell to digress and go down alleys and backroads, take a sightseeing tour in the country, and maintain the interest of the reader. Some of the greatest novels of all time are of this nature, *Huckleberry Finn*, *Moby Dick*, and *Don Quixote* spring to mind.

Raymond Chandler, who wrote a fine set of books about private detective Philip Marlowe, was really a storyteller, even though he was writing mysteries where plot is normally king. Chandler's plots were less than stellar, and if one were to break them down in a cold, calculating way, they wouldn't add up to much of anything that made sense.

In fact, Chandler, when his book *The Big Sleep* was being filmed, was asked who killed the chauffeur, they couldn't find it in the book. Chandler said he had no idea.

Finding the chauffeur's body seemed like a good scene, so he went for it. But, I would hasten to add that it works within the context of the story, because you have some idea who might have done it, and though it's never answered in the novel, it has a feeling of real life about it, not all things are explained to satisfaction.

Chandler's prose, his dialogue and wit and atmosphere, are the true invitation into the story, the thin plot is merely part of a fabric that holds it together, but the essence of the story comes from the depths of the primitive brain. A place we all recognize, filled with collective memories and raw emotions. It's why storytellers are so appealing to us.

Chandler's plots may not have been strong, but the character's motivations were tip-top. You believed them, and you believed Marlowe's voice. He wasn't the kind of guy you doubted. Chandler once said he wanted to write the kind of novel someone would read, even if they knew the last page was torn out, and he did just that.

In the same manner, though nowhere as good a stylist, dialogue writer, or developer of character, Edgar Rice Burroughs did the same. He involved you with the story, with the raw elements of intrigue and tremendous imagination. The story itself was the character. And at least in his early books, you believed the story, outrageous as it could be, because on some level, Burroughs believed it. He dreamed on paper, and our reading of what he wrote made us dream awake.

I think the true storyteller is often swelling inside with story, and feels a story more than knows it. It's like hearing music from afar. You know it's music, but you can't quite name the tune, so the storyteller gradually walks toward the sound, listening and recording all the way, until the sound is clear, and finally the storyteller can hum it; which means by then they can write it down. It's not exactly magic, but it sure feels like it when you are dreaming freely. You have to learn to listen to your inner self, hear that unique and personally profound music, and write from the subconscious, the source of the melody.

Analysis of what has been written, working out a few wrinkles and mistakes, is then the function of the conscious mind, but it's the red-hot passion of story that puts it on paper, and all the true elements are there from the start.

How do you tap into the primitive brain, the memories, instincts and bright colors and dark patches that make us who we are?

Practice.

We each find our own way, but let me tell you how I approach it. Perhaps it'll work for you.

I have already mentioned it, but let's investigate it a little more.

I write from the dream.

I discovered long ago, that to lead a life during the day that is not overwhelmed with writing, the first thing I did was cut my writing time down. When I wake up, I have my coffee and breakfast bar, and go to work. I try to do this before I wake up too much, before the real day shifts into the dream world I have recently left. I work while the ghost of those dreams is still with me. I sit down and write, and as soon as I feel I've said what I have to say for the day, I stop working. I do have the goal of managing at least three to five pages a day, but sometimes I manage more. My true work day, not business calls, managing life, but the work and joy of writing, is about three hours. I let the dream decipher itself. And when the edges of it become ragged, I stop.

I do this five to seven days a week, with a few minor exceptions, such as long travel days, or a time when I choose to take off for a couple days for whatever reason I feel is valid.

But when I work, which is most of the time, I don't believe in waiting for inspiration. I'm doing something I love, and because of that, inspiration becomes a constant companion.

I don't plot or outline, though I may take a few notes here and there, instead I let my dream world fill up each night with a segment of the story. I do this without worrying about it, or trying to force it, and when I wake up the dream bag is full, and I can go to my writing desk, and dream all over the page.

For me, correcting as I go is best. I don't like multiple drafts, but there is no telling how many drafts

I do, considering I don't have a trashcan full of paper. Instead I correct directly to the word processor. I finish my one draft, and then when I get to the end, I go through it again for a polish. Now and again, the polish may require more than usual, but for the most part, making my corrections as I go, or at the end of a session, allows me to finish a project closer to what I want, and not end up with multiple drafts, trying to figure which one is best, what to borrow from one or the other.

This is writing for the joy of it, the pleasant experience of telling a story. The reason we all became writers, storytellers, in the first place.

Another thing I like to keep in mind is a personal motto I have. Write like everyone you know is dead.

Don't try and write for anyone but yourself, because it's easy to quit being yourself, easy to push your dream aside, or defuse it, if you're trying to figure out what your friends, relatives, editors, agents and publishers might want.

Therein lies distraction and barriers.

You have to write as if everyone you know is dead to keep from writing in such a way that you're constantly editing yourself to fit what you believe will be the expectations of others, including the audience. When you finish, come out of the dream, polish the work so that it clearly states what you meant for it to say, but not to the extent that you brush the powder off the butterfly's wings.

At that point, you can hope others like it. But trying to write for someone is a losing game, because truly, no one really knows what anyone else wants. You have to appeal to the one audience member you know best. Yourself.

No one writer appeals to everyone, and you can't be universally admired, and you shouldn't try to.

A story should also rely on life-experience, the experience of others, research, and the constant habit of doing the work. And by writing in the dream, not outside of it, trying to recover some thread of it, writing will rarely seem like a job at all.

But, before I carry it too far, it's not all about dreaming. The dreams have to have a foundation under them. What makes a story work is the voice of the narrator, and the surer the voice is, the more believable it is. That comes from stacking your dream on a foundation of reality.

No matter how fantastical the story, true life experience gives it credibility. Dropping in elements of your own life, telling bits of detail borrowed from your memory bank, give the reader a feeling of assurance. It's the old story about how to tell a lie. Don't make it all up, tell the lie with large dollops of truth. The truth can give foundation to the most outrageous of lies.

The moments of "truth" have to blend, as well, and cannot be like a fruit salad. They have to be included as ingredients in such a way as to make a soup. That way a singular element doesn't stand conspicuously alone, but adds to the taste of the soup, as do the other ingredients, not tasted individually, but in such a way that their blending creates a unique taste for the reader.

Another component is research.

I'm not the kind of writer who likes to do a lot of conscious research, which is not the same as choosing not to do it. I follow my interests. If I'm interested in something, I will read about that subject for entertainment and knowledge. I may use that research, and I may never use it. I enjoy myself, and sometimes, after a dip in the pool of one subject, I may instantly use that new-found information, or it may remain in the pool, perhaps becoming almost stagnant. But if it is interesting enough to me, it just might resurface and stir the waters fresh.

On occasion, this research might add tidbits to a story or novel, or it may be the foundation for a story, and therefore, have a larger role to play. I have always been interested in the Old West, and have read a ton of material about it for my entertainment. But as the years went on, that material began to stir in my metaphorical pool, and eventually, like a small evolutionary creature, it grew legs and came ashore, ready to stand on its own.

I've been amazed at how reading I did years before, stimulated a book or story long after. I might then have to return to that research, to validate certain dates or events, but if I found the material interesting, the mood of the first reading tended to stay with me for years, like the remembered verses of a catchy tune.

The rest of storytelling is the characters, and once again, they are informed by your personal autobiography, or that of others you know about, and the research. A story can not only grow out of research, so can a character.

A character is simply put, someone you believe and have either an interest or concern about, or both. I do not hold to the idea that you have to have a likable character, but I do hold to the point that you have to have an interesting one.

Another knack of the true storyteller is to realize

that everyone in a story or a book is a character. Some of those characters may get more attention than others, but even the smallest roles deserve consideration.

Film is a great example of this. Frequently, among the best performances, are those given by character actors. These roles, though smaller, are at their best defining, and give the story even more verisimilitude, as well as enhance the believability of the main characters. Smart film stars know that one way to make a film better, more interesting and believable, to actually enhance their own performance, is to surround themselves with strong character actors.

Sometimes the character actors can steal the show, however, and in novels I've had these minor characters blossom and take on larger roles, and a character who was originally a walk-on, can become so interesting I feel it's necessary that they should play a larger role.

In a series of books, I have been writing for twenty-five years, about a duo called Hap and Leonard, Leonard was originally a secondary character that I intended to drop in briefly, and then focus more on Hap. But instantly, that character became as much of a lead as the original hero I had in mind, and even though Hap narrates their stories in first person, Leonard is not a sidekick. He is just as important and valuable a character as the narrator.

Dialogue is another component, and a really important one. Dialogue is not always about how people actually talk. It's about making the reader believe this is how they talk. It's dialogue that is engaging, revealing not only of story information, but character as well. Dialogue reveals how a character views the world.

To write good dialogue, you have to develop a recorder's ear, trying to catch the rhythms of natural speech, but not being bound by it. As a writer, you get to cheat. You get to spend time polishing the dialogue, making it wittier, more revealing and ironic, than real dialogue might be. You get to customize it.

It, along with the other elements I've mentioned, is my idea of what makes a story great, and what constitutes the making of a true storyteller; someone who speaks directly to the reader's dreams with dreams of their own.

A-Z OF HORROR

CLIVE BARKER

MOST HORROR, whether it's real or fictitious, literary or cinematic, deals with the eruption of chaos into human existence (or else the revelation of its constant, unseen presence). Between these covers, the title suggests, is all you need to know, as soon as we begin to delve into the nature of horror, or attempt to list its manifestations in our culture, the sheer scale of the beast becomes apparent.

Horror is everywhere. It's in fairy tales and the evening headlines; it's in street corner gossip and the incontrovertible facts of history. It's in playground ditties ("Ring-a-ring o' roses" is a sweet little plague song); it's in the doctor's surgery ("I've some bad news, I'm afraid . . . "); it's on the altar, bleeding for our sins ("Forgive them, Father, for they know not what they do"); it is so much a part of our lives (and deaths) that a hundred volumes could not fully detail its presence.

This isn't to say we should give up on the endeavor. After all, don't we make everything in our lives—art, love, children—in the certainty that what we create will be flawed? Let's make the lists anyway, knowing they're arbitrary. Let's pretend at least for a little while—that we consider the subject authoritatively covered. Let's even ask a few questions of ourselves, as though there might be some kind of answer to be had.

We must inevitably begin with the root question: what is horror? We can all point to its presence. It's in black-jacketed books and lurid movie posters. It's in police reports from murder sites and tearful recollections from battlefields. It's in our nightmares. It's in our secret ambitions. But is there any common thread of subject matter that connects all these manifestations? Maybe. Perhaps the body and its vulnerability. Perhaps the mind and its brittleness. Perhaps love and its absence.

What becomes apparent, however, the more closely we study the issue, is how misleading the term actually is, describing as it does a response rather than a subject. Horror elicits far more complex responses than gasps and giddiness. It can shame us into recognizing our own capacity for cruelty; it can arouse us, making plain the connection between death and sexual feeling; it can inspire our imaginations, removing us to places where our most sacred taboos may be challenged and overturned.

Do I believe it will make converts of the bunkered commentators who think that horror—particularly if it takes the form of popular entertainment—is sick or likely to degrade fine minds? No, I'm afraid not. I was, at the beginning of my career, a passionate believer in the need to convince people to re-evaluate horror, particularly in its literary form. After all, I argued, the best of science-fiction novels and spy thrillers are now viewed as literature, so why should the same respect not be paid to a fictional form that uses supernatural conceits to debate and illuminate the dark side of our personal planets? Much of the work in the genre is, of course, sheer sensationalism, but then there are a thousand disposable hackworks for every book by John le Carré or Frank Herbert. Shouldn't we judge a genre by its finest members, not by its runts? That was the core of my position. But over the years I've largely given up on the debate. People will come to the point of view in their own time or not at all.

(Of course, there's the "guilty pleasure" aspect of all this: that while I love well-turned phrases and great cinema, I also have a sentimental fondness for the literary or cinematic equivalent of Titus Andronicus. Indeed, there are times when the sheer artlessness of a Z-grade zombie flick can tellingly reveal the root of the genre's fascination in a fashion that a more sophisticated piece of work may conceal.)

Here—while we're talking about horror's appeal— may be an appropriate spot to discuss its enduring popularity. I have no new answers to the puzzle, only the strengthening sense that, as our century advances and the casual cruelty of our world becomes ever more visible through the medium of television, we seem to take comfort in fantastications of that cruelty; fictions in which we may savor the very subjects that distress us in the real world. Does it empower us to do so; give us a sense of control over forces that, in truth, threaten to overwhelm us? Or are we simply warming ourselves at the blaze that's burning our culture down? I suspect a little of both.

Bathing for a time in the red rivers of violence and retribution that feed the heart of this fiction may indeed wash away some part of our insanity; discharging our anger by indulging our private monsters. But if it doesn't—if we're simply making ourselves all the crazier by inflaming these appetites—then I humbly suggest that it's the way of the world, and perhaps our culture, in its fall from faith and certainty, needs to go through a dark night of the soul, in which the atrocities of street and battlefront, and those conjured by storytellers, become one seamless nightmare . . .

Only this seems certain: the subject is part of our psyche from childhood, enshrined in innumerable tales as a force that helps us understand the primal battle of our natures. The abomination, whether it comes in the form of a fairy tale dragon, a serial killer, a piece of special effects, or a crazed terrorist, is a necessary part of the human story.

It defines what the best in us despise; and reminds us how close to it we come in our most forbidden thoughts. There are countless interpretations of this enigma.

Think of it, perhaps, as footnotes to the grand encyclopedia that we are, each of us, amassing as we pass through our lives. That book will contain a number of entries under bliss, I hope, and love. But there will almost inevitably be a whole host of entries under horror. If these footnotes help illuminate the moments of dread and despair that inevitably come into our lives, however careful or sheltered an existence we lead, then it has found a fine purpose. And if such a high flown intention offends you, try reading the book in the bath. You'll find upon emerging that after a certain age—say, eighteen—the mirror may remind you how much we need the comfort of another's misery.

WHY HORROR?

MARK ALAN MILLER

WHY HORROR? It's a simple enough question, and it's certainly asked often enough. Though I think the reason the question comes up so frequently is because it's not a very easy one to answer. And it only complicates matters that every time I ask myself the very question, I seem to find a new answer.

I've done my homework, believe you me. I've logged more hours in horror than anyone ever asked of me. I've read every work published by Stephen King and written by Clive Barker. I've watched as many anthologies and franchises as I can find. I try to read or watch anything that's recommended to me. And I'll even digest things that I'm recommended to avoid, but if I'm being honest, it's sometimes because I was recommended to stay away! I've digested fiction, non-fiction, horror theory, the psychology of horror, essays and reviews on the different sub-genres and what each of them means. And even through all of these different forms and outlets from myriad minds, a lot of people seem to come up with a lot of the same theories.

Perhaps the most predominant one is that horror, more than any other genre, is the blackest crude of our subconscious bubbling to the surface. I've heard it said more times than I can count that if you look at an iconic or popular horror work (film/television/ novel/etc.) from any given year, you'll find what issues the country (or world at large) was working out at that time.

If you look at *The Twilight Zone*, which first broadcast in 1959 during the tail end of McCarthyism and the beginning of the Civil Rights movement, the show delves into the idea of nuclear war, mistrust of your neighbor, and what it means to be human. Hell, the episode "The Big Tall Wish" even won the Unity Award for Outstanding Contributions to Better Race Relations. So there is certainly something to that theory.

First of all, it would explain why there are so many Frankenstein iterations. Seemingly there's a new Frankenstein book or movie that comes out every year, each one altering the technology or adjusting for cultural settings. And is it any wonder? Science is evolving by leaps and bounds every day, and our world is in a constant state of flux, so the source material is evergreen, to be sure. We didn't know much as a culture back when Karloff donned the bolts, but we knew he was both to be feared and pitied. A recent re-imagining by Bernard Rose has Frankenstein's monster in contemporary Los Angeles, wandering the shanty towns of the increasing homeless population found in the riverbeds. Same monster, different world.

Hell, even franchises change with the times. The first *Texas Chainsaw Massacre* was a protestation about Vietnam. It's one of the most effective and damning statements on war, the effects PTSD, and what it's like coming back from the brink with nothing left—not even your sanity. And then 12 years later, *Texas Chainsaw Massacre 2* came out and was a scathing indictment on Reaganomics and the excess of the 80s. The two topics couldn't be more different, and the same can be said about the films. The first Chainsaw is a dizzying descent into madness; the second a delirious and often hysterically pitch-black satire.

Why horror? Because the greatest horror holds a mirror to our world and makes us look long and hard at our plights. What's interesting, though, is that most of the theorists seem content to stop there. However, for those delving a bit deeper, looking to move beyond the simplicity of the simple theory of the shadow, it's also been said that the genre allows for the richest metaphors. When you're mining the realm of the fantastic, you're getting into the stuff that dreams are made of. A drama can only be about the subject at hand. But a horror film can be about, well, anything at all. And a drama cannot be a horror film. Nor can it be a comedy. But horror can be a comedy, a drama, a thriller, a fantasy. You get idea. Let's talk examples. In the film *Still Alice*, Julianne Moore plays a woman diagnosed with early onset Alzheimer's. There's no metaphor here, only a reflection of a tragic reality we all potentially face, whether it's personally or relationally. The same is true for all films tackling the hard subjects. *A Beautiful Mind* deals with the difficulties walking the tightrope between genius and insanity. And it explored the truth that even our titans are human. There's no doubt these films are important works. But on the whole, their field of vision is often singular and quite narrow.

Even the more metaphysical dramas fall prey to this limitation. Look at a film like *Tree of Life*. While it is undoubtedly a masterpiece, it never transcends the prison of the abusive family unit. That's not an indictment of its effectiveness, however. The film resonated with me in a way few films have. While watching it, I was transported to a different time in my life—one that I'm happy I no longer have access to, save for in my memories. All that being said, it never got close to the emotional resonance of another family melodrama: the love it or hate it critical darling *The Babadook*.

I've never found myself in more arguments about any other film in existence. On the surface, it's about a family being haunted by an evil spirit. But under that single-layer façade is one of the richest pieces of storytelling I've ever had the discomfort of enduring. Again: not a criticism. I adore the film. But for me it's heavy going. And not because it's so terrifying, rather because it's a film that is so emotionally intelligent that it's painful. The movie, to me, is about depression, and the beast that grabs hold of you—literally haunts you—and takes control of your life. In the grip of a crippling depression, everything is upended—everything is in jeopardy—and you're at the whim of this dark visitor you feel will never leave. Taken as a beautiful Jungian dream interpretation, the mother's journey with her monster is one of the most cathartic cinematic experiences ever captured. It's also an awesome horror film, and it works on that level alone, to be sure. But on top of that, it's a beautiful, agonizing film that's about so much more than a creepy guy stalking a family. And, in part, it answers the question at hand.

Why horror? Because life is horrible sometimes, and working through those horrors is the only way we can make sense of it when everything else has failed us.

I think both answers are right, actually. But I don't think they fully answer the question. And the one that I've discovered—the one that resonates as possibly the third part of this whole—is related to the aforementioned agonies represented by *The Babadook* and every horror film like it that tells the story of what it means to be human. Another prime example is the film *Starry Eyes*. It's about one aspiring starlet's journey to realize her dream. On the surface, it's just a story following a young woman, adrift in a strange city, who gets taken advantage of until there's nothing left. But it's very much a parable of what it means to gain the world only after selling your soul. And, worse yet, how sometimes the selling of that soul becomes necessary just to survive in a cold world. The film is a marvelous, layered work that bears repeating!

Why horror? The world is harsh. And cruel. And full of pain. And films like *Still Alice*, or *A Beautiful Mind* tap into that, yes, but they don't provide an escape in the process, only the cold hard reality of the ways the body can turn on us.

I came to this realization while watching the television series *13 Reasons Why*. The series begins with the narration of a girl who, we learn, has killed herself. Every episode is narrated by her, as she takes us on the journey of every reason she decided to end her life, laid out on 13 cassette tapes. And it's the 13th episode, after we've heard all the reasons, and gone through the journey with her, that an unblinking camera watches her slit her wrists and bleed out in a bathtub. It was during both the lead up and the payoff to this moment that the question was answered for me. *13 Reasons Why* was so depressingly bleak that it gave me the answer I was looking for without even knowing it. Why horror? Because life is filled with loss every day. The news is depressing. The world is at war. People starve. Humans are cruel. And the bad guys win. In a world like this—a world filled with actual horrors—I turn to heightened horrors, wrapped in metaphors that work out the things I'm feeling, because I find that it provides hope, escape, and exorcism of the day's demons all at the same time.

13 Reasons Why was too true to life. It was that aforementioned drama which was only about the thing it was about. And it was brilliant at being about that. But it was also almost punishing for the viewer. There was no catharsis. There was no redemption. There was no metaphor. There was only one girl's sadness, and everyone's loss. Sometimes even the bleakest of horror films have an undercurrent of something fantastical. Why horror? Because it is the only genre that is unapologetically supernatural. And in a world where the natural order of things is a constant reminder of our slow and ineffable march toward death, I find the most comfort in what's considered the darkest of genres, because even the darkest, deadliest, most terrifying horror film is steeped in the tradition of survival and resurrection. In horror films, anything is possible, and there's always a chance to bring someone back.

Life is a terrifying prospect, and a zero sum game, to quote George Carlin. And while watching *13 Reasons Why* or *Still Alice*, there is no hope to be had.

I wanted Hannah to come back. I wanted Alice to have her life again. But like in life, they never would. So why did I spend 15 hours with them to be reminded of this? Freddy, Jason, and Pinhead, on the other hand, will always be there no matter how many times they explode, are set on fire, or are banished back to the hell from whence they came. And, in the process of those experiences, we exorcise our demons, we enrich the metaphors in our lives, and we're visited by familiar friends who will never leave us. Not bad for a genre that's often stigmatized as being the most irredeemable. That, my friends, is why horror.

PIXELATED SHADOWS:

Urban Lore And The Rise Of Creepypasta

MICHAEL PAUL GONZALEZ

PICTURE A LARGE clearing in a forest. Spread throughout the area, cleverly disguised, are small thatch huts and lean-tos, protecting the three dozen or so people gathered there. Some of them sleep while others stand watch, their backs to the few small campfires scattered in the area. They're wary of the world lying beyond the edge of the light, and out there in the gathering darkness, they hear the sounds of life stirring. They feel the weight of eyes upon them. They stay awake and alert, and they tell each other stories.

Some of these are tales of their exploits on their current and past travels, while others are larger and more fanciful ponderings on their place in the universe. These tales are important in preserving the history and culture of their people. It is how lessons are passed from generation to generation. When the stories are exhausted, when the night grows darker and colder, they begin to tell stories about what they don't know.

What are those shining green eyes moving through the bushes out there? What is that song they hear, and what's making it? The mood of the stories shifts from fanciful tales of why those nightbirds sing to dire warnings of what happened the last time one of their hunters ventured into the shadows to confront the unknown. Fact begins to mix with fiction as a man recounts finding the remains of one of his friends after a particularly dark and rainy night, half his body missing, his bones washed clean of blood, his eyes still fixed on some unknown horror. Somewhere between the truth and the horrific fantasy of the shadow world, stories are told to teach lessons about hunting at night, about wondering how much bigger the known world could be. Eventually those lessons became common knowledge, and though the stories no longer served a purpose, they remained.

Over time, those grass structures evolve to mud huts, to wooden shacks, to complex stone dwellings. The small campfires are replaced by hearths and candlelight. The darkness would be pushed further and further from the realm of polite society, but the stories persisted.

Late at night, families gather to share tales and histories, and sometimes myths and folktales would invade their home. Tales were shared of what happened to a friend of someone they knew, warnings of murder and kidnapping were wrapped in a safe blanket of story to ensure people would remain inside and safe. When horror befell someone in the city beyond the vision of the waking world, answers were sought. Where none were found, monsters were invented as a cautionary tale. Wolves and bears and twisted creations would stand in as warnings for murderers, kidnappers, and rapists. These stories were teaching tools, but long after the need for the lessons had faded, the tales remained.

Society evolved further. Candlelight and hearth fire were replaced by incandescent bulbs and furnaces. Stone walls became lathe, wood, plaster. Streets were brightly lit, communication expanded to the airwaves. The boundaries of the dark unknown were pushed back still further.

People learned to communicate by letter, by telephone, and eventually, over the internet. Now, at our most advanced stage, when so much is known, when the causes of most bumps and groans in the night are easily discovered and catalogued, we no longer hide from the dark. We opt to push into the dark as explorers. The warm glow of a campfire has long been replaced by the cold glow of a computer screen, and safe behind that plastic light, we find new paths into the mysterious unknown.

Stories are a powerful force, the best of them transformative, vital, and almost always viral. Passing from generation to generation, the art of the story has been carried in five main forms: myths, saga, fables, folk tale, and fairy tales. The original purpose of these stories was an alchemical reaction that would simultaneously remind the listener who they were, where they came from, and what they could become. While rote lessons from a teacher were easily forgotten, the lessons learned from these tales were subtle, delivered quickly and sharply like a knife between the ribs, leaving an indelible impression on the listener.

The earliest extant stories we can find are myths, the legends that were forged in order to explain our place in the universe and the workings of the world. Humans are always happy to use fiction as a placeholder while we struggle to discover facts. Why does the sun rise every day? Why are there stars in the sky? Where does weather come from? Why are we here? In a broad sense, myths provided satisfactory answers to the bigger questions of life, the universe, and everything. Personal stories and enduring histories were passed from generation to generation in the form of the saga. These stories encompassed broader journeys across time, outlining lineage, successorship, heroic deeds, eternal shames, victories and defeats. Myths helped people understand where they were. Sagas allowed them to remember who they were. Where myths and sagas served a larger purpose in helping humanity understand itself on a macro scale, fables and folktales arose to explore the microcosms of daily life.

Although the terms are sometimes used interchangeably, fables typically involve non-human characters (anthropomorphic animals and other fanciful creatures) as a central focus. Almost all of these stories contain a focus on morals as part of the ending. Perhaps the most famous example of the fable genre is *Aesop's Fables*, where animals typically stand in for humans and learn lessons about greed, love, the pitfalls of pride and avarice.

Folktales focus primarily on humans and are typically used as a mechanism to root cultural experiences within families. Folktales sometimes offer a supernatural twist to help deliver a lesson and provide a cultural anchor point in history for people to remember where they came from. Think of Pecos Bill lassoing a tornado, John Henry driving steel and showing that the human spirit is stronger than any machine. The thing folktales and fables have in common is the oral tradition in passing them down from generation to generation. In doing so, slight tweaks and changes can be made to the story to help it remain relevant to its current audience without losing the importance of its historical significance.

The fairy tale continues the tradition of carrying lessons from generation to generation, but they differ by focusing more on action and adventure, and while a moral lesson may be learned at the end, the hero's quest becomes more memorable. In this sense, a fairy tale almost becomes the product of the merging of myth, fable, and folk tale. While most people in the Western world are familiar with classic fairy tales like Red Riding Hood, Cinderella, and Snow White, they aren't as connected to the original lessons intended to come with the story. They remember the big bad wolf, the evil stepmother, and the maniacal queen, but they forget the focus on coming of age and warnings of sexual assault. We never mention the prayerful nature of Cinderella and the self-mutilation of the step-sisters to win love. We don't mention that the queen wanted Show White as a sacrifice, demanding her organs as proof that the hunter had done as he was bid. Fairy tales were mostly intended for children, but were an important tool to help them to begin to understand the path that lay ahead for them as they grew. They have softened over the years into diversions and entertainments with lighter lessons.

Where myth and saga can provide a more concrete structure to help its readers understand the past, many fables, fairy tales and folktales are deeply tied to the cultures that birth them. While a Chinese fairy tale might seem interesting to a foreigner, it might not resonate as much as it would with someone from that culture. Likewise, the story of John Henry carries a much deeper significance in the United States than it would in other countries.

All of these story archetypes have been shared by travelers around the world for eons. It's how human beings came to know one another and learn about (or sometimes learn to fear) each other. The oral tradition was the original viral story. Now, with the world so deeply interconnected, with most of the barriers to intercontinental communication removed, we still reach out to each other with stories. The oral tradition has morphed into a new breed of stories, universally-understandable multimedia pieces that are birthed in word and pixel, video and audio, sped digitally from computer to computer, person to person, nightmare to nightmare.

In the early 2000s, internet message boards (what eventually became social media) were the new town pubs, where weary travelers could come to relax after a long day of work, distract themselves from the real world, talk about their days, and tell stories. Stay in any pub long enough, stay awake long enough, and the stories are likely to take a sinister turn. In the past, scary stories were a useful tool to keep people inside and drinking, safe from what lurks in the dark. Now, from the safety of the LED glow of their monitor, people may still fear the dark, but they have a powerful need to populate it with tales of the unknown. Speculative horror has become our generation's most viable tradition of the passed story.

My first encounter with the genre that has come to be known as creepypasta was a Korean Webcomic commonly referred to as the Bongcheon-Dong Ghost. The premise: A girl walks home at night and encounters a strange woman. The woman asks her if she's seen her baby. The girl tries to ignore her and keep walking. And the rest? If you've seen the story online, you probably got the cold sweats right around the time I mentioned "Korean Webcomic." It needs to be experienced, preferably in the dark, and definitely with headphones. You've been warned. You can see the comic with a simple google search of the term "Bongcheon-Dong Ghost Comic."

To explore why the short horror works so well, we have to examine the genre of creepypasta itself, its roots, its place as the new campfire story, and how it's grown so popular so quickly.

Let's start with the name of the genre. Sure, Creepypasta sounds like something you'd get at a questionable buffet in a bad part of town, but its roots are simpler than that. Way back in the days before social media, when email and bulletin boards were the only sources of online communication, people would send each other short pieces—news items, jokes, stories, all of them copied and pasted into a new message. The shorthand for sharing these stories was the phrase copypasta, and when online forums and discussion groups started specializing in horror stories, the term creepypasta was coined and has stuck ever since.

Googling the term produces an endless supply of short horror fiction, some of it clunky, some of it horrible, and much of it so scary that you'll spend a few hours after encountering it doing further Google searches to reassure yourself that it's not true. The truly amazing thing about the genre is how pervasive it is, how quickly it spreads in all media—creepypasta can be found in short YouTube videos, copy-pasted fiction, video games, and sometimes hiding in places where most people wouldn't think (or have the ability) to look—programming code, HTML scripts, even inside of soundwaves in audio files!

The stories are usually quickly consumed and easily shared. Rather than relying on narrative story structure, they go for a gut-punch of visceral terror, something that inspires a desire in the audience to immediately share it with their friends.

The Internet—Frontier of Shadows

Now that the world is interconnected like never before, it has become harder to create speculative stories about the unknown. Over the past few decades, popular science fiction has turned its focus away from deep space opera and interplanetary exploration and returned to earth to investigate diseases and the electronic frontier. Horror has followed the same route, infusing the elements of everyday life with just enough of the supernatural to unsettle its readers. Today's reality-rooted science fiction tells readers this could happen. Today's reality-rooted horror leaves readers wondering did this happen?

We can compare and contrast what made old urban legends work so well, and examine how creepypasta takes what it needs, discards what it doesn't, and utilizes modern technology to make itself more pervasive and far-reaching.

Artifacts Make Story Starters

Older tales of lore and urban legends frequently begin with a found object or the remnants of an incident. A doll that's seen in numerous old photographs could someday be tied to rumors of ghosts and demonic possession. A lone tree that happened to grow in the right spot can become the nexus of rumors surrounding witches, hangings, and ghosts. In the case of the former, there is the legend of Robert the Doll, in the latter, the Devil's Tree in New Jersey. Robert was a doll owned by a painter, supposedly given to him by a servant that practiced black magic. Stories of Robert moving on his own, talking in a deep voice that only some could hear, and driving others mad abound. The doll is available for public viewing in Key West, Florida. Looking at its coal-black eyes, threadbare skin, and bare facial expression, it's easy to see how dark tales might become attached to what is a seemingly innocent object. The Devil's Tree in New Jersey is a lone oak tree in a vast field. It has sparse, gnarled limbs, some of which are long-dead. Legend says the tree was once used by the KKK to lynch people. Or perhaps it was the site of pagan ritualistic sacrifice. Or perhaps it was once on a farmstead, where the farmer went crazy and killed his family before hanging himself from one of its branches. Whatever story you choose, you'll find trace legends of the evils that befall people who come near the tree, or deface the tree, or even just speak ill of it.

Inanimate objects are some of the easiest places to start a legend, because they tell no tales and leave their histories almost entirely to the imagination of the beholder. How can this translate to creepypasta, a genre that lives entirely in a digital domain?

One of the common devices used in creepypasta stories is the inclusion of "discovered" artifacts. There are arcane stories and anecdotes with mundane backgrounds in every industry. Game engineers frequently hide images, sounds, or messages inside of their game code, most likely because they're bored or playing jokes on each other. Animators slip risqué images or bawdy slogans into single frames of animation, mostly to see if they can get away with it. You can spot examples of this in Disney's *The Rescuers*, where during a freefall outside of an apartment building, a poster of a naked woman can be spied through one of the open windows in the building. In *The Lion King*, when Simba lies down on a cliff face, a puff of flower petals lifts into the night sky, swirling away. The flowers briefly spell out (depending who you talk to) S-F-X, a nod to the visual department, or S-E-X. Tiny, blink-and-you'll-miss-it instances like this lead to the rise of urban legends surrounding animation studios. The movie adaptation of *Fight Club* took great advantage of this trope, weaving single-cells of Tyler Durden throughout the movie (and of course, giving one last naughty sendoff to the audience after the climax of the film).

There are several examples of creepypasta following the lost film archetype. *Mickey in Hell* or Suicidemouse.avi (Googling either should take you to a trove of retellings, and allegedly, the cartoon itself . . . if you dare.) is the story of an intern at a Disney animation factory who uncovered a short reel of an old Mickey cartoon. The first few minutes are the kind of standard looping animation you'd see in every cartoon back in the day, Mickey walking rhythmically down an anonymous city street. Then, the screen goes black for several minutes. When Mickey returns, the walking continues, but this time the music has been replaced by low, gurgling sounds and muffled screaming. As the screams grow louder over the next few minutes, the picture begins to distort and stretch. Mickey's placid expression turns increasingly demonic, his mouth gaping into a sinister leer, his eye sockets stretching so far that his eyeballs fall out of his skull. The gurgling sound changes to ear-splitting screams, sustained for almost two minutes. Colors leech into the frame, a technology that wouldn't have existed when the black and white reel was created. Finally, the screen goes black again, replaced by the familiar smiling mouse face that was under the credits of every Disney short. The viewer was forced to stare into Mickey's menacing grimace for 30 seconds, accompanied by hellish screams. Legend held that anyone who viewed those crucial seconds would leave the viewing room, proclaiming to have an understanding of hell and suffering, and quickly committing suicide thereafter. The fact that there are multiple versions of this purported film floating around don't serve to lessen the creep factor.

Another popular example is Squidward's Suicide, where a dour, put-upon character in Spongebob Squarepants finally succumbs to the darkness inside of himself. The show is renowned for its use of non-sequitur humor and quick cuts to hyper-detailed images for comedic effect. In this tale, a Nickelodeon intern recalls the time he was given an envelope with a tape to edit called "Squidward's Suicide." The tape consisted of Squidward sitting on his bed, deeply depressed and sobbing. This footage was intercut with split-second clips of graphic, gory scenes involving children. The images intensify, and a low voice begins to creep into the audio, murmuring commands to Squidward to do it . . . do it . . . do it. Squidward's face begins to blacken, his eyes turn photorealistic, filling with blood. He stares at the camera as the voice continues to command him, the black pits of his eyes deepening. He raises a pistol into the frame, a single gunshot is heard, and the camera is coated in a fine red mist. The cartoon cuts abruptly. The intern, shocked at what he sees tries to find out more about the tape. None of the animators recall working on any of the images and nobody had a package delivered to this intern. Rumors abound that the video machine itself may be haunted or possessed by a demonic entity. Those with the misfortune to work on that particular machine all meet untimely ends.

Sometimes, creative forces move in the opposite direction, and a bit of creepypasta is transformed into mainstream studio fare. Candle Cove was first found on an internet nostalgia board, where users talked about the shows they used to watch as a kid. The creepypasta unfolds as a dialogue narrative, with several users discussing their favorite shows. A few of them mention a show called *Candle Cove*, about a girl named Janice who befriends a group of pirates. The pirates were all puppets, and the show was generally the type of fare you'd expect. Some of the users had odd memories about some of the puppets, including one called the skin-taker, a skeleton pirate who wore clothing made from children's skin. Another user recalls a bizarre episode that consisted only of the pirates screaming and flailing their arms for the duration of the show. The story closes with one of the users mentioning the show to his mother, who was always baffled at the kid's fondness for *Candle Cove*. While the children recounted numerous episodes and adventures, the mother could only remember that she saw nothing but static on the TV screen while they claimed to be watching the show.

Candle Cove works because it's treated as found footage, legitimized by dozens of people on a forum having a conversation about the same thing. Those who stumbled into it blindly would think they were witnessing a real conversation. It is hailed as one of the best examples of creepypasta available, and has since been optioned by the Syfy network and launched as *Channel Zero: Candle Cove*.

All of these examples rely on small bits of true information—found artwork, discarded portraits from animators never meant to see the light of day. Finding a kernel of truth, an undeniable and easily-researched artifact or event, can lend a tremendous amount of weight—and horror—to your story.

Based on True Events

Urban legends often spring up around real historical events. Most children in the Western world might not know who Mary Tudor was, but they've almost all heard of the legend of what happens when people try to invoke her spirit in a mirror by saying Bloody Mary three times. Walk outside of the Biograph Theater in

Chicago on the right night at the right time, and you might bump into the ghost of outlaw John Dillinger, who died there in a shootout with police.

The found object aspect of creepypasta is what makes it more enjoyable, the story-beyond-the-story, physical evidence that exists because of the community of creepypasta devotees rather than savvy viral marketers or studio execs. We live in a world where urban legends can be quickly rendered to audio or video, where objects can be 3D printed, rendered and assembled as totemic objects from another realm. Horror as a visual genre has always been the realm of people with low budgets and high creativity, and now the cost of entry barrier sinks lower every day, opening the door for a new generation of creators. With the advent of the internet, practitioners of creepypasta can effectively create traces of the real historical events they need to start their story.

Hollywood has a long history of movies being made on a shoestring budget that go on to gross hundreds of millions of dollars, becoming cultural icons along the way and changing the way stories are told. Recent low-budget films like *The Blair Witch Project, Paranormal Activity*, and *The Exorcism of Emily Rose* all traded on sleight of hand and low-key creeps to deliver a huge impact.

In one way or another, these films utilized marketing campaigns that deposited them into the world as real things. *Blair Witch* got heavy buzz at Sundance after posters were placed around the town featuring missing posters of the three lead characters in the film. The studio launched websites months in advance, posting photos and short video clips to start laying a trail of evidence of the film's events. The IMDB listing for the film cited the actors as "missing, presumed dead." When the film made the festival circuit, some patrons reported being near tears meeting the actors, hugging them and expressing relief that they were unharmed. The movie blazed a trail for the phenomenon that has since been named viral marketing.

The appeal of the modern urban legend thus becomes an evolution from a spooky campfire tale (Have you heard the story of . . . ?) to a presentation of near-fact (Let me show you the story of . . .). Horror once challenged readers to stay with the story, to confront the monsters lurking in the shadows and find catharsis in the ending of the story. Now, the story oozes from the page, creeping like a low black fog into our everyday lives.

Two examples of creepypasta made manifest can be found in video game lore. The legend of the retro-arcade cabinet POLYBIUS has become so pervasive that it has shown up in numerous films and TV shows, as well as appearing here and there in the real world. In 1988, the website coinop.org, dedicated to cataloging the old quarter-munching machines that 80s kids know so well, gained a new entry about a cabinet created in 1981 called Polybius. The legend has it that the machine made its debut in the Pacific Northwest, where it became fiercely popular. Long lines would form with people sometimes fighting each other for a chance to play the game. They would play, entranced for hours, and when the arcade closed, strange men in black would arrive to extract data from the machines. Fans of the game would report varying symptoms after playing—nausea, sleep loss, night terrors and hallucinations, ultimately culminating in some players completely losing their minds, turning into babbling maniacs. The machine was pulled from arcades only weeks later in 1981. The company that supposedly created the game was called Sinneslöschen, a German phrase roughly translating to sensory deprivation or loss of sensation. There are playable ROMs of the game floating around the internet, and physical versions of the cabinet appear and disappear at arcades and pop-up events.

Like all good legends, this one was rooted in some truth. When the arcade game Tempest was originally released, some players complained of nausea and vertigo caused by the strobing lights and flashing colors. PC development company Rogue Synapse has since registered the name Sinneslöschen and created a cabinet version of Polybius that was based on the numerous accounts of the urban legend (with a disclaimer that it's not the real thing, only a faithful emulation).

Sometimes, a small adjustment from a game publisher can lead to the birth of a dark legend. Pokémon, one of the world's most popular games, is a turn-based role-playing game where you (a Pokémon trainer) travel from town to town, collecting Pokémon and pitting them against other trainers to see who's the very best (sorry if that gets the theme song stuck in your head). Your trainer will visit numerous locales, including a gloomy, secluded spot called Lavender Town. In the game, Lavender Town is where trainers go to mourn their dead Pokémon. The music changes to an extremely somber, mournful dirge (sample that by Googling Original Lavender Town theme at your own risk). The chiptune melody contains high-pitched, jarring chords that were purportedly binaural audio programmed to affect the mind. Children aged seven to twelve would experience nosebleeds, irritability, or sometimes outright rage. The Lavender Town theme was eventually changed, allegedly after claims of over one hundred children in Japan killed themselves after hearing the original tune began to circulate online. Outside of the legend, people who've listened to the music for a prolonged period have indeed reported feeling dread or slight nausea. Couple that with the difficulty in tracking down unsubstantiated rumors in a foreign country, and you have a story plausible enough to become a creepypasta legend. What makes it effective is a trifecta of real-world occurrences: the original score was real. It was removed from production. And most importantly, Pokémon had, in the past, been involved in incidents where children were harmed as a result of watching it. The original cartoon in Japan contained scenes of flashing lights and colors so intense that some children went into seizure from watching, some of them losing consciousness or even vomiting blood. It might be the rare occurrence that reality was more frightening than creepypasta.

Today's publishing environment puts more of the onus on authors to carry some of the weight of their promotional material. Finding a way to bring elements of your story into the real world, be it a blog, a giveaway trinket, a "buried" account online that suddenly surfaces to reinforce your story, can help your story reach a wider audience. People are more likely to pass around short snippets of information, creepy photos, links to short stories or copy-pasted emails. Writing an effective tie-in piece of creepypasta could help your story market itself. A word of warning there—most people can sense marketing and buried ads from a mile away, and they tend to reject it. If you're going to try this with one of your stories, make it irresistible. Even if they never buy your work, the legend you create might last for years and take on a life of its own.

Staring Too Long into The Abyss

What happens when people take their devotion to urban legends too far?

In its early days, the video sharing site YouTube was primarily used to host short music videos and comedic clips pulled from TV and movies. Before the site shifted to monetizing user-driven content, a small band of pioneers began releasing serial short films online under the guise of found footage. These films were so convincing that they birthed a new genre, the Alternate-Reality Experience (ARE). Viewers flocked to these video diaries, expertly crafted to look like real footage from real people.

The most infamous piece of creepypasta lore was popularized in numerous photos, stories, and media online, in particular the ARE series *Marble Hornets*. While movies, books, and TV shows have given pop culture numerous icons of fright, it wasn't until *Marble Hornets* widened the popularity of the creature known as Slenderman that creepypasta found its first multimedia star.

Marble Hornets is an episodic YouTube series telling the story of Alex Kralie, a student filmmaker who lost himself in a project in 2006. He was creating a short film called *Marble Hornets* and had a troubled production that lasted over three months. His crew complained of high stress and irritability surrounding the shoot, and eventually Alex pulled the plug on the project just as it was nearing its conclusion. When Alex's friend asks what he plans to do with the tapes, Alex tells him, "Burn them." He convinces Alex to hand over the works to him to see if there's anything he can do with them. Something about the tapes disturbs the student, and he stores them in a closet, uncovering them three years later. He decides to go through the footage to see if he can discover what happened. The tapes are all unnumbered and lacking timestamps of any kind. The student uses his YouTube account to upload anything he finds of interest so that it can live in the public record.

The first clip uploaded to the YouTube channel had the audio removed or muted. Instead of taking place on a film set, it's shot inside of Alex Kralie's house. The camera lurches frantically, desperately, as if the person shooting is looking for someone or possibly trying to hide. Peeking out of the curtain, the camera captures a brief glimpse of a tall, pale being in a dark suit. Its head is formless and completely lacking in features, yet it seems to be watching him: it is Slenderman.

It's a rare thing to be able to trace a piece of urban folklore back to not only its creator, but the day and date it was born. The website forums on SomethingAwful.com hosted a Photoshop contest, challenging users to edit everyday photos and add paranormal elements. On June 10, 2009, user Eric Knudsen combined images of children with an eerie, spectral figure. Hidden in the background (or sometimes dead center in the image) was an unusually tall being with long arms and legs, apparently dressed in a black suit, with a bright, white, featureless head. Referred to as The Slender Man or Slenderman, the creature would appear shortly before the abductions or murders of children in an area. Knudsen posted simple captions under the photos, suggesting that the photographers had somehow taken part in the kidnappings and ritual slayings against their will.

From these simple origins, the legend of Slenderman grew, until he was featured in books, movies, comics, and video games. In 2014, concern began to surround the legend of Slenderman as several acts of violence in the real world were credited as being inspired by the legend. In Wisconsin, two teenage girls stabbed a 12-year-old girl nineteen times, claiming they were attempting to become proxies of Slenderman. Later that same year, a mother reported that her daughter had attempted to stab her several times after reading Slenderman stories online. There was also a rash of suicide attempts on the Pine Ridge Indian Reservation by young people aged twelve to twenty-four who had all been deeply interested in Slenderman stories.

Levels of moral panic surrounding violent pop culture images were nothing new, but for the first time, there seemed to be a direct link between a piece of artistic fiction and numerous unrelated acts of violence.

Back to Darkness

In the past, only two things were required for urban legends to thrive and survive—an unexplainable object or event and someone to share the story. Through fault of memory, legends could spread, evolve, and mutate. With the advent of online technology, it's become more difficult to sustain certain urban legends. It's become easier to research events, deaths, and catastrophes. Debunking phenomena captured on film or audio is simply a matter of uploading it to YouTube and asking experts for an explanation. It's become easier than ever to find the unknown, and harder than ever to stay there.

This is where creepypasta gains its strength. Incidents and events can be linked disparately through unrelated articles. Unexplained murders and deaths can be connected tenuously to elements of creepypasta stories. If there's enough evidence to suggest something happened, but not enough of a trail to investigate it, the reader is left to fill in the blanks in their imagination. Once a story takes root in their brain, its work is done. Trees in the park take on sinister life, glitches in a program signal impending doom, and a familiar childhood doll fallen to the floor becomes the work of demonic possession.

Horror writers can increase their arsenal of tricks by studying creepypasta and urban lore to find ways to capture an audience's attention immediately, terrify them instantaneously, and haunt them for days after they've finished the story.

LIKE FARTS AND CURSES

RAY GARTON

"**WHERE DO YOU** get your ideas?"

The question is inevitable, and writers dread it. It is probably the question most commonly asked of writers. It is, without a doubt, the question writers hate most because there is no good answer. Well, there may be one:

We don't know.

Really. We never know where they're going to come from. I don't know a single writer who has a system for coming up with ideas. There are systems for processing ideas, making the most of ideas, shaping ideas into stories or novels—but first, you must have the idea. That is systemless.

David Lynch said, "Ideas are like fish. And you don't make a fish, you catch a fish. You desiring an idea is like putting a bait on a hook and lowering it into the water."

Unfortunately, there are no lakes stocked with ideas. There are no idea bars where you can go to meet ideas and, if you're lucky, go home with the idea of your choice. There are no red idea districts where you can pull your car over to the curb and, for the right price, pick up an idea even though you don't know

44

where it's been. Writers can't go to an idea hunting preserve to stalk and kill ideas and take them home and cut them up into pieces of fiction.

Ideas don't come when you call them. They just float around all over the place, silent and invisible, like farts and curses, and we have to hope that, every now and then, we're lucky enough to catch one.

There may be no places where ideas gather and can easily be found, but some writers have places they go to find the inspiration that might lead to ideas. The sweet spot for screenwriter and novelist Dalton Trumbo, for example, was a bathtub. He often worked at night in a tub of water with a typewriter on a tray in front of him.

I used to find inspiration in all-night coffee shops, where I would write longhand in a notebook (we didn't have laptops back then) and drink coffee while writing and people-watching. The simple act of quietly observing people, I've found, can stir up ideas.

It was while sitting at the coffee counter in the 76 Truck Stop in Redding, California, late one night where I overheard a couple of truckers at the coffee counter talking about "lot lizards." I had never heard the term before, so I asked them what a "lot lizard" was.

"That's a truck stop hooker," one of the truckers said.

The other shook his head and said, "Nothin' but trouble. Buncha drug addicts and thieves."

I jotted down the term and started turning it over in my head. Over the following months, as I returned almost nightly to that truck stop, I wrote *Lot Lizards* (even better than that, I met my wife there, where she managed the gift shop on the graveyard shift). That novella exists only because of that overheard conversation and the curious question I asked those two truckers. Had I not been a late-night coffee shop writer, that novella never would have been written. I would have written something else inspired by some other experience.

When I lived in the San Fernando Valley in southern California, my usual spot was Tiny Naylor's on Ventura Boulevard, now gone, where I would occasionally break from writing to look around at the parade of character actors from movies and TV, drag queens from the Queen Mary nightclub up the street, and porn stars from the nearby adult film studios, in addition to an endlessly colorful cast of characters lining up to populate my books and stories—unknown to them, of course.

That was where I wrote much of *Crucifax*, a novel that grew out of the location in which I lived. North Hollywood and the surrounding towns were crawling with teenagers who seemed to have nowhere to go day or night, nothing to do except perhaps play pinball and video games at convenience stores in strip malls, sit in coffee shops, or hang out on sidewalks. I began to wonder about them, especially when I saw them wandering the streets aimlessly in the wee hours of school nights. I know my parents would have been apoplectic, and I wondered what their parents thought. Did they know where their children were? Did they care?

The more I wondered, the more I felt a faint but familiar tightness in my chest, a tension, like encroaching anxiety. That's my clue that something is worth following—if it's not an idea yet, it probably will lead to one. That feeling means I have stumbled upon something worth examining more closely. In this case, it led to a whole novel.

I suspect every writer has one of those clues, whatever it might be—a sign that there's a potential story or book hiding somewhere nearby. Once you discover what that is, always trust it and always follow it. Respond like a bloodhound that's just picked up a scent and track it down.

It's rare, but sometimes an idea will drop fully formed into your head unexpectedly, like a block of frozen waste plunging from the toilet of a passing jetliner high overhead. *Live Girls* happened that way for me on my first visit to Times Square in the mid-1980s.

I worked up the courage to go into one of the many peep shows that could be found in Times Square back then. Such places existed far, far outside my realm of experience and made me more than a little nervous, but I was curious. After getting some tokens at the entrance, I entered one of the booths and dropped a token into the box on the wall. A panel slid up over a dirty rectangular window to reveal a gaunt young woman who was naked, seemingly wasted, and probably not in the best of the health judging by her appearance. Below the window was a slot through which to slip tips to the dancers. But this slot had a crude circular opening cut into the center of it. The faint light coming through from the other side fell on ridges in the edges of that slot. I thought to myself, 'That looks almost like it was . . . chewed open.' And BAM! There it was! In my head! An idea, a hell of an exciting idea that I did not think had been done before. I left the booth immediately and hurried out of Times Square in search of a notepad, a typewriter, something—I needed to write.

The thing about ideas, though, is that, like a frigid church lady, sometimes they just don't come. No matter what you do, where you go, what you eat the night before, how much sunshine and exercise you get, the ideas stay far away. They fly off to other places and drop in on other writers while you sit with your head in your hands, thinking, reaching, searching for one of them, invisible and mercurial and maddening. At times like that, you may be tempted to force an idea to come, to bear down and grunt and groan and try to squeeze one out.

Allow me to tell you a cautionary tale.

Before I ever sold a novel, I was introduced to a literary agent by some friends. I was in far northern California and he was at the other end of the state in the Los Angeles area. I sent him a few short stories. In a phone call, he responded favorably but said he did not sell short stories. Did I have a novel I could show him?

I said, "I'm working on one now and should be done soon. When it's ready, I'll send it to you."

I was relieved that he did not ask what it was about because my work in progress was, of course, a lie. I was not working on a novel. But suddenly I was gripped with a sense of urgency. I had an agent who was interested and, so far, had liked the short stories he had read. I could not let him get away. I had written two or three novels by then, but they were not suitable to send to an agent. I had written them mostly for practice. This had to be something new. I needed an idea.

I read an interview with Stephen King in which he mentioned that he had not yet been able to work vagina dentata into any of his fiction yet but he would keep trying, or something to that effect.

I was a twenty-year-old college dropout with a Seventh-day Adventist education, which meant that I had to look up "vagina dentata" because I had no idea what it was. Suddenly, I was gripped with a sense of urgency. I had to beat Stephen King to fanged vaginas! I had to come up with a vagina dentata novel! I was determined to be the champion in an exciting race to the vagina dentata finish line of which Stephen King was, of course, blissfully unaware. I set about doing this in the only way I knew how—I sat down at my Brother typewriter and began to write.

It was like trying to pass a bowling ball through my colon, and nowhere is that more obvious than on the pages of the quickly-written book that resulted, my first published novel, *Seductions*. I console myself with the fact that I was a kid and truly did not know what I was doing (which, to some extent, remains true to this day because every writing project is new and I'm never quite sure what I'm doing), but it makes the book no more readable in my opinion. It isn't even about fanged vaginas, it's just a horror novel with lots of sex and gore into which I managed to work a fanged vagina or two.

Trying to force ideas is . . . well, a bad idea. Whenever a writer forces something, it shows. You can't hide it. Mark me down as being opposed to forcing ideas. However, I am not opposed to building ideas.

Just because you lack a solid idea doesn't mean you shouldn't start writing. Ideas are not simply a goal of writers, something we seek out, they are also tools. Most ideas come in fragments, and those fragments typically have more creative value than we might think at first, so it's always a good idea to keep them around for later. Idea fragments can be used to build whole ideas, or they can contribute to and enrich other ideas. It's possible to begin with the vaguest of notions and then, with some goal in mind, build a whole idea around that notion. That was how I wrote the novel *Sex and Violence in Hollywood*.

As a writer of horror fiction, I'm sensitive to the way people respond to violence, which is a common element of the genre. When I was a kid, everybody was afraid of what violence on TV was doing to children. After the controversy that exploded when NBC aired a TV movie in which Linda Blair was raped in prison with a broom handle—the highest-rated TV movie of the year, incidentally—the networks agreed to program shows with violent content only after nine in the evening. The eight-to-nine prime time slot was designated the Family Hour—safe viewing for families, children, old ladies, and small animals. But that ended in 1977.

People used to respond to violence in movies and on TV with outrage. Now they only respond that way to sex. Violence . . . not so much.

"Would your books be appropriate for my thirteen-year-old?" a woman asked me once.

"Probably not," I said, "because they usually contain explicit violence and—"

"Oh, I don't mind violence. He can handle that. I just don't want him to be messed up by a bunch of sex."

I've had many such exchanges over the last twenty years or so and the parent almost always says the same thing: violence is okay, but no sex. The same attitude is applied to TV and even feature films. You can kill all the people you want, torture them, eviscerate them, dismember them. But if you show so much as a nipple, you're going to have some upset people on your hands. This baffles me.

I'm not one of those indignant moralists who says violence in the media turns kids into killers, not at all. But there's something weird about this attitude, don't you think? I don't keep up with TV like I used to, but sometimes I'll surf the channels and come across graphic lingering shots of gutted corpses and dismembered limbs—and that's just NCIS. That's not on HBO or Showtime or some other pay channel. It's on CBS, the Tiffany network, of all places. To me, that means explicit depictions of violence have become a part of our everyday lives. The kind of stuff that I used to have to watch in secret as a kid is now everywhere, even on the Tiffany network.

A common remark heard from eyewitnesses of violence has become, "It didn't look real." Why? Because it didn't look the way it does in the movies or on TV. There, when someone gets shot in the head, the skull explodes and blood and brain matter go everywhere and blood spurts from the remaining stump of neck, all in slow motion. When it happens in life, it's fast. The gun pops the victim drops. That's it. Sure, there's blood, but not like on the screen. It's not surprising, then, that when people see it happen, it doesn't look "real" because movies and TV have become more real to us than reality. For that reason, you'll see some strange responses to actual violence and death. Like laughter.

All of this had been stewing in my head for a while. At the same time, I had been itching to write a novel about movies that was set in the movie industry. I decided to try combining these two things. I sat down and began to write. What followed was my most enjoyable writing experience ever. The result was *Sex and Violence in Hollywood*.

My meditations on violence in media, our fascination with it, and how it might subtly affect our own views on violence are some of the book's ingredients. That is mixed with a comic thriller involving blackmail, murder, and a spectacular celebrity trial that captures the nation's attention. The book is made up of whole ideas, idea fragments that came in handy, and a lot of brand new stuff that bubbled up during the writing. It's not a horror novel and maybe that's the reason it didn't sell very well at first. People have come to expect a certain kind of fiction from me and this did not quite fit those expectations. In spite of that, it remains my personal favorite of all my novels.

People who become writers tend to be people who get a lot of ideas. These days, after more than thirty years of writing full time, I find that ideas are everywhere. Life is an onslaught of ideas. It's frustrating because I know I'll never live long enough to make use of more than a tiny fraction of them. I think this is the case with most writers. Everything is material for fiction.

Most of the writers I've known have said that, like me, they have to write. We don't have a choice. We would write in every spare moment if that was all the time we had. Even Stephen King has said that if he didn't get paid for it, he would write for free. The thing that fuels that need to write is an idea that we have to get out. Maybe it's a character, or an appealing plot, or simply a particular emotion—whatever it is, it forms an idea that we must put on the page.

When asked where he gets his ideas, Harlan Ellison has often said, "Schenectady."

We have to come up with smartass responses like that because it's the only way to answer that unanswerable question. Asking a writer where he gets his ideas is like asking someone "How does your spleen feel right now?" or "What does your pain smell like?" Huh? What? I have no idea. I don't know how to answer that question. Why would you ask such a thing?

That's what the question feels like. Ideas are so much a part of what we do and who we are that we cannot pinpoint a source. Like the Force, ideas surround us, penetrate us, and bind the galaxy together. They're all over the place—outside of us, inside of us, and sometimes both at once. They come from nowhere and everywhere. They are invisible mercury, the ghosts of creativity, and part of the fabric of virtually everything we know. Everything begins with an idea.

If you ever figure out where they come from, let me know, because I'm curious, too.

HOW TO GET YOUR SCARE ON

Finding Your Inspiration and Muse in Horror

S.G. BROWNE

In·spi·ra·tion

1 a) a divine influence or action on a person believed to qualify him or her to receive and communicate sacred revelation; b) the action or power of moving the intellect or emotions; c) the act of influencing or suggesting opinions
2 the act of drawing in; specifically, the drawing of air into the lungs
3 a) the quality or state of being inspired; b) something that is inspired
4 an inspiring agent or influence
—Merriam-Webster Dictionary

WE'RE ALL FAMILIAR with the various definitions of inspiration. But where, exactly, does inspiration come from? And what do we mean when we talk about finding it? Is it some ephemeral concept that's only attainable for those who practice meditation or who collect honey on the Himalayan cliffs of Nepal? Or is it something solid that can be found by those who practice using their imaginations or who collect signatures from celebrities on the panels at Comic-Con?

Frequently, people think of inspiration as something that just happens: a transcendent moment when your creative mind and spirit are inspired beyond their default setting. Some people claim that when inspiration strikes in this manner, it's accompanied by a slowing down of time and a heightening of the senses, along with the thrill of discovering that there is something greater to be achieved: an awareness of a reality or idea not previously understood.

This is the lightning bolt version of inspiration: a moment of clarity that is often overwhelming in its power. When in the grips of this type of inspiration, where nothing else seems to matter but the idea and doing something with it, writers often speak of a sense of transcendence, as if someone or something else is speaking through them. That's The Muse talking, but we'll get to her (or him) in a bit.

Most writers will tell you that the lightning bolt version of inspiration doesn't hit very often, if at all. It's a fairy tale writers tell themselves as an excuse for not getting any writing done. If you're waiting for inspiration to hit before you sit down to start writing, then you're probably not getting much writing done.

For most writers, horror and otherwise, inspiration is something that happens after you've been sitting in front of your computer, staring at a blank screen for an hour or two as the clock ticks inexorably toward your deadline, trying to remember why you're bothering to do this in the first place. In this instance, the inspiration is more panic and survival instinct than a creative epiphany. But that still begs the question as to where inspiration can be found.

The answer is simple: everywhere.

Inspiration for stories can be found at the supermarket, on the bus, at an office party, or in a movie theater. It can be found on vacation, in a hotel lobby, at the post office, or in a fast-food restaurant. And when it comes to finding inspiration for horror, as someone once said, "If you want to read a horror story, all you have to do is pick up a newspaper."

From terrorism, global warming, and nuclear missile tests, to child abductions, deadly viruses, and just about anything that happens in Florida, horror is front-page news. Of course, most people today don't get their news delivered to their doorstep but instead devour it while surfing the internet on their phones, laptops, and tablets, which creates an entirely new set of technological horrors.

Computer viruses. Cyberstalkers. Internet trolls. Phishing. Ransomware. Online dating.

Horror is a pervasive presence in our world. You can't go anywhere without encountering it. Kind of like Starbucks. So if you're having trouble finding inspiration for writing horror, you're probably not paying attention. Either that or you need to get out more.

Let's go back to the various definitions of inspiration for a moment.

1 a) a divine influence or action on a person believed to qualify him or her to receive and communicate sacred revelation; b) the action or power of moving the intellect or emotions

2 the act of drawing in; specifically, the drawing of air into the lungs

In a manner of speaking, all inspiration is a divine influence. While not necessarily sacred or holy, inspiration is a whispering into the subconscious of an idea that can move the intellect or emotions to create something that transcends the ordinary and transforms perception (again, this is The Muse knocking on the door, but we're not ready to answer it just yet). It's the job of the writer to convey this experience, this divine influence, and use that inspiration to move the intellect and emotions of the reader. And it all starts with processing that inspiration into an idea.

Likewise, the second definition of inspiration—the physical drawing of air into the lungs—applies to the process of writing, as inspiration is as necessary to creativity as oxygen is to breathing. The writer breathes in ideas from his or her environment and consumes them in order to breathe life into his or her creations.

As it's already been pointed out, when it comes to horror, the news is a never-ending source of material for the consumption of ideas and inspiration. But the horror in the pages of the newspaper isn't always what translates to the horror on the page of your story or novel. It's up to the writer to find the horror that matters to him or her.

Back in the late 1990s—when internet access was dial-up and the news arrived every morning at the foot of your driveway—I read a short article in the national section of my local newspaper about a man on a weekend camping trip who decapitated his sons with a hunting knife before turning the knife on himself.

This was a horrific story all by itself and didn't require any embellishment to make it any more horrific. But as a writer—specifically as a horror writer—I wanted to know what had compelled the father to behead his sons. Did he have a history of mental illness? Had he consumed something that caused him to experience hallucinations? Was there any kind of outside influence involved?

The article in the newspaper was all of ten lines, with no explanation for the father's actions or his medical history. The fact that the father had been found dead a short time later from a self-inflicted knife wound only made me wonder even more.

So the inspiration the news article provided was for me to find an answer to those questions, or at least to formulate an answer. And I did so by writing a story that began with that article, or a facsimile of it, before telling the story of another father who commits similar atrocities and suffers a similar fate. The story ended with a second news article about the fictional father that mirrored the opening.

But the article wasn't the only inspiration that helped to give birth to the story. I also found inspiration for the story from an afternoon spent cutting down a couple of small dead shrubs in the backyard of my home while I listened to Pink Floyd's "Welcome to the Machine." There may or may not have been recreational drugs involved.

The point is that while real-life horror from the news was the initial catalyst, several other influences inspired the eventual creation of the story, including a personal experience, a song about the music industry as a moneymaking machine rather than a forum of artistic expression, and several bong hits.

Now I'm not advocating that you go out and get a medical marijuana card or develop a drug habit in order to get your creative mojo on, although Ernest Hemingway, Charles Bukowski, Edgar Allen Poe, Raymond Chandler, Ian Fleming, Oscar Wilde, and Hunter S. Thompson might have something to say on the matter. History is rife with writers who claim to have found inspiration at the bottom of a bottle.

But alcoholism aside, I believe that personal experience is essential when it comes to finding inspiration. You can sit inside your office or apartment or hotel room all day long with your muse, reading or watching the news and coming up with ideas, but nothing beats interacting with your environment and having new experiences to stimulate your creativity.

> "I shall live badly if I do not write, and I shall write badly if I do not live."
> — Françoise Sagan

A number of my earliest short stories were inspired by personal experiences or activities I witnessed first-hand: watching birds dive across street traffic, being stranded sixty miles south of the Mexican border, and repeatedly losing to my best friend while playing Nintendo video games. In addition, I wrote several stories that were inspired while traveling, including a Lovecraftian tale that takes place in a small English town in the Cotswolds and another story that takes place on an airplane while sitting in front of a little girl who kept chanting, "I win the game."

None of these events or experiences were horrific in and of themselves, but they inspired stories that became horrific or at least contained an element of horror.

So if you're looking for inspiration, get out of your comfort zone. Explore a different neighborhood. Go for a drive. Ride the bus. Spend the day at the beach or in the mountains or wandering around a small town or a big city. Eat at a new restaurant. Listen to people speak another language. Talk to a stranger. Do something, do anything that enriches and nourishes your mind and nurtures your creative soul. Then sit down and write about the experience and any tangential feelings or ideas it evokes.

Of course, finding inspiration and making good use of it are two entirely different processes. The former simply requires that you keep your eyes open and your ears tuned for the seeds of ideas, while the latter demands that you nourish your inspiration with the thoughtfulness and dedication that will help those ideas grow into short stories, novellas, and books.

This, of course, is where The Muse comes in.

The Greeks believed The Muses to be the source of the knowledge that gave birth to poetry, songs, and myths. They were the daughters of Zeus and divine in nature, which ties back to the whole divine aspect of inspiration. Although in modern day a muse can be a specific real-life person who inspires the writer, for the sake of argument and of this article we'll refer to The Muse as a creative entity we invoke for inspiration when we sit down to write.

The problem with invoking The Muse is that she's not an on-demand service. She requires devotion and appreciation. Expecting her to show up whenever you need her services is tantamount to treating her like an indentured servant who is required to do your bidding. You need to nurture your relationship with your muse, creating a regular, comfortable routine for her so that when she arrives, she's ready to get to work.

The best way to nourish this relationship is to set up a schedule. Set aside the same time each day to write, whether that's one hour, two hours, or fifteen minutes in the morning, afternoon, or evening. Sticking with a routine helps to cultivate creativity and The Muse thrives best in fertile, creative soil. Of course, the enemy of creativity is distraction, and distractions are an ever-growing problem for the modern day writer.

It used to be that The Muse only had to contend with simple distractions like pets and children and spouses, maybe a landline phone ringing or a solicitor knocking at the door or some mindless channel surfing on cable TV. Now with smartphones and laptops and tablets that provide constant access to streaming services and social networks and people who demand our attention from the other side of the country or halfway around the world, our muses have to deal with distractions that follow us no matter where we go.

Facebook and Twitter and Instagram.

Netflix and YouTube and Tinder.

Email and voicemail and text messages.

All of these conspire to distract us from our purpose, from putting pen to paper and words to screen. And expecting The Muse to serve as a source of creativity with all of these distractions is unrealistic. So we need to disconnect from our phones and apps and social networks in order to connect with our muse. The same way that answering your cell phone while you're out to dinner with a friend is like turning your back on that person, when you go on Facebook or check email while you're supposed to be spending time with your muse, you're ignoring her. And creative hell hath no fury like a muse scorned.

So silence your cell phone. Install internet access blocking software and apps like Freedom, Self Control, or Cold Turkey. Or take a break from your laptop or tablet and write in a journal the old-fashioned way to avoid the allure of technological distractions. This includes doing research. As much as you feel as though you need to find some relevant bit of information for your story to work, research distracts from your writing and inevitably leads you down a rabbit hole of websites and articles and, more than likely, the temptation of checking your email or your Facebook profile or the baseball scores on ESPN.

So during your scheduled time with your muse, remember that she is the only thing that matters. Everything else can wait. You can always check your email or do your research later when your muse's talents aren't required.

Likewise, when you sit down to work with your muse, you need to realize that she might not show up on time. That doesn't mean you can check your Twitter feed or stream videos on Amazon Prime while you're waiting. Sometimes you need to start doing the work before she makes an appearance. Your muse can be fickle and temperamental. When you make demands of your muse, she might just decide to have other plans. So treat your muse with respect, listen to her when she whispers ideas and phrases and characters in your ear, pay attention when she speaks to you, and you will be rewarded with words.

But just because your muse fills your head with ideas doesn't mean you should follow blindly along, chasing after every potential story or novel. You have to prioritize your projects and encourage your muse to lead you in the direction of your deadlines, be they external deadlines for a publisher or an anthology or your own personal goals. Leaving stories or novels unfinished to chase after bright shining objects leads to a collection of unfinished novels and stories. And there's nothing worse than a writer who never finishes what he or she started.

So rather than following your muse wherever she leads, you and your muse should have a symbiotic relationship, each of you working together for the mutual benefit of the other. Yes, this might sound weird considering that your muse is an imaginary being imbued with the gift of words by the ancient Greeks. But we're talking about the act of writing, which involves spending a lot of time alone creating imaginary stories about imaginary people.

Here are some additional tips on how to work with your muse so that you get the most out of the relationship:

- Make your muse feel welcome. Burn candles or incense if that's what she likes. Play classical music or death metal if that's what gets her creative juices flowing. The idea is to create the best possible environment for ideas and words to flourish.

- Praise your muse for her help. Give her credit for a job well done. Let her know that she's appreciated. A happy muse is a helpful muse.
- Don't chase after perfection. Muses aren't interested in perfection. They're interested in making messes. Let your muse make a mess. You can always clean it up later. That's what the editing process is for.
- Take your muse on a date. Go to the movies or take in a ballgame. Spend an afternoon at an art gallery. Have dinner at a new restaurant. Explore a local park. Learn another language or how to play a musical instrument. The more stimuli your muse gets, the more ideas she'll be able to provide.
- Give your muse a break. Expecting her to deliver for hours on end day after day and week after week will burn her out. Give her room to relax and reenergize.
- Avoid comparing your muse to other muses. Just because one writer is pumping out 3,000 words a day or another writer is publishing two novels a year doesn't mean your muse is any less helpful. She just works at her own pace.
- Finally, even when on a deadline, try to enjoy the creative journey. If you're only focused on the destination, your muse will likely abandon you. Or at the very least, she won't give you her full attention.

The Muse can be both a source of frustration as well as a source of inspiration. Knowing when to embrace her and when to back off and give her space is the key to keeping the relationship healthy. And like most relationships, you need to learn how to be respectful and accepting of your muse while encouraging positive interactions. While her job may be to inspire your creative endeavors, she's not your employee. She's your partner in crime. Or, in this case, horror. But she's there to inspire you so that you, in your own way, can inspire others, which brings us back to the third and fourth definitions of inspiration:

3 a) the quality or state of being inspired; b) something that is inspired

4 an inspiring agent or influence

Inspiration is contagious. When people become inspired by an idea, they can be compelled to take a leap toward something they wouldn't have otherwise considered, often creating their own ideas that inspire others. So when you're inspired to write a story or a novel—by an idea, a news article, or a book—others who read your story might, in turn, be inspired by your writing, either to read more of your writing, to read other books or stories similar to yours, or to write something themselves.

I don't know of any writer who hasn't read a story or novel that inspired them to take up the pen and pursue a hobby or a career or a lifetime of creating his or her own stories. I was inspired to follow my muse down the writing path after reading *The Talisman* by Stephen King and Peter Straub. While not my favorite book by either author, this was the first time I'd become so lost in the story unfolding on the pages that the world outside of the novel ceased to exist. And I enjoyed the feeling so much that I realized I wanted to make other people feel the same way.

It's a powerful and life-changing experience that can compel someone to spend every spare moment they can find sitting alone at a typewriter or in front of a computer while eschewing the company of friends and family. And then to have your own writing inspire someone else is like paying the muse forward, compelling others to follow their own writing path, and so on down the line. It's almost a form of writer procreation.

So go forth and create. And procreate. Find the inspiration for your own stories and inspire others to do the same. Your readers, and your muse, will be pleased.

STORYTELLING TECHNIQUES:

The Many Faces Of Horror

RICHARD THOMAS

W HEN IT COMES to telling scary stories there are
a number of ways to get under our skin, but it's never
an easy thing to do. When I talk to my students about
technique, there are three genres, or emotions, that I
think are the most difficult to do well—horror, humor,
and erotica. Why? Well, what scares one person, does
absolutely nothing for the next. The same goes for
humor—what makes you laugh, somebody else may
think is stupid. And as far as arousal and erotic
passages in fiction? Obviously we all have our own
unique turn-ons and turn-offs, not to mention the
wide range of fetishes out there. So how can you tell a
scary story with horror? Here are a few ideas.

1. Be Sincere

I think one of the best ways you can scare somebody is
to speak from the heart—write about the things that
scare you. In the horror class I taught at the University
of Iowa a few summers ago, I made each author sit
down and list off ten things that scared them. And then

I listed my own, as well. The range of phobias, personal experiences, broad, and specific fears was pretty compelling. There were creatures of course—spiders, snakes, wolves, and bears. And there were supernatural monsters, as well—demons, ghosts, and other mythic creatures. There were the various ways we can die—drowning, heights, fire, knives, guns, etc. And there were broader horrors—a fear of failure, a fear of being unimportant, a fear of your legacy being entirely forgotten. I personally have an issue with mirrors. So when it comes to writing horror, tap into your base fears, and your broader worries, as well. If it weren't for Jack Ketchum suggesting to me that I do this very thing, I never would have written my second novel, *Disintegration*. My greatest fear was to see my wife and kids killed in a car accident in front of me, and that's the inciting incident for that story—and then down the rabbit hole I went. It was a dark, unsettling, and upsetting journey that left me shaking, crying, and on the verge of vomiting when I finally finished writing it. But I left it all on the page, held nothing back. It was intense.

2. Speak with Authority

Another way that horror can really resonate is to speak from a place of authority. Whatever jobs you've had, use them to create an air of believability—whether you work in advertising, as a waiter, at a university, or in a morgue. Think of the places you've lived, as well. Where has Stephen King set so many of his stories? Maine, right? Castle Rock, Derry, and Jerusalem's Lot are fictional places, but they're very close to Bangor, where he lives, and Portland, where he was born. He writes about the places he has lived, and it comes through in his stories and novels. The same could be said about Benjamin Percy and the Pacific Northwest, a rural voice that truly resonates. I've set many stories and novels in my old apartment in the Bucktown/Wicker Park area of Chicago. That neighborhood is seared into my brain, and it comes through in my writing. And what about the tragedies in your life? Those moments can spill onto the page, as well—every accident you've seen, every time you've been hurt, every death that has seeped into your life. I often wonder if seeing a man parachute to his death at the base of the St. Louis Arch, as a child, was part of the reason I started writing horror. I can picture that moment in horrifyingly vivid details—from his shredded orange jumper, to the sheen of blood that spanned the leg of the metallic structure. It stays with you.

3. Consider Size and Scope

When it comes to horror I like to think of it in two terms—the broad, and the specific. The best stories to me are the ones that bleed off the page, that speak to universal truths, beyond the one moment captured in time. I think that's why so much of Lovecraft's work resonates with readers—we're talking about ancient horrors, and cosmic wonder, the unfurling of terror happening in grand, chaotic ways. But as powerful as those huge, expansive, overwhelming moments are, when you pair that with the specific, it adds depth, nuance, and personality. It's not just the creature—

furry, scaly, or covered in tentacles—that scares us, it's the myriad of horrible details we see as the camera closes in. It's the suckers on the tentacles, and the yellow tusks splitting the gaping maw; it's the bunch of eyes pushed into a pile atop its head; and it's the trail of viscous black liquid that trails behind it. These are usually the last things your protagonist, or secondary characters will see, before meeting their timely death. Make them worth showing.

4. Quiet Vs. Violent—Choose Your Moments

There has always been an air of violence to horror, it's hard to avoid. When there is a werewolf or a vampire on the page, as silver miner Daniel Plainview said, "There will be blood." So I want you to think about how you distribute your violence, and where you place your silence. Think about how most every horror film starts—it's the quiet before the storm, it's the safe neighborhood, the cabin in the woods surrounded by chirping birds and the rustle of leaves. And then something horrible happens, right? But we don't just keep hammering you with the violence (unless you're writing a slasher flick or Splatterpunk story). We need to allow the audience time to breathe, to relax between the horrors. Why? Well, so we can scare them again! So we make them think they are safe, when they are not. So we can go deeper, and darker with the next scene, the horrors just beginning. And if you want to write horror stories that avoid violence entirely? Is that possible? Sure it is. It can happen off the page, or it can happen in the past, or it can be told quickly as we move forward, into the psychological horrors that unfold afterward—the consequences, and damage done, the aftermath still resonating. There is a brilliant story in the most recent *Best Horror of the Year*, entitled "Hippocampus," by Adam Nevill. It is one hell of a slow burn that only shows a quiet sea-going vessel, and over time we are shown clues, bits and pieces (literally) of the horror that we THINK happened, the truth taking several pages to reveal itself. It's a masterful exercise in restraint, not the gunshot we hear, merely the echo after, the smell of gunpowder in the air. What's the line in the opening to Will Christopher Baer's *Kiss Me, Judas*? "I must be dead for there is nothing but blue snow and the furious silence of a gunshot." Use both to great effect—in doses, large and small.

5. Get Us to Care About Your Characters

It's essential in every story you tell, but I think especially so in horror. If you are going to tell us a long, complicated story—an epic tale—across cities, highways, and lost continents, over mountains, rivers and barren wastelands—and then torture, maim, and destroy your main characters—we have to care, or none of it matters. When those horror films are starting up, in addition to that quiet before the storm, what else are they doing? They're showing us the happy couple, the domestic family setting, the group of friends—and everything they're doing is to establish the relationships, and get us to care. You have to build it up before you tear it down. Think of how we care about Jake in The Dark Tower series (especially in *The Gunslinger*, the first book in the series). Think about how we need to get to know Danny Torrance in *The Shining*. Even in a literary story like *Of Mice and Men*, how we see Lennie, and the horrors that slowly happen over time—accidents, and then on purpose. And on the opposite end of the spectrum, if you want us to HATE somebody, we have to care first, right? We have to feel something. The opposite of love is not hate; they are actually related, close together. In order to hate, you really have to love first, have strong feelings about a person, place, or thing. The opposite of love is apathy— a lack of caring. So for your bad guys, we need to feel strong emotions, as well. Before you can inflict the horror, we have to care about your characters, and deeply. And that takes time—a sentence, a paragraph, a page, a scene, or an entire novel.

6. Innovate

When telling horror stories, think of ways that you can be fresh, different, and unique. Sure, there are expectations of the genre, and if you don't get certain things (thrills, chills and spills, right?) then you won't be satisfied. If you go out to buy a cheeseburger, you want the meat, and cheese, and toppings. You don't want a handful of rice or a bowl of fruit. But when it comes to burgers there is a wide range—from fast food to the local diner to the bistro to the gourmet restaurant (complete with a fried egg on top). So while you still need to fulfill the promises of your story, if you're calling it horror, look for ways to take old, tired formulas, settings, creatures, and plots and do something new with them. See the aforementioned story by Adam Nevill. Look at how Sara Gran has a new take on possession with *Come Closer* (the same being said for Paul Tremblay and *A Head Full of Ghosts*). Look at Ben Percy with *Red Moon*. I think of the constantly unique stories by Stephen Graham Jones, Brian Evenson, Livia Llewellyn, and Seanan McGuire. If you're going to write werewolves and vampires, bring something new to the page. Even better, find a new monster, a new mythology, something we haven't seen before—maybe a Barghest, an Abaddon, or a Jorogumo, instead. Likewise, we see so much Greco-Roman mythology—why not Aztec, Mayan, African, Japanese, or Australian? Do some research, or make up something entirely new, all your own. This can also apply to how you cast your story (against sex or type), the location (please, no more standard haunted houses or asylums), or the structure (first person plural or epistolary maybe). Just find a way to do something new.

7. Leave Room for Your Readers

I was talking to Stephen Graham Jones in one of my classes a few weeks ago about his story, "Father, Son, Holy Rabbit" (which I reprinted in *The New Black*) and how much detail he puts into describing his characters, and we realized that he didn't really show the father and son all that much. Which, in many ways, is pretty amazing. He said he always pictures his characters as a Native American Indian, because that's what he is (Blackfoot) and how he sees them, but he doesn't go to great lengths to pencil in all of those details. So, what this does, is leave room for the readers to insert themselves into the narrative, or, to paint a picture with characters they can relate to, and see. So when sketching in the framework of a haunted forest, or when describing your protagonist, don't feel that you have to give us every single detail. Let the character of your protagonist shine through in their actions. Sure, you may mention their shirt or boots as they appear—kicking in a door, or cutting off a hunk of fabric to make a tourniquet—but focus more on how we feel, what the main character is doing (internal and external conflict) so that we can care about them (see the aforementioned technique), and then root for or against the people in your stories. I'm all for sensory detail, I love heavy setting, and places where you feel like you are actually there, immersed in the place and time, but find a way to sketch in the details while leaving room for your audience, and they'll empathize and sympathize in ways you might not anticipate.

8. Tap into The Psychological

Beyond the visceral horror of dark stories, I think what really gets under my skin more than the unfurling of some violent moment, or the scene where the bad thing catches up to the good guys, is the way that I can be mentally manipulated—psychological horror and dark fiction is the kind of writing that truly stays with me. While I certainly have an appreciation for a film like *The Texas Chainsaw Massacre*, the moments that really got to me were the quieter sections where we panned across the living room or basement, where we came to a conclusion about what is really happening here, the horrific details adding up, and the kind of mind that must be behind these atrocities—that's what bothered me the most. It's the subtle way that Sara Gran shows us possession and a mind that is slipping in the aforementioned *Come Closer*. It's the way that we are manipulated in the doppelganger flick, *Enemy*, with Jake Gyllenhaal. It's the mental and emotional battle that the biologist goes through in Jeff VanderMeer's brilliant novel, *Annihilation*. When I look at the stories that I've accepted at *Gamut*, or that I took in the past at Dark House Press, I'm willing to bet that there was a psychological component in just about every story I said yes to—manipulated by the author, my feelings and emotions bubbling up to the surface, my mind straining to grasp the truth (that can't be what's really going on here, can it?), the conclusion and understanding a powerful epiphany that can inspire as well as depress. Make us feel something—the human condition is what we find most compelling under all of the violence, gore, and suspense. Without that depth (mental, physical, and emotional) your story can only take us so far.

9. Let Atmosphere Help You on Your Journey

I think I've said before that I'm a huge fan of putting sensory detail in my writing—heavy setting and atmosphere. And while that's important in just about every genre, in my opinion, it's especially so in horror. Think of every haunted house, asylum, forest, basement, barren wasteland, and circle of hell you've read about—what do they all have in common? If done right, the atmosphere will add another layer to your story, putting you in the moment, no way to escape, the response almost something primal. It's not just using all five senses—sight the most common, with sound and smell right behind it, touch and taste used less often. Definitely do that when it's appropriate. If you're cooking a grand meal, I better smell the roast, the garlic, the spices and sauces that fill the room. If you're in an alley in the hot Arizona heat, it better be horrible—spoiled meat, sour milk, acrid urine, and rotting vegetation. But above and beyond that, the atmosphere you create needs to be unpacked in places where it matters and dialed back where it doesn't. If you're traveling across country, while I definitely want to see what's out the window, what may be more important is the discussion in the car—especially if one of the characters is held captive. It's when you stop for the night, and the fire is flickering in the darkness, and the sounds of the nightlife fill in around us—slow down for that. Show us this place and time, and allow us to sit in that tension, or peace, as you give us hints of what's coming—nature closing in, magic and darkness playing out in surprising ways, your savior just over the next hill, perhaps.

10. Use Theme and Symbolism to Hint at The Big Picture

I talk a lot about Freytag's Pyramid (or Triangle) in my classes, and those are certainly essential elements to telling any story, but another key component that is especially important to horror is the development of a theme, and the use of symbolism in your writing. You can look at the use of food and hunger in Alyssa Wong's Nebula-winning story, "Hungry Daughters of

Starving Mothers" for instance. So much of that story is viewed through a lens of hunger and desire, as well as that appetite for destruction. I can think of the color blue in Kate Braverman's literary story, "Tall Tales from the Mekong Delta," and how it represents sadness and depression, a trigger for her addiction, and mental state. I recently read a story by one of my students where she used the idea of disease, destruction, and rot to show how the world of her protagonist was falling apart, the psychological damage that was unfolding, and the actual setting in the real world. I did similar things in my novel, *Disintegration*, showing how everything was less than it had been—no mirrors, no contact with the outside world, no name for the protagonist, fugue states, an unreliable narrator, and a slippery reality. Stephen King says, about the Dark Tower series, "All things serve the beam," and that can be applied to your story here as well, in relation to the plot, and the theme (or themes) you are using to support it, the symbolism that appears out every window, in every cup of soup, in the sounds of the forest all around us. Be subtle, and it'll help your readers to figure out what's going on, a trail of bread crumbs leading up to the truth.

In Conclusion

The techniques you use to tell your horror stories are very personal—so take my advice on whatever works for you, and ignore the rest. We all have our own unique ways of creating, of building worlds, of course. We have developed our voices through the influence of those that came before us, those that shape and inform us now, and the ways we want to be seen, heard, and recognized. As we weave these dark tales of loss, suffering, and terror we seek to be a part of the landscape of horror and dark fiction, and while it's important to know what came before us, to honor and then innovate, our voices are the unique amalgamation of the universal truths we have seen and come to understand, paired with our own unique perspectives. There is only one of you (as far as YOU know), so what you put on the page needs to show that special mix of good and bad, lost and found, fear and hope, darkness and light that only you can tell. That moment in the woods when the glowing orbs darted around the trees, leaving burn marks on the bark? Nobody else was there. That conversation with God, or a ghost, or a flickering faerie in the garden—only you were there. The accident you saw, the fight you were in, the dark nights that spilled across your apartment as you contemplated your own demise—those emotions are yours, and only yours. So tap into the darkness, put it on the page, and exorcise your demons. We don't mind. In fact, we'll pull up a seat, and bear witness to your suffering. May there be a cleansing in your absolution.

HORROR IS A STATE OF MIND

TIM WAGGONER

ONE OF THE biggest mistakes beginning horror writers make is to write their stories from the outside in. What I mean by this is first they develop the Dark Thing—the person, entity, place, or situation—that will serve as the primary conflict for their tale, then they try to create a character who will encounter the Dark Thing and be horrified by it (and probably munched or sliced and diced by it as well). And what the character experiences—the actual horror—comes last. But you're writing a horror story, right? The horror should come first. Your story should grow from the twisted seed of horror, and the best way to make this happen is to understand that horror arises from consciousness. Horror is an emotion, a reaction to something that violates our sense of what we believe to be our normal and (mostly) safe reality. In other words, horror begins inside a character's head. The story isn't about what happens. It's about what a character perceives to be happening, and how that perception impacts the character. What follows are some techniques to help you create effective inside-out horror.

Know Your Character

You don't have to create full-fledged biographies for your characters, although you certainly can if you find that helpful. Since horror stories are reaction stories, you need to know how your character responds to stress, to threats, to the nightmarish and unreal. For example, a character like Shaggy in the *Scooby Doo* cartoons will react much differently to a shadowy figure approaching him in a graveyard than a character like Sherlock Holmes would. Shaggy is nervous and scared much of the time. He'd already be frightened simply by being in a graveyard even before the shadowy figure appeared. And when that stranger started coming toward him, he would absolutely lose his shit, shriek, and run like hell. Holmes, on the other, is the epitome of controlled intellect. He would feel nothing, except perhaps a certain wariness. As the stranger approached him, he'd be busy taking in details about this person and beginning to formulate theories. So knowing how your particular character will react to the Dark Thing in your story is the first—and most important—quality about them that you need to know. Will your character freeze? Scream? Run? Deny its existence? Seek to confront it, either from bravery or from a moth-like attraction to its dark flame? Will the character seek the aid of others or go it alone? Will the character doubt his or her sanity? Once you know the answer to these kind of questions, once you know how your character will react, then you'll be able to more effectively plot your story.

See Through Your Character's Eyes

Ask yourself what sort of details your character would pay attention to in a particular scene. In the graveyard, Shaggy's attention would be drawn to details that heighten the fear he already feels—a spooky owl hoot, a cold gust of wind, a leafless tree whose branches look like a multitude of grasping hands . . . And don't just focus on external details. What's happening inside your character, both mentally and physically? What is your character conscious of inside themselves? A chill rippling down the spine? A watery feeling in the bowels? A flashback to a similar event? An almost psychic sense of baleful power gathering? These are the sort of details that horror stories are built from.

Hello Darkness, My Old Friend

Horror is strongest when characters have a connection to whatever Dark Thing plagues them. This is most obvious with ghost stories, where the haunting often has a link to a character's past—a person they lost (or killed), a place that's important to them, etc. But a character's consciousness can be fertile ground for creating a deeper, more psychologically impactful Dark Thing. For example, Pennywise in Stephen King's It is the archetypal scary clown, a sinister figure that frightens the story's child protagonists. But when they're adults, they see what lies behind the clown and they see it's something they can fight. Pennywise is a manifestation of a child's consciousness, but what lies behind the mask of Pennywise is a manifestation of adult consciousness—problems are real, and while they may be dangerous, they can be fought. In "The Monkey's Paw" by W.W. Jacobs, the couple in the story are grieving for their dead son, and more than anything they wish for him to be returned to them. But when that wish is granted, their son isn't the same as they remember. One parent hopes, one fears, and the resurrected son is the manifestation of their two minds, in a symbolic if not literal sense. The unnamed narrator in Edgar Allan Poe's "The Tell-Tale Heart" suffers from what he claims is an over-acuteness of the senses. So what bedevils him in the story? A sound— the pounding heartbeat of the old man he killed. In the film *The Babadook*, the monster is—perhaps literally— a manifestation of the main character's conflicted feelings about motherhood. The Babadook is a creepy figure from a children's book, representing how something that should be innocent (such as a child) is an actuality threatening. So think about your characters' deepest fears and desires, ones so deep even they might not be aware of them, and use them to create the darkest of Dark Things for them to contend with.

Bad Places

A character's consciousness can also shape your story's setting. Earlier, I suggested using a character's consciousness as a focus, or perhaps filter, for selecting descriptive details. But you can take this principle even further and blend the character's consciousness with the setting. In other words, the character's inner world is the outer world—in a symbolic sense at least. Is your character gripped with paranoia? Then portray the setting as covertly observing and plotting against your character. Every eye—human, animal, real or manufactured (a doll, a statue, a photograph)—is trained upon your character. Every sound—a voice, a baby's gurgle, a gust of wind, a dog's whine—is part of a secret conversation about your character. Every traffic light that turns red before the character can drive through an intersection, every empty ketchup dispenser at a fast-food joint is part of the conspiracy against your character. If you have another character, one filled with restless energy, the hum of an air-conditioning system, the vibrations in the concrete sidewalk as a city bus rumbles by, a too-loud, too-fast pop song on the radio . . . all of these details reflect and magnify the character's inner state.

This technique allows you to develop a setting that stylistically fits the story you're trying to tell, while intensifying the emotional aspect of your character. It also instills a stronger sense of that emotional state in your reader. All good fiction can use this technique to enhance setting, of course, but it's especially effective in horror, which—even if it's based in reality—should feel nightmarish to readers. Perhaps the ultimate example of this technique is Ambrose Bierce's "An Occurrence at Owl Creek Bridge," which literally merges the character's inner and outer worlds.

(I don't want to give away the ending to this classic story by saying anything more. If you haven't read it, do so ASAP, and you'll understand what I mean when I say almost every aspect of the story arises from the character's consciousness.)

I've already mentioned "The Tell-Tale Heart," but it's worth revisiting the story because it's a perfect example of how a character's consciousness is an effective filter for telling a story, and it shows how awareness of this filter can affect all the narrative elements: character, setting, description, conflict, and plot. It's a master class in using consciousness in fiction (and just as with "An Occurrence at Owl Creek Bridge," if you haven't read "The Tell-Tale Heart," do so before proceeding further).

The narrator in "The Tell-Tale Heart" is revealed to us as a consciousness that possesses several important qualities: an over-acuteness of the senses (which the narrator believes is his main problem), an obsessive nature, the ability to meticulously plan, and a need to be viewed by others (in this case, readers) as sane. There is nothing else to this character. The narrator *is* his consciousness.

The setting for the story is presented to readers through the filter of the character's consciousness. Readers get only the details of the setting that matter to the character: the house and the old man's room where the murder is committed. Using the filter of consciousness allowed Poe to decide which details of the setting, and how much of them, to present to his readers. The narrator is obsessed with his or her perceptions and emotions—his internal world—so the outer world receives little attention. The narrator's consciousness is the real setting.

The description flows from three of the narrator's main attributes: heightened senses, obsessiveness, and a need for meticulous planning. The first part of the story presents details focused on the character's almost inhuman sight and hearing, as well as describing in depth the object of his or her obsession:

the old man's eye. The second part of the story provides details drawn from the narrator's need to plan, with the narrator showing us the steps he takes in order to conceal the murder and then the steps he takes to make the police believe nothing untoward has occurred. And in the end, the story returns to providing details from the narrator's senses, this time his uncanny hearing, as the narrator believes the old man's heart has begun to beat again.

The conflict in the story derives from the narrator's discomfort with his highly acute senses and propensity for obsessiveness. The narrator might be obsessed with any number of things, leading to any number of actions. But the old man's eye—an overlarge sensory organ—mirrors the narrator's heightened senses. Symbolically, the narrator seeks to destroy his own hated senses by killing the old man. For a time, it seems to work. The narrator is relaxed and calm as he goes about dismembering the old man's body and concealing it, and the narrator is unworried when speaking to the police. But then the main conflict—the narrator's senses—returns to plague him, leading to the story's climax.

The narrator's consciousness plays a huge role in determining both the plot and structure of the story. By this point, I think it's obvious how the narrator's personality shapes the events of the story: the obsession, the murder, the concealment, the confrontation with the police, and the confession (in which the narrator hopes to end the horrible sound tormenting him or her). But the character's consciousness also guided Poe in making a number of other narrative choices. First person is the perfect point of view for this story. Readers are given direct access to the narrator's distorted consciousness, which is where the real horror in the tale is found. The narrator tells us at the beginning of the story that his motivation for relating these events to us is to prove that he's sane. How could a madman have carried out such a meticulous plan? Poe has the narrator tell us the events of the murder and attempted concealment in detail, while all the time asking us to judge him as sane. I've already spoken of how the narrator's heightened senses appear at the beginning, get worse as his obsession grows, seem to quiet after the murder, only to return in full force at the end. This provides the structural underpinning of the story. And at the end of the story, the narrator loses control of his emotions—and the narrative itself—and cries out for the horrible heart to be silenced, providing the climax. There is no more to the tale. The narrator has struggled to hold onto sanity throughout the story only to lose his battle in the end.

So the next time you belly up to your computer to work on a story, don't just write about characters. Get into their heads and take a good look around. Use their consciousness as the lens through which to view your story, and you'll create tales of dread and terror beyond your most fevered imaginings—and readers will love you for it.

BRINGING AN IDEA TO LIFE THROUGH LANGUAGE

MERCEDES M. YARDLEY

ONCE UPON A TIME there was a girl, and she was dead.

Perhaps that isn't quite right.

In a land far, far away, there was a dead girl.

Maybe that isn't quite right, either.

There was a girl. She had been alive once, a beautiful thing with starry eyes and deep dimples, but that was before A Great Something happened. This Great Something was swift and it was sure, and now the shiny girl had become something else entirely. She had become a dimpled corpse.

I find it deliciously ironic that I'm writing an article about bringing stories to life when my livelihood depends on killing literary characters. Death of those we love, especially the innocent, is something that's gripping, horrifying and yet strangely beautiful all at once. That's my particular niche: rich language and lush beauty. What is one way to bring an idea to life? Why, through language, of course!

We learn language from the time we're very young, and quite often we aren't even conscious of it. We know the words that get us what we want. If we want milk, we ask for milk. If we want to sit on granddaddy's shoulders, we ask to be lifted up. If we want to learn about a boat, we ask about a boat. This is all well and good when we're small. Keep it simple. Use the language for its basic use. There are few frills and certainly no bells and whistles.

But when we become older? Ah! We learn so much more, and words become our playground. For example, perhaps you want to learn more about that boat.

"Tell me about a boat," you say.

"Which boat?" I ask.

"The red boat."

So perhaps I tell you of the little red boat's history, where it was built and by who. Maybe we discuss the sails and wood and all the wonderful things that created this boat. It is a small red boat. It has had many wonderful adventures.

"No, not this red boat. Tell me about a ship."

A ship is different than a boat. So now I know that you don't want to hear about Cousin Lucky's Little Red Boat. You want to hear about a ship, which is bigger and grander. Shall we discuss steel? Are you interested in how steam engines work? What about the way the ocean parts to let the ship through? The ocean is a sentient thing, you see, and it wants so badly to get out of the way so this ship can continue its exciting travels. Perhaps it carries ore or food or coal or any number of useful things.

"I'd really like to hear about a grand ship," you tell me, and again, your words guide me in a different direction. A grand ship doesn't carry things as much as it carries people. It is full of lights and electricity and perhaps places to swim. Isn't swimming on a ship luxurious? There are shows where artists show their work and musicians play for the crowds. Do the passengers dress up? Do they wear finery? What are they drinking out of? Do they sip or swill from fine fluted glasses or directly from the bottle? What merriment do they experience? There are all sorts of things on a fine, grand ship.

"Please tell me about the Titanic," you say softly, and now my face falls. It was a big boat, even a grand ship, but when I think of it, I'm not thinking of dance halls and the ladies in fine hats. I'm thinking of human beings floundering in the ocean, being pulled beneath by their beautiful, heavy skirts. I think of mothers watching their children struggle in the water and fathers screaming up and down the hallways for their families. The story I tell you will be a very different one than when you originally asked me, "Tell me about a boat."

The power of language is an astronomical thing. We have refined it to a science. Each beautiful word has a precise meaning. Some words are lovely and make you feel at ease. Daisy. Comfort. Kitten. Some words conjure up feelings of loss. Widower. Bereft. Casket. Some words are charged and make you attentive simply by reading them. Abortion. Political. Street fight.

Words are everywhere. We're constantly surrounded by them, simply awash in them. They patter over us like rain, they soothe us like the sea, they slam into us like verbal bullets. How have you used your words? Have you ever used them to calm somebody? "I love you, you'll be all right, I'm here for you, we'll get through this." Have you ever used them to cut? Sharpened them just right to spill the most blood? "I'm ashamed of you, you're disgusting, your work is worthless, he's not even your child." The power behind a well-placed word is dizzying. You realize this because you've spent time searching for the right words or phrases yourself. How do you talk to a dear friend about his self-destructive behavior? How do you word that email to your mother just right? How do you approach your boss without getting fired? This is nothing new to this. We do it every day. So why aren't we using our language in our writing?

We should be. The way we speak and communicate is part of who we are. The way we wield our words like weapons or offer them gently says so much about us. They reflect the different parts of our personalities. Human beings are deliciously multifaceted. Do you perhaps behave differently at work than you do at home? How does your language reflect this?

"I'll get it to you right away," you say respectfully to your boss.

"Timothy, can you please get that as soon as possible?" you ask your secretary politely. (You'd better be asking him politely. Don't be THAT GUY who doesn't.)

"Love you," you say to your wife as you kiss her.

"Way to go, buddy!" you yell to your kiddo as you play catch.

"Window Cobblepot, Prince of Barkness, you get back here!" you screech at your dog as he rips his leash out of your hand and runs away.

(This was the name of my dog, and yes, it was a mouthful. But compared to our bunny Sir Reginald

Bunnington the III, of the Cottontail Bunningtons, or our cat Taco Truck Van Fuzzlebottom, I'd say Window was pretty lucky.)

Different words for different situations. Different words for different people. We call them different names, address them in different ways. Perhaps you wouldn't call your boss "Darling," or your wife "Buddy" or your father "Hey, you," or "Dudebro." Then again, perhaps you would. Different strokes for different folks.

But these words, these terms, quickly and easily demonstrate not only who you are and what your role is, but they introduce you as a writer. Different writers have different voices. They use the same letters of the alphabet, jumble them up, and come up with something completely unique. "This is me," their prose says. "Do you see how I am? See how easily I show you?"

Think of James Ellroy. Pick up one of his books, especially his later works, and you can tell you're reading an Ellroy book without even looking at his name on the cover. How can this be? It's because his writing style is terribly distinctive. His prose rings out like machine gun fire. Rata-tat-tat. His sentences are short. He eliminates connectives. His prose is quick. It's fierce. It flows. It's terse. Your heart beats fast. It will scare you. Time is short. His sentences are shorter.

The way he crafts his words makes your blood run quicker. It's like reading something that is sweeping you down the river, faster and faster, without a break. The intensity is nearly overwhelming. It's beautifully effective and quickly distinguishes him from fellow authors.

Then again, imagine that you're rolly-pollying in the splendiferous world of Roald Dahl! Oh, the magic! The charm and whimsy! You're in a book where poverty-stricken, poorly-treated children see gloriumptious things like chocolate factories, taste snozzberries (which are so much better than snozzcumbers), and run from vermicious knids. What wild and fanciful language! They're jumbly, to be sure, but they're absolutely whoopsy whiffling at the same time.

Here are two examples of language utilized by two very different authors, but they do the same thing: they let you know who that author is. They tell the story by the way they sound as well as the picture they paint. Did you feel the heart-pounding urgency in Ellroy's work? Pick up *The Black Dahlia* or *White Jazz* and read it. Did you feel the tumbling joy and fancy from Dahl's language? You'll find that in *Charlie and the Chocolate Factory* or my favorite, *The BFG*.

The language is characteristic of these two writers, but does that mean that a writer always stays with one voice? Absolutely not. Write with the words that fit the story. See what language shines through. Experiment and see what fits.

I tend to have two separate voices. If I'm writing something poetic and rich with language, like *Pretty Little Dead Girls: A Novel of Murder and Whimsy*, then I choose to use a lusher language. It fits the characters. It tends to be a little more Neil Gaiman-esque, if I'm going to make a comparison. I choose fanciful words that fit the protagonist and situation. These are words like "exquisite," or "diamonding," or "broken" and "fallen." It's a chance to be more verbose, which I adore. I use the words that are deep in my heart but sometimes I don't unleash in everyday conversation lest the cashier at the grocery store looks at me askance.

I hate when people look at me askance.

When writing *Nameless: The Darkness Comes*, the point of view is from a rather prickly girl who would rather cut off her fingers than use the word "exquisite." She has a knife in her boot and yells at people, calling them "freaks" and "weirdos." The flowery language doesn't fit her at all. It isn't her personality. If I tried to use the same voice to write her as I used in the other novel, it would be a massive failure.

So how do you decide which voice to use in your work? If we're singing the praises of language, how do we make sure we're using the correct language? It's quite simple, actually. You let your characters tell you.

That's all. These are your characters, your creations. What do they say? How do they speak? If he's in the military, what language does he use? Is he strict? Does he get off on military lingo? Does he speak poetically? Is he mute? Does he cuss every time he opens his mouth? Does he call people by their correct names, or by nicknames he makes up on the spot?

If you're still getting to know your character, a great exercise is to fill out a sheet of paper that says, "This character is the kind of person who . . . "

This character is the kind of person who says to a woman, "Let's get you out of those wet things," when her clothes are completely dry.

This character is the kind of person who closes his eyes before walking into a crowded room.

This character is the kind of person who cleans her gun every night before going to sleep.

Now that you're familiar with the character, you'll be able to see how he or she speaks. Write up a conversation between them and somebody else. Even better, write a conversation between them and you.

Your character walks in, sees you sitting at your computer and says . . . what? Does he comment on your hair? Demand a bigger part in your novels? Does she help you hang a shelf? Petulantly ask why you don't have anything good in the fridge?

Do they mock you? I mean, come on. Do they really? You're their creator. Do they push back? Accept it? Tell you they aren't into the romantic lead you gave them?

What words do they use? Your female character thinks you're lazy and don't give her enough interesting things to do. What name does she call you by?

Your male character thinks, but won't say aloud, that you remind him of his abusive parent. How does he convey that?

They'll tell you what they want to say and how they want to say it. This, in turn, will guide you on what language to use when you create your voice.

Pick your favorite words, ones that you use in conversation. Use the ones that you squirrel away for special occasions. Let them fall from your mouth like pearls, because they are, indeed, that precious. Nobody speaks exactly like you. Nobody writes exactly like you. The key is to peel the top layer from your own personal vernacular and let the real you, the guts and brains of the author, all of those tricky red parts, spill out onto the page. By being your true self and using the linguistic tics and tricks that you, yourself, use, you'll not only personalize your work, but you'll bring the characters and situations to life in a way that nobody else can.

THE PROCESS OF A TALE

RAMSEY CAMPBELL

IDEAS FOR TALES come easily to me, and the hard work follows. Very occasionally a tale has virtually told itself, but almost always the process is effortful and prolonged—intermittent, even. I'm going to take a story of mine—"Holding the Light," first published in 2011—and examine the process in detail.

Some ideas leap out of a situation, and this was one such case. While holidaying on Rhodes, my wife and I took a guided tour around the island. One stop was Efta Piges, an irrigation system constructed during the Italian occupation, and venturesome tourists were offered the experience of walking through an underground tunnel several hundred yards long in darkness unrelieved except by a central shaft. I'd experienced absolute darkness once before, in 1967 during a tour of caves, an experience that gave me the basis of "The End of a Summer's Day" (1968). The Efta Piges visit could hardly have been more opportune, since the splendid Pete Crowther of PS Publishing had asked me to write a story to be released as a Halloween chapbook. I always carry notebooks, though my phone increasingly does duty as one. I believe I started making notes pretty well as soon as I left the tunnel, and here they are:

> *Efta Piges tunnel*
> *—boyhood dare?*
> *when you meet someone coming other*
> *way, sometimes human*
> *when not, you realise they aren't stooping*
> *although you have to*
> *you touch top of a head, which moves*
> *altogether too readily for a cranium*
> *Halloween dare (other Halloween*
> *traditions having been done away with*
> *locally)*
> *you must go all the way through, turn and*
> *come back*
> *suspicion friends have crossed above*
> *ground and are lurking at your back*
> *their whispers at your back—then you*
> *realise it's down shaft from hatch*

I believe I scribbled all this down in just a few minutes. It includes good developments, some of which made their way into the tale, but it's also typical of this phase of the proceedings: a few glimpses of narrative awaiting characters to give them shape or alter them. (Alongside writing the present essay I'm starting to develop a new novel, which reminds me how much these early stages feel like limbo, where I grope through a colourless region of my mind in search of hints of the characters.) The next two notebook pages are devoted to ideas for other work, and then I returned to this tale:

> *weeds underfoot and on walls*
> *you trip, fall headlong*
> *hear someone running towards you in*

pitch dark—sound of wet objects slapping walls—they squelch
whatever you fall on slithers away
staying with cousin?
you take turns to shine flashlight down inspection shaft for others to see
—he calls up something—then flurry below—you have to go down—eventually suspect he said that light was "keeping it away"

I'd also been commissioned to write a tale in tribute to Ray Bradbury, and notes for this and other passing notions intervene. I'd done the Bradbury tribute ("The Page") before I returned to the tale under discussion, eleven notebook pages later. In a bid to grasp the characters I named them Joe and Russell.

cousins living close?
Joe the only one Russell's parents trust?
adolescent—too old for Halloween games—say they're going to film?
parents told Joe to stay away from tunnel—someone killed himself there—must have fallen down shaft or hanged himself there
BEYOND THE LIGHT
HOLDING THE LIGHT
suicide pact, or one died and then other followed out of teenage grief
suicides: sex before steady relationship, mixed up with drugs
flashlight falls down shaft—Joe thinks it's thrown to him?

By this stage I'm circling with red ink notes I plan to use, which doesn't always mean they're used. Despite its red mark, the next one appears to have fallen by the narrative wayside:

denizens of tunnel object to anyone else? or trying to make them join them? or conveying their own terror at dark they have to stay in

A good deal of my method is instinctive, particularly when I come to actually telling the tale. Even ideas that looked promising in note form may fail to find a context (though some have shown up in a different tale). In the case of this idea, perhaps my instincts told me that I was concentrating too much on spectral motivation, insufficiently on the living characters. I haven't plotted in advance for many years, preferring to gather material until I feel I have enough to energise the story. There are fifteen more pages of notes.

I try out an opening—*They were too old for ducking apples—They had been for years*—that ultimately finds no home. Since Russell has been bullied at school, Joe is delegated to take care of him despite thinking his cousin has provoked the treatment. By now I'm sending them to a Halloween show at the cinema. There they encounter girls Joe knows from school, but Russell puts them off, not least by refusing to go to a film rated as suitable for viewers older than he is. I'm starting to grasp the nature of the central duo and in particular of their relationship— therefore, why they act as they do. More thoughts pass without finding a place in the narrative—*"Don't see anything depressing,"* one of Joe's parents' counsels—

and here's a second stab at an opening: *As Joe followed his cousin into the lobby of the Frugoplex he saw two girls he knew. They were giggling at costumes, and so he laughed as well.* By the time I've built up six pages of this more concentrated set of notes I've started writing the actual story, and most of the subsequent notes relate to specific passages about to be written. Oddly, the characters retain the names they started with until the very end of the notes, where Russell becomes Donald and Joe turns into Tom. Nothing is fixed, we'll find.

I never sit down to write until I've composed at least the first sentence of the session in my head or noted down a version. I'm at work by six every morning—Christmas and my birthday too. When I'm working on a first draft I'll never take a day off. I once waited to continue work on a story until I felt inspired, only to burden myself with a writer's block that lasted six months. Once the first draft is done I may avoid rereading it for months, and then comes the rewrite. All the same, do be aware that I mean none of this prescriptively. My method may not work for you. Other writers have other methods, and you should find the one that's best for you, perhaps by trial and error.

The first draft of "Holding the Light" begins thus:

As his cousin followed him into the Frugoplex lobby, Joe saw two girls from school. Out of uniform and in startlingly short skirts they looked several years older, and he hoped his leather jacket had performed that trick for him. They were giggling at the cinema staff, who were dressed as witches or Halloween characters, and so he made sure

*the girls saw him laugh. "Hey, Lezly," he said
in his deepest voice. "Hey, Dianne."*

For the record, that's handwritten, like virtually all
the first drafts of my fiction. When I reread them I tend
to grow dissatisfied but generally fall short of
identifying exactly where improvements should be
made. In this case I made just a couple:

*As his cousin followed him into the
Frugoplex lobby Tom saw two girls from
school. Out of uniform and in startlingly short
skirts they looked several years older. He
hoped his leather jacket performed that trick
for him, in contrast to the duffle coat Lucas
was wearing. Since the girls were giggling at
the cinema staff dressed as Halloween
characters, he let them see him laugh too.
"Hey, Lezly," he said in his deepest voice. "Hey,
Dianne."*

Early in my career I approached revisions with a
view to keeping as much of the first draft as I could. At
some stage I graduated to challenging that draft to
justify every aspect of itself and to refining or deleting
all the prose I felt deserved it. That's the spirit in which
I rewrite onto the computer now. The girls propose
watching *Cheerleads with Guts*, but Lucas protests
loudly that nobody under fifteen is allowed in. In
previous years the boys' parents have sent them out to
play Halloween games, where his cousin's clumsiness
has embarrassed Joe (Tom). Now Lucas proposes they
and the girls visit nearby Grinfields, where a teenage
couple killed themselves. Dianne is prompted to ask

"Why do you want us to go there, Russ?"

"Who's Russ?"

"I told you," Joe said in some desperation, "he's like that."

"No I'm not, I'm like Russell."

At times such as this Joe felt he understood all too well why his cousin was bullied at school. There was also Russell's habit of staring at anybody unfamiliar as if he expected them to wait until he'd made up his mind about them. Joe couldn't imagine this had endeared his cousin to the girls, and there was Russell's pasty face too, far spottier than his and topped with unruly red hair. Nevertheless Dianne seemed about to speak until her friend said "Come on whoever's coming. I don't want to miss any of my film."

"Are you sure you don't want to see it?" Dianne said.

She was speaking to Joe, but his cousin responded. "We can't. We've been told."

"I haven't," Joe muttered, which was no kind of compensation. He watched the girls join the queue at the ticket desk manned by a tastefully drooling vampire in a cloak, and then he turned on Russell. "Let's go, since you've put them off."

He let Russell wander towards the queue full of chattering children before he said "Not there. We aren't going to the kids' film."

The declaration was intended mostly for the girls, but he didn't think they heard. "Which one, then?" Russell complained.

"None of them. We'll go where you wanted." Joe made for the exit as spilled popcorn squeaked beneath his feet, and then he swung around, not only to ensure Russell was trailing after him. "We need to switch our phones off," he said.

Russell's frown creased his pudgy forehead. "Why?"

"We're in the cinema."

Accuracy mattered most to Lucas, and he did as he was told. Joe was only making certain that their parents thought they were in the Frugoplex and couldn't interrupt their adventure. He deadened his mobile, and as soon as Russell pocketed his, Joe led the way out into the Frugall retail park.

More cars and larger vehicles than he thought he could have counted in a weekend were lined up beneath towering lamps as colourless as the moon. In that light people's faces looked as pallid as Russell's. They seemed to take on colour once they reached the shops, half a mile of which surrounded the perimeter. Joe dodged through the crowd on the pavement but had to keep glancing back if not halting for his cousin to keep up. "Get it moving," he muttered without much caring whether he was heard. At least as he loitered outside a Frugelectric store he was able to realise "We'll need a light."

Russell peered at the nearest lanky floodlight, and not by any means for the first time Joe wondered what was going on inside his cousin's head. "A torch," he said with all the resentment that had built up inside him.

"There's one at home."

"That's too far." Before Russell could suspect he didn't want their parents to learn where the boys would be Joe said "You'll have to buy one."

He stared at his cousin and pointed at the shop until even Russell couldn't misunderstand. It was Russell's choice of an activity, and he could pay for it, not to mention for putting the girls off. Joe watched him select the cheapest flashlight on a shelf and drop a ten-pound note beside the till so as to avoid touching the checkout girl's hand. He made her place his change there for him to scoop up while Joe took the flashlight wrapped in a flimsy plastic bag. "That's mine. I bought it," Russell said at once.

"You hold it then, baby." Tom stopped just short of uttering the last word, though his face was hot again. He was tempted to give the checkout girl at least a meaningful glance, but thrust the flashlight at Russell instead. "Look after it," he said like a parent and stalked out of the shop.

So much for the first draft. This became

"Why do you want us to go there, Luke?" Dianne said.

"Who's Luke?"

"I told you," Tom said in some desperation, "he's like that."

"No I'm not, I'm like Lucas."

At such times Tom understood all too well why his cousin was bullied at school. There was also the way Lucas stared at anybody unfamiliar as if they had to wait for him to make up his mind about them, and just now his pasty face—far spottier than Tom's and topped with unruly red hair—was a further drawback. Nevertheless Dianne said "Are you sure you don't want to see our film?"

She was speaking to Tom, but Lucas responded. "We can't. We've been told."

"I haven't," Tom muttered. He watched the girls join the queue for the ticket desk manned by a tastefully drooling vampire in a cloak, and then he turned on Lucas. "We need to switch our phones off. We're in the cinema."

Accuracy mattered most to Lucas. Once he'd done as he was told Tom said "Let's go, and not to the kids' film either."

A frown creased Lucas's pudgy forehead. "Which one, then?"

"None of them. We'll go where you wanted," Tom said, leading the way out into the Frugall retail park.

More vehicles than he thought he could count in a weekend were lined up beneath towering lamps as white as the moon. In that light people's faces looked as pallid as Lucas's, but took on colour once they reached the shops, half a mile of which surrounded the perimeter. As Tom came abreast of a Frugelectric store he said "We'll need a light."

Lucas peered at the lanky lamps, and yet

again Tom wondered what went on inside his cousin's head. "A torch," he resented having to elucidate.

"There's one at home."

"That's too far." Before Lucas could suspect he didn't want their parents learning where the boys would be Tom said "You'll have to buy one."

He was determined his cousin would pay, not least for putting the girls off. He watched Lucas select the cheapest flashlight and load it with batteries, then drop a ten-pound note beside the till so as to avoid touching the checkout girl's hand. He made her place his change there for him to scoop up while Tom took the flashlight wrapped in a flimsy plastic bag. "That's mine. I bought it," Lucas said at once.

"You hold it then, baby." Tom stopped just short of uttering the last word, though his face was hot again. "Look after it," he said and stalked out of the shop.

The boys make their way through a gap in the fence around the retail park to a path that leads through woods to an abandoned tunnel. A tree that overhangs an inspection shaft is said to be where a teenager hanged himself, after which his girlfriend threw herself down the shaft. By this stage of the writing I have a general sense of subsequent events—more so in a short story than a novel—but I like to surprise myself with the writing. There doesn't seem much point in writing just what you already know. Often enough the characters bring the surprises by acting as their nature makes them.

He followed Russell down the increasingly steep path and saw the flashlight beam snag on the curve of a stone arch protruding from the earth beside the track. It was the end of the irrigation tunnel that had once brought water to the fields beyond the ridge. Now the fields were overgrown and the tunnel was boarded up—at any rate, it had been, but someone had torn the boards down. As Russell poked the flashlight beam into the tunnel he said "Where's the bell?"

Joe's best guess was that the slow dull metallic notes were the little that was audible of some music from a car in the distance. He didn't mean to reassure his cousin with that, and so he said "Is it in the tunnel?"

Russell stooped under the arch, which wasn't quite as tall as either of the boys. "Listen," he said. "That's where."

Joe heard a last reverberation as he arrived at the foot of the path. He had no chance to place the sound, but surely it was just his cousin's gaze that made him wonder if it had indeed come from the tunnel. Or had someone followed them into the woods to play a Halloween joke? Suppose the girls had decided they were more interesting than the film—that Joe was, at any rate—and were on the ridge, hitting the ladder in the shaft with some object? In his hopelessly limited experience this didn't seem the kind of thing

*girls did, especially while keeping quiet as
well. The thought of the girls resurrected all
his discontent with his cousin, and he said
"Better go and see, then."*

*Russell stepped into the tunnel at once. In
another moment his silhouette blotted out
most of the way ahead—the stone floor
scattered with sodden leaves, the walls and
curved roof glistening with moss, a few weeds
drooping from cracks in the stone. The low
passage was barely wider than his elbows as
he held them by his sides—so narrow that the
flashlight bumped against the wall with a soft
moist thud when he swung around to point the
beam at Joe.*

This becomes

*He followed Lucas down the increasingly
steep path and saw the flashlight beam snag on
the curve of a stone arch protruding from the
earth beside the track. It was the end of the
tunnel, which had once helped irrigate the fields
beyond the ridge. Now the fields were overgrown
and the tunnel was barricaded, or rather it had
been until somebody tore the boards down. As
Lucas poked the flashlight beam into the entrance
he said "Where's the bell?"*

*Tom thought the slow dull metallic notes
came from a car radio in the distance, but said
"Is it in the tunnel?"*

*Lucas stooped under the arch, which
wasn't quite as tall as either of the boys.
"Listen," he said. "That's where."*

Tom heard a last reverberation as he stepped off the path. Surely it was just his cousin's gaze that made him wonder if the noise had indeed come from the tunnel, unless someone was playing a Halloween joke. Suppose the girls had followed them from the cinema and were sending the sound down from the ridge? In his hopelessly limited experience this didn't seem the kind of thing girls did, especially while keeping quiet as well. The thought of them revived his discontent, and he said "Better go and see."

Lucas advanced into the tunnel at once. His silhouette blotted out most of the way ahead, the stone floor scattered with sodden leaves, the walls and curved roof glistening with moss, a few weeds drooping out of cracks. The low passage was barely wider than his elbows as he held them at his sides—so narrow that the flashlight bumped against one wall with a soft moist thud as he turned to point the beam at Tom.

Lucas insists that while he's exploring the tunnel by himself in search of scariness his cousin should shine the light down the inspection tunnel.

He marched to the shaft and sent the beam down to the tunnel, where he seemed to glimpse movement—a dim shape like a scrawny limb or an even thinner item retreating at speed into the dark. It must have been a shadow cast by the ladder. "Come on," he called. "I'm here."

"I'm coming."

It was disconcerting to hear Russell's shout resound along the tunnel while it also came from beyond the ridge. Joe strained his eyes but couldn't judge how far the flashlight beam reached. The glare from the retail park was still hindering his vision, and he dodged around the entrance to the shaft to face away from the problem. Now he was able to see that the cheap flashlight fell short of illuminating the tunnel itself, and was unexpectedly anxious for Russell, even if all this had been his cousin's idea. "Can you see the light?" he called.

"I can see something, I think."

Joe thought this wilfully vague. "What?" he yelled.

"It must be you."

This was vaguer still, particularly for Russell. Was he trying to make his cousin nervous? In that case Joe wouldn't be. He peered down the shaft, waiting for Russell to dart or totter into view in a feeble attempt to alarm him. Or did Russell mean to worry him by staying out of sight longer than he should? He wouldn't be forced to call to Russell again, but he was on the edge of yielding to the compulsion when an ill-defined figure appeared at the foot of the shaft. He didn't really need it to turn its glimmering face upwards to prove it was Russell. "What do you want me to do now?" he resented having to ask.

"Stay there till I say," Lucas told him and stooped into the other section of the tunnel.

Presumably glancing over his shoulder at whatever hint of light was visible would provide him with some reassurance. Joe tried to listen to his cousin's receding footsteps, but could hear nothing at all—at least, only the sound he'd taken earlier for the rustle of plastic. Perhaps the bag in his cousin's pocket was brushing against the wall of the tunnel, except that Joe seemed to hear the sound behind him. Had Russell sneaked out of the far end of the tunnel to creep up and pounce on him? Surely his shadow would give him away, and when Joe twisted around, nothing was silhouetted against the glare from the retail park except the trees. He'd kept the flashlight beam trained down the shaft on the basis that he might have misjudged Russell, but how long would he have to wait to hear from his cousin? He had a sudden furious idea that, having left the tunnel, Russell was on his way home. "Where are you now?" he shouted.

"Here," Lucas declared, appearing at the bottom of the shaft.

So he'd been playing a different trick—waiting until his cousin was anxious. "Finished with the light?" Tom only just bothered to ask.

"Go and meet me at the end," Lucas said before ducking into the dark.

This ends up as

He marched to the opening and sent the beam down to the tunnel, where he seemed to glimpse movement—a dim shape like a scrawny limb or an even thinner item retreating at speed into the dark. It must have been a shadow cast by the ladder. "Come on," he called. "I'm here."

"I'm coming."

Tom was disconcerted to hear his cousin's shout resound along the tunnel while it also came from beyond the ridge. Despite straining his eyes he couldn't judge how far the flashlight beam reached; the glare from the retail park was still hindering his vision. He dodged around the shaft to turn his back on the problem, and saw that the beam of the cheap flashlight fell short of illuminating the tunnel itself. "Can you see the light?" he called.

"I see something."

Tom found this wilfully vague. "What?" he yelled.

"Must be you."

This was vaguer still, particularly for Lucas. Was he trying to unnerve his cousin? Tom peered into the shaft, waiting for Lucas to dart into view in a feeble attempt to alarm him. Or did Lucas mean to worry him by staying out of sight? Tom vowed not to call out again, but he was on the edge of yielding to the compulsion when an ill-defined figure appeared at the bottom of the shaft. He didn't really need it to turn its dim face upwards to show it was Lucas. "What am I doing now?" Tom grudged having to ask.

"Holding the light."

"I'm saying," Tom said more bitterly still, "what do you want me to do?"

"Stay there till I say," Lucas told him and stooped into the other section of the tunnel.

Tom tried to listen to his receding footsteps but soon could hear nothing at all—or rather, just the sound he'd previously ascribed to plastic. Perhaps the bag in his cousin's pocket was brushing against the wall, except that Tom seemed to hear the noise behind him. Had Lucas sneaked out of the far end of the tunnel to creep up and pounce on him? Surely his shadow would give him away, and when Tom swung around, only the trees were silhouetted against the glare from the retail park. He'd kept the flashlight beam trained down the shaft on the basis that he might have misjudged Lucas, but how long would he have to wait to hear from him? He had a sudden furious idea that, having left the tunnel, Lucas was on his way home. "Where are you now?" he shouted.

"Here," Lucas declared, appearing at the foot of the shaft.

So he'd been playing a different trick—staying out of sight until Tom grew nervous. "Finished with the light?" Tom only just bothered to ask.

"Go and meet me at the end," Lucas said before ducking into the dark.

Once he emerges, it's Tom's turn. I rather think I didn't know until I came to write it that when Russell shouts from his post by the inspection shaft—"It's waiting"—the words seem to come from two places at once, as though another voice is imitating his. Tom makes his way to the centre of the tunnel, and Russell shouts down:

"When you've been through the rest you have to come back this way."

He might have, but that needn't mean Joe did. Russell hadn't had his scare yet, which was among the reasons why Joe meant to leave the tunnel by the far end and tiptoe up behind him. He lowered his head and shut his eyes to ready them as far as he could for the dark. He hadn't opened them when Russell called "Are you scared to go in?"

That did away with any reservations Joe might have had about frightening him, and Joe ducked into the tunnel. He wouldn't have believed the blackness could grow thicker, but now it seemed not just to coat his eyes—it filled them to the limit. He'd taken a very few steps, which felt shackled by his wariness, when his foot collided with another heap of leaves. He heard twigs if not small branches snap as he trod several times on it—the yielding heap must be almost as long as he was tall. Once he was past it the floor seemed clear, but how far did he have to shuffle to catch even a glimpse of the night beyond the tunnel? It couldn't be so dark out there that it was indistinguishable from the underground passage. He was stretching his eyes wide, which only served to let more of the darkness into them, when his foot struck a hindrance more solid than leaves—an object that his groping fingers found to be the height and the width of the tunnel. It was composed of planks. This end of the passage was boarded up.

So Russell hadn't just been setting out the rules of the game. Perhaps he'd thought it was plain that he was informing his cousin there was no way out of this end of the tunnel.

And here's the rewrite.

"When you've been through the rest you have to come back this way."

That he had needn't mean Tom should. Lucas wasn't frightened yet, which was among the reasons why Tom intended to leave the tunnel by the far end so as to tiptoe up behind him. He shut his eyes to ready them for the darkness as far as he could. He hadn't opened them when Lucas enraged him by calling "Are you scared to go in?"

Tom lowered his head as if he meant to butt the dark and advanced into the tunnel. He wouldn't have believed the blackness could grow thicker, but now it didn't just smother his eyes—it filled them to the limit. He'd taken a very few steps, which felt shackled by his wariness, when his foot collided with another heap of leaves. He heard twigs if not small branches snap as he trod several times on the yielding heap, which must be almost as long as he was tall. Once he was past it the floor seemed clear, but how far did he have to shuffle to catch his first glimpse of the night outside? It couldn't be so dark out there that it was indistinguishable from the underground passage. He was stretching his eyes wide, which only served to let more of the darkness into them, when his foot struck a hindrance more solid than leaves—an object that his groping fingers found to be as high and wide as the tunnel. The entrance was boarded up.

So Lucas hadn't just been setting out the rules of the game. Perhaps he'd believed he was making it plain that Tom couldn't leave the tunnel at this end.

Let me analyse this a little. Some of the changes bring succinctness or add force to the prose. I also believe that the effect of such a passage in an uncanny tale depends not just on the selection of language but on its rhythm. I tend to hear that in my head, which is one reason my tales seem to read well aloud. The odd small edit takes care of inadvertent rhyming, an element I dislike: hence "leave the tunnel by the far end and tiptoe up behind him" becomes "leave the tunnel by the far end so as to tiptoe up behind him." Indeed, even in the present paragraph I originally wrote "one reason why my tales seem to read well aloud."

One more extract, after Tom has been too careless in the tunnel: an extra image sprang upon me like a denizen of the dark. I originally wrote

Between him and the way out, someone was running through the absolute blackness as if they had no need of light—as if they welcomed its absence.

For a moment that seemed to have no end Joe felt the darkness had claimed him, and then he lunged at the ladder and clutched at a rung and hauled himself desperately upwards.

This becomes

Between him and the way out, someone was running through the absolute blackness as if they had no need of light—as if they welcomed its absence.

For a moment that seemed endless Tom felt the darkness claim him, and then he shied the flashlight in the direction of the sodden flopping footsteps. He clutched at the ladder and hauled himself desperately upwards.

Let me leave the tale there. Tom belatedly realises that the one friend Russell said he had was Tom himself, but does this connection come too late? I know only as much about their fate as the reader will. I hope this analysis of the mechanics has been of use. I should mention that I print out the final draft and reread it in that form, always finding minor changes still to make, and then out it goes into the world. The published story can be found in various anthologies and in a collection of mine.

GREAT HORROR IS SOMETHING ALIEN

MICHAEL BAILEY

IN HIS INTRODUCTION to *Chiral Mad 3*, "Observations on Horror Burnout," Chuck Palahniuk states, "For a writer, the greatest achievement is to create the next great monster. For that is to foresee the future. To be the truest truth teller." The next great monster he speaks of is the unknown, the thing that is not yet thought of, or the mysterious and perhaps nameless idea with the potential to scare us most. And for an editor, the next great monster is what we seek— something new, something capable of scaring readers, something that avoids tropes; something completely original; something alien; for that is what makes great horror.

Whenever I hear the word "horror" I think of Ridley Scott's film *Alien* from 1979 (arguably a science fiction, but also horror), which debuted the year I was born and was my first exposure to the special blending that can happen with genres. I find this movie relates well when discussing what I'm looking for when reading either horror or science fiction.

In *Alien*, the Xenomorph—a word that literarily translates to "alien form"—was, at the time, the next great monster, a highly-aggressive extraterrestrial, endoparasitoid species so new that it rocked the box office, even by today's standards.

Part of what made *Alien* so special was the story's origin and the creature's stages of life. The alien, in this case, enters life through an Ovomorph, which literally translates to "egg form," a complicated organism with a symbiotic relationship to the Facehugger nestled within its shell. The egg is seemingly inert, yet has the ability to sense the approach of potential hosts, and upon touch or another creature passing by, the top of the Ovomorph opens like curling flower petals before it dies, and out launches a yellowish spider-like ribcage of a creature with a long tail, latching onto the face of its host, appendages wrapping around the head, tail strangling like a coiled snake around the neck. It has the ability to release acid to create a cavity if one does not exist, releases a cyanose-based paralytic substance to render the host unconscious, and inserts a proboscis down the throat. This second stage of parasitoid alien life exists solely to implant an embryo, via mouth or via acid-burned cavity, to make way for what will become the third stage of alien life: the Chestburster. Once the embryo is in place, the Facehugger detaches, skitters away, and eventually dies, like the egg, while the infant form of the Xenomorph gestates within its host. Upon maturation, the Chestburster, like its name implies, violently erupts from the host's chest cavity, thus beginning a fourth stage of life. Within hours the creature molts into an adult through a dramatic growth spurt, transforming to perhaps the most frightening of forms. The apex and fifth stage of this creature's life is the Xenomorph Queen. Much like the queen bee, or queen ant, the Xenomorph Queen is capable of birthing an incredible amount of Ovomorph sacs, thus repeating the cycle and rapidly populating the alien species. The wheel of alien life rotates, each stage repeated, and the endless cycle brings forth new life over and over again at an exponential rate.

The chest-bursting alien was inspired by real-life monsters, however: parasitoid wasps, which include multiple species. The parasitoid wasps lay their eggs in similar fashion to the Facehuggers in *Alien*, forcing their embryos into caterpillars and various insects; when the eggs hatch, offspring chew their way out of their living incubators. Dinocampus coccinellae, one species of wasp, specifically targets ladybugs, the insects sitting zombielike over the wasp larvae, partially paralyzed.

So was *Alien* original?

The film was not entirely Ridley Scott's baby. The screenplay was written by Dan O'Bannon, based on a story he co-wrote with Ronal Shusett, a story much influenced by other works of science fiction and horror. The idea for the parasitic creature/host relationship, for example, may have been inspired by the parasitoid wasps, but think of also the creation that went into the alien design. The eponymous alien and its various stages of life were originally designed by H.R. Giger, a Swiss artist, part of the special effects team that later earned an Academy Award for Best Achievement in Visual Effects. Ron Cobb and Chris Foss, artists O'Bannon had worked with on projects like *Dark Star* and *Dune*, created sketches of both the interiors and exteriors of the spaceship, both inspired by and named after the novel *Nostromo* (1904) by

Joseph Conrad, and the escape shuttle, Narcissus, named after Conrad's 1897 novella. And let's not forget the film may never have happened had *Star Wars* not been so successful in making science fiction such a hot genre at the time. "They wanted to follow through on *Star Wars*, and they wanted to follow through fast, and the only spaceship script they had sitting on their desk was *Alien*." And the film may never have happened if Dan O'Bannon, who said those words, had not beforehand taken an offer to work on the film adaptation of *Dune*, a project that fell apart like sand under his feet. Yet not working on *Dune* sparked a trip to Paris, and introduced him to artists whose works inspired an original science fiction story that became *Alien*—people like Chris Foss, who had created science fiction book covers, and H.R. Giger, whose work he found both horrifying and beautiful. And so O'Bannon went on to write a script about one of Giger's monsters, and moved to Los Angeles to live with Shusett, who suggested he work on his World War II story about gremlins infiltrating a B-17 bomber, but to change the setting to a spaceship, a project they coined Star Beast. The title then became *Alien* after realizing how often the word appeared in the script, a more fitting title that could mean both adjective and noun. Shusett came up with the idea of a crew member getting implanted with an alien embryo as a plot device in order to bring the creature aboard the spacecraft, and so on.

It was quite the collaboration, but was the movie all that original? It was more than that; it was a collaboration of many original concepts and inspired ideas, and perhaps a few stolen ones, or perhaps borrowed abstractions of ideas.

Mark Twain was noted as saying, "There is no such thing as a new idea. It is impossible. We simply take a lot of old ideas and put them into a sort of mental kaleidoscope. We give them a turn and they make new and curious combinations. We keep on turning and making new combinations indefinitely, but they are the same old pieces of colored glass that have been in use through all the ages."

Alien is a great horror story, perhaps one of the best, and it is a great science fiction story, but it wasn't entirely original; it was a kaleidoscope of colored glass turning and turning until the film hit the screen.

Even Ridley Scott, after taking on the role to direct the film and convincing 20th Century Fox to double the initial budget, had storyboards created that included designs inspired by *Star Wars*, and *2001: A Space Odyssey*, with designs for the spaceship and spacesuits influenced by those films. He described *Alien* as "*The Texas Chain Saw Massacre* of science fiction." O'Bannon then went on to introduce Scott to Giger's artwork, and together they felt his painting, Necronom IV, was the alien they were looking for and brought Giger in as a designer.

When asked about writing the script, O'Bannon admitted the script drew inspiration from previous works. The claustrophobic environment and idea of being pursued by a deadly alien creature was inspired by *The Thing from Another World* (1951); the discovery of a chamber full of eggs was inspired by a short story written by Clifford D. Simak called "Junkyard," which was published in 1953; the idea for crew members being killed off one-by-one by an unknown creature after warned not to land their spacecraft was inspired by *Forbidden Planet* (1956); the idea for alien reproduction was inspired by *Strange Relations*, a novel by Philip Farmer (1960); the discovery of a giant alien skeleton was inspired by *Planet of the Vampires* (1965); not to mention various horror titles from EC Comics about monsters eating their way out of people.

"I didn't steal *Alien* from anybody," O'Bannon said, when asked about his creation, "I stole it from everybody!"

Even when presented to studio execs, the movie was pitched as "*Jaws* in space" in order to find it a home. And of course Hollywood did its thing, both making the script worse and adding to it. Two of the movie's producers, David Giler and Walter Hill, put the script through eight revisions, trimming much of the alien planetoid sequences, naturalizing the dialogue, and adding what O'Bannon thought was an unnecessary subplot—an android character named Ash, which Shusett later claimed was "one of the best things in the movie." Many fans of *Alien* agree; some disagree.

So was the Xenomorph the next great monster of its time? Most definitely. Was *Alien* original? Not entirely, but that doesn't matter in the grand scheme of things. It was a movie that spawned from idea after idea, from a great pool of collective thought and imaginative minds. And that is why the movie works so well, even now, nearly forty years later.

If you look at Giger's painting of Necronom IV, you will see the Xenomorph that was eventually conceptualized in the film, but even Giger's inspiration for that painting had to come from somewhere.

Creators draw inspiration from other stories, other paintings, other movies, pulling from everything and everyone around them.

The creator's mind is much like Twain's kaleidoscope, using every sense to create something new—not out of nothing, but from many small somethings.

So what does all of this have to do with what makes for a great horror story?

I guess what I'm trying to say is that I agree with both Mark Twain and Chuck Palahniuk. Great horror is not thrown together haphazardly, or created out of thin air. Great horror relies on inspiration, the ability to create originality out of unoriginality—perhaps a mosaic of horror mosaics. The next great monster Palahniuk wrote about, what editors of horror fiction are constantly searching for (the creation every writer may be trying to achieve) seems unobtainable based on Twain's quote on originality, yet we are finding and creating new monsters every day, and the kaleidoscope of creation constantly turns, birthing horror after horror.

The egg sac is birthed, its petals curl, the Facehugger hugs face, its embryo placed, the Chestburster bursts from the chest, and the Xenomorph feeds and replicates ad infinitum.

But the alien, the monster in this case, is not the only thing that makes *Alien* such a great film, and likewise the next great monster is not the only thing that makes great horror fiction.

Terror is often evoked by what is not seen—in fiction what the reader is manipulated to envision—and by creating a certain level of claustrophobia.

The *Alien* film accomplishes both of these feats. There is not a lot of screen time for the alien in its various stages of life; with an original theatrical runtime of just under two hours, the alien life is mostly off-screen, out of view, hiding in shadows, lurking down an empty tunnel, or sometimes hinted at with a flash of glossy black or a swipe of tail—a directing technique Ridley Scott perhaps borrowed from fellow director Stanley Kubrick.

Horror is often created by what is not seen, and I also look for that in fiction. Once a monster is seen, or envisioned by a reader, magic is lost and fear fizzles.

In Andy Muschietti's film *Mama* (2013), the first two acts focus on not showing the monster—the witch—and the first half of the film is an incredible piece of filmmaking and scary as hell; the second half, however, ruins the entire feel of the movie with the monster having much screen time during the third act in the form of bad CGI, and the film ultimately fails.

In the novel *Birdbox*, Josh Malerman accomplishes the opposite effect. He creates what I'd consider the next great monster of books published during that particular year. He kept his monster hidden from the story's characters—which are well-developed and blindfolded throughout—and also kept his monster hidden from the reader. *Birdbox* created a claustrophobic atmosphere from beginning to end, Malerman never cheating the reader, and he created loveable/hateable characters.

The most important part of any work of fiction is character. As readers, we need to understand who we are rooting for and who we are rooting against. We need to love them and to hate them. We need to feel them and feel for them. We need emotion. Characters need to be well-developed, but not overly-developed, and we need to experience a story through them, not by looking over their shoulders. We need to care.

At the time of *Alien*'s release, action movie stars were predominately men, with women often portrayed as weaker individuals. Argue all you want, but watch any action movie from the late seventies and early eighties and action stars were predominately sweaty muscular men. The script for *Alien* was a bit different, all characters written as unisex, and each referred to only by last name: Ripley, Dallas, Kane, Ash. Once Sigourney Weaver landed the starring role, we were suddenly given a new type of character to root for: a motherly figure battling odds of survival against exposure to an uber-threatening alien race . . . on a spaceship, with a cat named Jones.

When reading for anthologies, and when reading in general, I am constantly searching for the character. Do I feel compassion? Do I care? Are the characters real, and unique, or are they the same type of characters we've already seen recycled through plots?

Characterization, plot, setting, atmosphere, point-of-view, dialogue, voice, tone, style, structure; all of these are important in creating great fiction, but character is the most vital.

I've read thousands upon thousands of stories for dark science fiction and horror anthologies, for the Chiral Mad series, *Qualia Nous*, *The Library of the Dead*, and most recently *You, Human* and *Adam's Ladder*, and for other books uncredited. I have read hundreds of books within a particular year for jury award consideration, and spend most of my free time reading countless unpublished manuscripts from writers seeking publishers, and of course I sometimes even read books for pleasure. What I have discovered over the years is that every writer is, in fact, searching for that next great monster, but most are going about it incorrectly.

I used to read submissions in their entirety, every single one, but given the volume of work I've had to handle recently, I've cut back significantly. If I'm not pulled into a story by page one, I'm out, and move on to the next. The first sentence needs to ensnare, the first paragraph needs to entrap, and every paragraph thereafter needs to be as strong as—or stronger than—its predecessor. A reader should be able to randomly flip to any page in a writer's work, to any paragraph, start reading, and be captivated. If I find my mind wandering at any time during a story, I'm out, and move on to the next, always searching. With longer works, I may give a story more time, but with thousands of short story manuscripts submitted to anthologies year after year, and only a handful of slots available in a particular table of content, there is no room for mediocre. I don't have time for that. I read stories and find the ones I love and set them aside until I have what I believe are the strongest of submissions, maybe forty or fifty for each anthology. If I skim through the stack and a story jumps out at me, like one of the Facehuggers in *Alien*, and I remember everything about that story by a few simple words on the page—what had held me so captivated that first go around—or perhaps by the title, these I find have the highest rate of survival. These are the Xenomorphs.

Slush piles are full of potential Ovomorphs, some

flowering open, some not; and out of these a handful of Facehuggers emerge, some able to latch on, others too weak and incapable of holding the reader; and out of these a few embryos are able to make it down the reader's throat, some that gestate, some that don't, and out of these a few Chestbursters may develop and burst forth from the page, some capable of becoming spectacular, like the Xenomorph, and some that wither away in a corner and die. Slush piles are full of stories in various stages of life, and our job as editors is to find those capable of greatness.

What I've found in my relatively short time as an editor is that writers are often trying to cheat the process of creation, or skipping stages. They are showing us their monsters, over-describing them, putting them right there on the page instead of slightly off-page or out of focus. Writers are creating two-dimensional characters we've all seen before (mostly experienced from film), creating formulaic storylines, shoving setting in our face, down our throats, forcing plot through dialogue, or through unnecessary data dumps, or using their own inner voice instead of creating new ones with their characters. Writers are forcing readers away from relying on imagination, which is the source of all book magic.

Those new to the horror writing scene, or so I've noticed lately, are mimicking other horror writers, reproducing what they may have seen on screen or read in other books instead of attempting originality. Perhaps new writers are trying to take the easier way in order to make a quick buck, and copying what's already been done countless times before instead of pulling from the giant pool of horror available and letting inspiration run its evolutionary course. Editors see through this, however, and rather quickly.

Editors spend most of their time reading unpublished work—an entirely different world than most are used to with fiction or nonfiction. We've seen all sorts of tricks from new writers—even veterans— and seen all sorts of copycats and style-shadowing and plagiarizing. We can tell good writing from bad in a matter of words. It's sad to say most of us are looking for the bad before the good, for reasons not to publish, weeding to make way for the good because time is our biggest enemy and we don't have time for ordinary.

We've seen your monsters before. We know your plot. We know your cookie-cutter characters. So why not give us something new?

There are writers, and then there are typists, and the difference between the two is simple: writers survive the gamut that is successful, publishable storytelling; typists don't.

All creation requires a certain level of evolution. Horror writers, good ones, reach their tendrils farther. They try harder. They pull from what's already available, yet they pull correctly, allowing existing ideas and "monsters" to inspire and spark new life into their own ideas and their own monsters. Horror writers and editors publishing horror should always be searching for the next great monster, whatever it may be—as long as it's new and fresh and unknown— because great horror is always something alien.

A HORRIFICALLY HAPPY MEDIUM

Choosing the Right Medium for Your Story and Yourself

TAYLOR GRANT

YOU HAVE AN intriguing horror concept, unique plot, or fascinating character you are ready to explore. You may already have a format or medium in mind. And quite often your instinct for the medium of your story may be right. But have you stopped to consider which medium would best serve your story? In my experience, choosing the right medium is not only crucial to the story, but also for the writer as an individual.

Let me explain.

I was asked to write this article because over the past three decades I have written in a wide variety of mediums, including feature films, short films, live action television, animation for television, prose fiction, comic books, video games, one-act plays, stand-up comedy, music videos, and web animation. I've also written for national magazines, newspapers, the web, and radio.

A big takeaway from all of my experiences is that some stories are better suited to specific mediums, not only from a storytelling perspective, but also because a particular medium may not align with a writer's goals, priorities, or even personality. An often overlooked fact is that the writing process in one medium may not be as gratifying to you as it is in another.

Each medium offers different storytelling opportunities and also unique personal and professional challenges. Some story ideas can work across multiple mediums, others will not translate as well.

When choosing the best medium for a story, I consider these four important questions:

1 Which medium best serves my story creatively?
2 Which medium do I enjoy writing in and/or want to explore?
3 Which medium offers the highest probability of a sale?
4 What is the ratio of passion, to time commitment, to money?

I suspect the fourth question will prove controversial for some, but it requires some context. For that, let's take a look at some of the mediums you may be considering for your horror story.

The mediums discussed in this article are film, television, stage, comics, novels and related prose formats. Some industries are notoriously difficult to break into, but all of them present unique challenges for you, both as a creator and a businessperson.

Generally speaking, the more collaborative the work, and the higher the cost of creating it, the more challenges you will face seeing it produced and/or published.

Writing, in whatever medium you choose, can be a rewarding, heartbreaking, sometimes joyous experience, but one thing it will never be, is easy.

Film

The allure of writing a Hollywood film is understandable. Movies tend to reach much wider audiences than say, novels, graphic novels, or stage plays. Screenplays also usually require far less time to write than a novel and from an industry perspective, in terms of ROI (return on investment), horror films top the list of all genres. Plus, we've all heard those stories of screenwriters making a six or seven-figure deal.

I got my start as a professional screenwriter. And for several years that was how I paid the rent. But the job didn't turn out to be anything like I'd imagined.

Let's separate fantasy from reality.

Firstly, the experience of reading and writing a screenplay is much different than writing prose. While scripts require some prose to set the tone, hint at atmosphere, describe setting and action, the language used isn't the thrust of the form.

Brevity in screenplay descriptions is essential. Whereas prose fiction allows a deep appreciation for a particular style which is expressed through word choice, diction, tone, and the use of imaginative language, such as metaphor, simile, alliteration, and lyricism.

This isn't to say that prose in screenplays isn't

important—it is. However, the artistic gratification of crafting perfect prose is better suited to authors than it is to screenwriters or playwrights.

If writing dialogue is one of your strengths, then screenwriting (and, of course, playwriting) are formats you may enjoy. In film, it is central to propelling the plot and developing character. Dialogue must sound natural, and not expositional. It should also be character-specific. Too often I have read screenplays where all of the characters sound the same. Each character needs to have different vocabularies, mannerisms and personalities.

A film emphasizes the camera, visuals and sounds. It shows what's happening on the outside, as it were, of its characters. Novels, novellas, novelettes and short stories show what's happening on the inside. So if your story relies heavily on the inner thoughts of your protagonist or other characters, your story may not work well as a film.

Ask yourself if you will be able to tell your story in one hundred and ten pages (optimal) or one hundred and twenty pages (absolute maximum). Can your story be told visually? If your story is highly visual and you are imagining sound or music as having a large influence on the story, then obviously your story is well-suited for film.

What is the setting? This is important due to budget. When writing a novel or graphic novel, there are no budgetary considerations. Your story can span centuries, different countries, and generations of characters. But getting your screenplay sold will be infinitely more difficult if the setting and/or story requires a massive budget.

Consider creative ways to reduce the budget. Does your car chase need to be in a big city? Could it work in a desolate area? Does your story truly require that many special effects? Don't give buyers reasons to pass on your great story simply due to budget.

Does your story have a good hook? If you're writing a haunted house story, strong characters are important, but that's not going to get you the sale. You need to develop a unique premise that makes the haunted house story feel fresh, easy to market, with mass appeal.

But beyond the format, techniques and commercial appeal necessary for a saleable screenplay, there are also the realities of working in a *collaborative* medium.

The life of a Hollywood screenwriter isn't for everyone.

For example, how will you feel if your story gets eviscerated—as often happens—by the buyers or potential buyers? How will you feel when other writers are hired to rewrite your script, which is common practice?

Are you the type who doesn't like to make changes to your story or characters based on the whims of the buyer? Is your story deeply personal and not something you would like to alter? Be honest with yourself. There is nothing wrong with that. You have a great deal of creative control over the story in a novel or graphic novel. However, this is the exact opposite of what you can expect as a professional screenwriter.

You're going to be taking notes. Endless notes. From agents, managers, story editors, producers, production company executives, and studios. And if you're lucky enough to make it into production, you'll take ongoing notes from the director, more producers, and even actors at times. Ask yourself if this is something you think you would enjoy.

Of course, this is assuming you will actually sell your script.

I was fortunate in that I had five movie deals in a row (with the likes of studios such as Imagine Entertainment, Universal Studios and Lionsgate Films). It is possible to make money at this. And I was thrilled to be paid for my work. However, none of these projects have been produced (yet). This is common and has nothing to do with the quality of a script. Often, the reasons films are made (or not made) are completely arbitrary.

What many aspiring screenwriters don't realize is that most sold scripts will never see the light of day. There are screenwriters who have made a good deal of money, but have never had a script produced. This came as a big (and painful) shock to me. Of course, I was delighted to be paid, but it can be soul crushing to spend years working on various scripts, making countless creative compromises, and putting your heart and soul into pages that will never make it farther than a desk drawer.

Eventually, my feature horror film (*The Muse*) and two shorts (*The Vanished* and *Sticks and Stones*) were produced due to my own efforts. My shorts premiered at the Short Film Corner of the Cannes Film Festival in France, and received worldwide distribution through Shorts TV. And yes, seeing my work come to life was incredibly gratifying.

Look, I believe in dreams and ambitious goals.

They are important. And if yours is to sell a screenplay then nothing I say should deter you. However, having worked in Hollywood for many years, I would be doing you a serious disservice to sugar-coat anything. The purpose of this article is to aid you in choosing the right medium for your story, but I also believe it's just as important to choose the right medium for *you*.

Many won't like to hear this, but the truth is that the likelihood of selling a screenplay is remarkably low. The chances of selling a novel are far greater. An unproduced screenplay will never be read, but a novel can always be published (by a large, medium, small, micro-publisher, or yourself).

As you're deciding which medium is best, it's important to look at the sometimes harsh realities of the screenwriting business. This is not to dissuade you from being a screenwriter. It is merely to give you a reality check so that you can make your decision based on facts—not misconceptions (of which there are many).

1 If this is your first screenplay, don't expect to sell it. Seriously. Like any craft, it takes time to hone your skills, instincts or style. Most great screenwriters wrote multiple scripts before they had the skills necessary to write a saleable screenplay (yes, this applies even if you're adapting a novel).

2 Pitches don't sell. The heydays of the 90s are long over. Ideas are a dime a dozen. The handful of pitches that sell these days are from established moneymakers.

3 The market for "spec" or "speculative" scripts (meaning a non-commissioned, unsolicited

screenplay) is about the toughest it's ever been. It has been on a steady decline since the financial crisis of 2008. To give you some perspective, the best source I could find showed that approximately 75 spec scripts were sold at the studio level in 2016. Even if that low figure isn't exact, when you consider that anywhere between 50,000 to 100,000 *new* scripts are registered and copyrighted every year, it will give you some perspective on the odds.

4 Piquing the interest of top literary agents in Hollywood is extremely difficult, and many are not in the business of discovering and nurturing new talent. Most of them already have a stable of writers that they need to manage. However, if you live in Los Angeles, and to some degree, New York, here is where relationships can really help. If you don't have any connections, don't be disheartened. You can't throw a rock in L.A. without hitting someone who knows someone in the industry. Get out there and network. Meeting people who can assist you is mission critical. Salesmanship is important in Hollywood. It is a skill you will have to develop.

5 Lastly, there is self-expression. This isn't talked about enough when people choose their writing path. There is less opportunity for self-expression in the world of screenwriting than writing a novel, or even a graphic novel. Authors such as Cormac McCarthy, Gabriel Garcia-Marquez, Toni Morrison, Neil Gaiman, Virginia Wolfe, William Faulkner, D.H. Lawrence, and many other great authors have a distinct and unique style and voice.

But try to guess who wrote a screenplay? With the exceptions of Quentin Tarantino, David Mamet or Charlie Kaufman it will be virtually impossible.

Most of what we've covered so far relates to films produced within the Hollywood system. But there may also be opportunities for you to sell your screenplay to independent producers and/or production companies. Horror remains one of the most bankable and common genres in film. A lot of independent horror films are produced every year, and the tier structure ranges from $50,000 micro budget films to $1 million and up.

Now back to the original four questions:

1 Which medium best serves my story creatively? We've taken a look at why some stories are better suited for film.
2 Which medium offers the highest probability of a sale? Knowing the odds of selling a screenplay are much lower than a novel, this *must* be taken into consideration.
3 Which format do I enjoy writing in and/or want to explore? Although I started my professional career as a screenwriter, there is no question I enjoy the process of writing prose and comic books more. For me, self-expression is a critical component of why I write.

However, there may come a time when you simply want to stretch your wings and try a new medium. Obviously, that is a perfectly good reason, and you may find that writing a screenplay gives you a completely different perspective on your story. It is certainly a fantastic way to learn three-act structure, write more concisely, and discover how to show rather than tell.

If you are still determined to be a screenwriter, I highly recommend writing and producing a short film. These days, almost anyone can afford to produce a 5 to 10 minute short. It will empower you as a storyteller. You don't have to ask for permission or wait for someone to produce your art. Sure, you can certainly follow the old Hollywood paradigm of trying to "break in." But that doesn't mean you can't simultaneously create your own shorts.

With the advances in prosumer technology, creating your first short film is easier than it's ever been. And if you end up creating something quite good, you'll have a finished product to garner attention, instead of just a spec script.

4 What is the ratio of passion, to time commitment, to money? As I mentioned previously, this question might be controversial for some (art vs. commerce). But if you value your time as much as I do, this is an important question to ask yourself. How passionate are you about your story? Or the medium itself? And how does that balance against what you can expect to earn for the level of effort? Writing for the hopes of riches is the worst reason to become a screenwriter.

When I first read of the terrible odds against selling a screenplay, I was completely deflated for a few days. But I had this burning desire to write for the screen, and so I ignored those odds. I was fortunate to see several of my scripts and treatments produced for television and have had the experience of seeing my work come to life. I was also paid by major studios for several feature film projects—two in the horror genre.

And yet none of the features I was paid for were produced. That's the business. It is a roll of the dice.

What exactly is the time commitment? In the past, several of my ideas could have been turned into a screenplay or expanded into a novel. But when I was honest with myself, I knew I'd never get to them all. So I chose to bring some of them to life as short stories, as I knew the time commitment for each would likely be six weeks or less.

I'm pleased to say that all of those stories have since been published. I was able to satisfy my muse, get paid, and do it with a relatively short time commitment. Sure, no one gets rich writing short stories. But as an artist seeking self-expression, I found the experience to be priceless!

I do have some good news for you, though. Selling your spec (unsolicited) script isn't the only way to make your screenwriting dream a reality. It is more common for spec scripts to be seen as "writing samples." What this means is that your script may get you writing assignments or script doctoring work.

So while your original script may never get produced, it *can* get you noticed—and hired to write other films. And that wouldn't be so bad, now would it?

Television

Horror, of course, has proven to be quite successful on television the past few years, with shows as diverse as *The Walking Dead, Stranger Things, American Horror Story, Supernatural, True Blood, The Strain, iZombie, Grimm, The Vampire Diaries, Hannibal, Castlevania, Bates Motel* and several others proving very popular.

Historically, the odds of selling a spec TV movie or series pilot are even less than a feature film. But I say this with the caveat that with the proliferation of cable channels and Web outlets (Netflix, Amazon, Hulu, etc.) producing their own series, clearly there is a growing need for content. So, if writing for the small screen is your dream, there are unique opportunities now that didn't exist before this decade.

Creatively speaking, there are similarities in writing for film and TV, but there are important differences too. If your story would make a great TV series, for example, there is an established format, whether it's a half-hour or one-hour show. In network TV, there are true act breaks to allow for commercials, a limited number of recurring characters and sets, and internal guidelines about the types of stories allowed.

For the most part, writing for television is far more collaborative than film. There are more limits on structure, storyline, characters and tone. Often there is a group of writers that work under the supervision of a producer called the "showrunner." The pace at which you are expected to write is much faster than in film too. It's more akin to working a regular job, though the hours will be much longer. If you are the kind of writer that prefers to work in solitude, television is not for you.

Budgets for TV movies are almost always less than theatrical releases, so your intergalactic sci-fi blockbuster or sweeping fantasy epic would be better served as a theatrical release.

Much like in feature film writing, don't despair if your speculative TV script is never produced—it might be the thing to get you hired to write something else.

My advice is to network and try and connect with people in the industry who can help you package your project (like a TV producer or an agent, of course). If you have no contacts whatsoever, you can submit your script to contests that accept TV scripts. This is a way to bypass the system and get your script seen by Hollywood agents and producers. Also, keep in mind that an original script is less likely to open doors than a spec script for an existing show.

In fact, I broke into TV animation on the Tim Burton-produced series *Beetlejuice* due to my spec script for—wait for it—*Seinfeld*. After that, I continued to work in children's television for several years, bouncing between several TV series—both animated and live action horror/comedies. I also created a short-lived animated series called *Monster Farm* that aired on the Fox Family Channel.

On a positive note, while feature film writers have very little say in the final execution of the work, in television, the writer often overrules the director.

Stage

Live performance of stories has been a part of almost

every culture since the dawn of recorded history. Every medium discussed here is in some way a descendant of the stage play.

It has been said that modern horror films were born from Le Théâtre du Grand-Guignol, a Parisian institution from 1897 to the early sixties. Live shows featured deranged characters, buckets of blood and violence so macabre and brutal that audiences were known to vomit or even faint during performances.

And while horror isn't the most prevalent genre on stage, it does exist. Some examples of well-known modern horror plays include *The Pillowman*, the *Things that Go Bump Trilogy*, *The Weir*, *The Woman in Black*, *Sweeney Todd*, *Ghost Stories*, *The Exorcist*, *Phantom of the Opera*, and *Carrie*. However, it is with small theater companies or, say, a fringe festival, where you will most likely find opportunities as a horror playwright.

The fact that horror is not the most popular genre doesn't mean you shouldn't attempt it, if it makes sense for your story and your personal goals as an artist. Theater is an intimate setting, and in my opinion, perfect for the horror genre. I would love to see more of it produced.

As in any medium, character development, a compelling story and structure are essential, but think of your audience as eavesdropping on the characters. While a screenwriter divides the story into scenes, a playwright breaks it down into acts.

Your story should have minimal special effects, limited settings, and they tend to work best with more intimate tales. A play requires extremely well-written dialogue in order to reveal exposition organically.

A few years ago I wrote a one-act horror piece called "The Promise" that was produced in Los Angeles as part of a stage production called *Love in 3-D*. The limitations of budget forced me to create an intimate horror story within a single location.

For a writer, there is nothing quite like the live theater experience. There was one particular moment in "The Promise" when—after building suspense between the two main characters—there was a (planned) loud bang on the wall. When I heard those glorious screams coming from the audience, it was the ultimate thrill.

This one-act play proved to be a great example of a story that could be adapted into another medium. Years later, when I was invited to write a short story for a terrific anthology called *Drive-in Creature Feature*, I knew that the concept of "The Promise" was perfect for the book. I adapted my one-act play into a short story called "Static." The editors (including Eugene Johnson, co-editor of this fine book) seemed to agree, as it was published this year to my great delight.

What I love about playwriting is that language and sounds are dominant, and much of the story unfolds by what the audience hears. In a play it is difficult to focus on visual detail, as we can't rely on close-ups, and storytelling techniques like flashbacks are difficult to execute on stage.

Lessons learned in front of a live audience are invaluable, as it offers an immediate response to your work. In fact, doing staged readings (even if it's your family and friends) is highly recommended with playwriting. Feedback from actors can shed light on what you're trying to do and it provides a way to measure how well you are accomplishing that. A discussion can help you uncover specific elements that are not working the way you had intended.

Much like film and TV, getting your work produced can be quite challenging (noticing a pattern here?). It's difficult for many theaters to remain profitable so producing a play from a new playwright is a big risk. This is why the larger theaters tend to work with those who have proven track records.

However, smaller theaters are sometimes open to taking these risks, as long as the production budget is realistic. Fortunately, there are many theaters across the country and they produce plays all year round. You'll have to spend time researching the right theaters for your work. Check out the Dramatists Resource Directory and look into joining the Dramatists Guild. Join playwriting groups on Facebook and LinkedIn. Read theater magazines and blogs, such as *American Theater, The Dramatist,* and *HowlRound* to find out what's going on across the country.

Use the internet to search for small theater companies or festivals that are already producing horror, mysteries and dark material. They do exist.

Make sure to attend the theater often. Try seeking out those who are writing and producing darker material. Follow them on social media and take interest in their work. Theater is about connections and people. Go to shows of the artists you enjoy and pay attention to where they are being produced. See if you can find a graceful way to introduce yourself without forcing a connection.

Comic Books/Graphic Novels/Web Comics

Creating comics can be quite gratifying. Not only do you have a great deal of creative latitude and control, you also get to see your story, characters and dialogue come to life with the wonders of sequential art. And, of course, horror has deep roots in the comic book medium.

In film and TV, the question is always, "How can we bring down the budget?" But with comics there are no limits on your setting, so you won't have to compromise your vision based on what you can afford. Need to destroy a major city in your story? Create a post-apocalyptic New York? Have a military/monster battle? No problem. You have a limitless palette. While you can certainly write a quiet, horror tale in a single, intimate setting, you can also write what feels like a hundred million-dollar movie.

A few years ago I co-founded a small comic book publishing company called Evil Jester Comics. During my short tenure on staff, I co-wrote, edited, art directed and published a horror comic called *Evil Jester Presents* that received a fair amount of attention. To this day, I receive occasional messages from fans asking for more. It was certainly a joy to create. Later, I co-edited a wonderful and extremely creepy graphic novel called *Made Flesh*, from the dynamic duo of Lars Kramhøft and Tom Kristensen. Soon after, I acquired a terrific post-apocalyptic project called *The Last Companion* from the talented William Neal McPheeters.

Prior to that I was the Head Writer/Executive Editor for Stan Lee Media, where I wrote scripts and developed some of the very first superhero web series with comic book legends Stan Lee and Steve Gerber, and also wrote a few sports-related comic books for a couple of independent publishers.

Comics tend to be 24 pages long and graphic novels around 80-120 pages and there are different page sizes as well. Comic scripts are more malleable than the screenplay format, but they are similar. You will break your script into panels. As the writer (and this also goes for animation scripts), you are the director of the scenes in a way. However, a common mistake is to try and have a character doing too many actions within a single panel. You can't have your protagonist open a door, peek in, and step through into the darkened room in the same panel—you'll have to break it up into several.

Another common mistake is trying to fit too much dialogue into a single panel or too many panels on a single page. With the limited space available, one of the biggest challenges with comic book writing is telling a compelling story with a beginning, middle and end in a short amount of time.

While thinking visually is important with screenwriting, multiply that with comic writing. You'll have to think in visual terms, such as how your panels are going to be laid out. Also, writing dialogue that will be read is different than dialogue that will be heard.

Keep in mind that there are not a standardized number of frames and panels per page, which can be quite freeing. Just remember that they are designed so the eye can scan them in a downward left to right cascading pattern.

Much like screenplays, as a comic writer, one of

your goals is to entice the reader to turn the page. Though you will have less space to do it than screenplays, so you will have to write less dialogue, as they have to fit into speech bubbles. In fact, I encourage you to look for ways to take advantage of this graphic format to tell your story without any dialogue at all.

Thought balloons have long gone out of fashion, but I overcame this limitation by putting my protagonist's feelings in the caption boxes. Purely a stylistic choice on my part, but I was quite happy with it.

As in writing for the screen, comic book writing also requires collaboration. Unless, of course, you can pencil, ink, color and letter. Otherwise, you're going to work with one or several individuals to bring your comic, web comic or graphic novel to life.

As a novelist, you can go sit in a house for six months and have a finished story, but with comics you will have to collaborate. So keep this in mind when you're deciding if this medium is the right fit. Some people find that collaboration is highly motivating, so this may work to your benefit if you prefer bouncing around ideas with others—especially your artist.

Breaking into the comic book industry with established publishers is notoriously difficult. There is no single answer to this question, as almost every professional working in the industry has a different story of how they got their first gig.

But one common theme is that many comic book professionals created their own comic books or web comics *first*, developed their craft, and established credibility before they got their break.

The good news is that no one can stop you from creating a comic book if that's what you want to do. And with crowdfunding, you may be able to find an audience to invest in your project. This is what I did with *Evil Jester Presents*, and while it was a lot of work, we met our funding goal and produced a beautiful book.

Novels/Novellas/Novelettes/Short Stories

In prose writing, you are the primary creative artist. This is quite different to the previous mediums discussed. Meaning, while you may receive some notes from your editor (how much varies from publisher to publisher), ultimately, you are the single visionary behind your story.

It is an important distinction. And for some writers, it is the main reason they have chosen this medium for their stories. Another distinction is that with comics, plays and screenplays you have a finite number of pages, while a novel can be as long as you need to tell your story.

But, of course, there are other differences to consider. Film, TV, stage and comics offer visuals for the audience to experience. In prose, the author uses words to help the reader construct the visual images in their minds. And the importance of those words is perhaps the biggest differentiator in prose writing from all other mediums.

Prose offers you the satisfaction of creating exquisite sentences and lyrical language. You might create a metaphor that stuns your reader and makes them ponder its meaning. You have the opportunity to share your characters' thoughts with your reader, and as a result, the characterization can be deeper in a book. It is this inner life that is arguably one of the greatest storytelling advantages books have over the other mediums.

Much like graphic novels, with prose you need not be concerned about the budgetary restrictions that are part and parcel with film, TV and stage. You don't have to worry about the cost of sets, special effects, or the size of your cast. Your story can be intimate or as epic and sprawling as it needs to be.

With prose you have to make decisions you won't face as a screenwriter. What is the point of view? Third person omniscient? Third person limited? First person? Objective? And yet, those decisions can be creatively empowering.

How much will you tell through dialogue and how much from the distance of the observer or inside the character? Is there a single protagonist or multiple, interconnected stories?

Then there is the consideration of language. Are you aiming for eloquence or simplicity? Language is more demanding in novels than the other forms, and it takes a lot more time to perfect. In fact, tenacity is another differentiator from writing in the other mediums. You might be able to write the first draft of a comic or TV script in a week or two, and a feature screenplay in a few weeks or less. But a novel simply takes more time than any of the other forms. There is a higher level of perseverance required to reach the finish line. If you've never written a novel before, this is something to consider when determining your medium of choice.

But what about the other prose formats? Perhaps your plot idea or protagonist(s) would be better served in a novella, novelette—or even a short story?

If you're wondering what the difference in length is for these categories, the numbers below are *general* ranges:

- Short story—7,500 words or less
- Novelette—7,501—17,500 words
- Novella—17,501—40,000 words
- Novel—40,001 or more words

Some stories are better told in one category than another. Not only in terms of the crafting of the tale, but also with regard to the writer's goals and priorities.

For example, one of my published horror stories is called "The Dark at the End of the Tunnel," which later became the name of my first collection. However, it was originally conceived as a feature film called *Spectres*. In fact, when the story was first published in the anthology *Fear the Reaper*, it was titled "Spectres."

The story had started as a loose outline for a spec screenplay, but I knew it needed to be fleshed out quite a bit. The main story beats were there, but there wasn't much in the way of characterization or backstory. I have a thick backlog of these kinds of story ideas, and when I was honest with myself, I knew that the likelihood of turning it into a script was pretty much zero (for many of the reasons I mentioned earlier).

Fortunately, the plot ended up working quite well for a short story. I can't emphasize enough that sometimes it's not about the money. And while I was paid for this story, it was the satisfaction of seeing it published in a book alongside other great authors, and having readers tell me how much they enjoyed it, that made the experience priceless.

There are advantages and disadvantages when choosing a novel, novelette, novella and short story. The larger the scale the more time you're afforded to develop your ideas and characters. Your plots can be more intricate. And generally speaking, there is more money to be made in the longer forms.

However, if you're a new writer, the platform of a novel might be more than you're ready to handle. And it may be too broad of a framework for you to tell a story that has a narrow scope. This is why some ideas are better served as novelettes or short stories.

If you decide to try the shorter formats, you may find that it is easier if you have less characters and settings to deal with, so you may have stronger dramatic and thematic harmony. Short fiction is also a great place for new writers to start to build their reputation and possibly get a novel contract.

Currently, I am working on a novella that would also make a great TV series. But I have chosen to write the novella rather than a TV spec for the following reasons:

1 I enjoy writing prose more.
2 I pitched the concept to a successful publisher and they agreed to publish it.
3 I know that my chances of selling it as a TV series will be enhanced if I publish it first.

Another advantage of prose writing is that all you need is a pencil, paper and an idea. You don't need a company to put up 50 million dollars and you don't need an A-list actor attached to get the green light. You won't have an exec telling you write to the ages of 18 to 25 males or 12 to 22 females.

Ultimately, if you decide to write a novel, it is the equivalent of having a completed film under your arm that needs a distributor. It is a finished work of art. And while landing a major New York publisher is extremely rare, there are a plethora of independent, small, and even micro-publishers to choose from.

There is also self-publishing, which doesn't have the stigma it had in the past. And while not for everyone, it certainly beats a screenplay, teleplay or stage play collecting dust in a drawer.

Lastly there is the issue of creative control. For me, this is incredibly important. I have a long-in-the-works novel on the horizon that was originally a screenplay pitch a couple of successful producers wanted to option. But their vision for the story meant I would have had to change most of it.

I declined the offer.

I'm glad I did, because it will be a much better novel than the hackneyed screenplay it would have been had I agreed to their vision. Did I pass up some quick cash? Yes. But the story was too important to me to give it up for a few thousand dollars.

With a novel, I have the ability to tell the story with more flexibility, and not have to worry about a lot of the perceived, prevailing Hollywood wisdom about how a story is supposed to work. Of course, most novels will never reach the large audiences that films or TV will, but for those of you who value creative control, the tradeoff can be worth it.

As you can see, there are a great deal of options for you when deciding which medium is best for your story, and more importantly, which medium is best for you.

I wish you every success in your writing journey.

INTERVIEW WITH JOHN CONNOLLY

MARIE O'REGAN

JOHN CONNOLLY was born in Dublin, Ireland in 1968. He studied English at Trinity College, Dublin and journalism at Dublin City University, subsequently spending five years working as a freelance journalist for The Irish Times newspaper, to which he continues to contribute. John is based in Dublin but divides his time between his native city and the United States, where the Charlie Parker mysteries are set.

His first novel, *Every Dead Thing*, was published in 1999, and introduced the character of Charlie Parker, a former policeman hunting the killer of his wife and daughter. *Dark Hollow* followed in 2000. The third Parker novel, *The Killing Kind*, was published in 2001, with *The White Road* following in 2002. In 2003, John published his fifth novel—and first stand-alone book—*Bad Men*. In 2004, *Nocturnes*, a collection of novellas and short stories, was added to the list, and 2005 marked the publication of the fifth Charlie Parker novel, *The Black Angel*. John's seventh novel, *The Book of Lost Things*, a story about fairy stories and the power that books have to shape our world and our imaginations, was published in September 2006, followed by the next Parker novel, *The Unquiet*, in 2007; *The Reapers*, in 2008; *The Lovers*, in 2009; and *The Whisperers*, the ninth Charlie Parker novel, in 2010. The tenth Charlie Parker novel, *The Burning Soul*, was published in 2011, to be followed in 2012 by *The Wrath of Angels*. *The Wolf in Winter*, the twelfth Parker novel, was published in April 2014 in the UK and in October 2014 in the US. 2015 saw the publication of *A Song of Shadows*, the 13th Parker novel, and *Night Music: Nocturnes Volume 2*, the second collection of short stories. Charlie Parker returned in 2016's *A Time of Torment*, and made his 15th appearance in 2017 with *A Game of Ghosts*.

In 2009, John published *The Gates*, his first novel for young adults. A sequel was published in 2011 as *Hell's Bells* in the UK and *The Infernals* in the United States; the third in the Samuel Johnson trilogy, *The Creeps*, was published in 2013 in the UK and in 2014 in the US. DreamWorks Studios acquired the Samuel Johnson trilogy in 2015 for development as a possible franchise.

Books to Die For, a nonfiction anthology co-edited by John Connolly and Declan Burke, won the 2013 Agatha, Anthony and Macavity Awards for Best Critical/Biographical Book of the year.

With his partner, Jennifer Ridyard, John published *Conquest*, the first book in the Chronicles of the Invaders series for teenaged readers, in 2013. The second book in that series, *Empire*, followed in 2015, and the third, *Dominion*, in 2016.

Hodder published *he*, a literary novel based on the life of Stan Laurel, in August 2017.

John is the recipient of the Shamus Award for Best First P.I. Novel for *Every Dead Thing*; the Barry Award for Best British Crime Novel for *The White Road*, winner of the Agatha Award for Best Nonfiction and Anthony Award for Best Critical Nonfiction for *Books to Die For* (with Declan Burke), and the Edgar and Anthony Awards for Best Short Story for *The Caxton Private Lending Library and Book Depository*. He has also been nominated for many more. A big thank you to John, who kindly agreed to this interview by Marie O'Regan, on the subject of writing.

MOR: Who would you say was your greatest writing influence?

JC: Gosh, that's so hard to answer. I've read so many books, and I'd like to think I've absorbed lessons from a lot of writers: James Lee Burke, Ross Macdonald, M.R. James, P.G. Wodehouse, Dumas, Dickens—although that risks making me sound as though I think I can hold a candle to any of them, and I can't. ("Yeah, I am a bit like Dickens, actually. We both liked facial hair . . . ")

Burke was an influence in terms of the beauty of his writing, and his unwillingness to accept that genre, by its nature, should be the poor relative of literary fiction when it comes to quality of prose. I've always found that distinction between genre fiction and literary fiction to be largely arbitrary anyway. All fiction should aspire to the condition of literature. Macdonald, meanwhile, is the great poet of empathy in the mystery genre, and a writer who gradually came to realise that the series of novels he was writing about the private detective Lew Archer weren't some stopgap, or means to make money, while he was planning his great literary work. These books would be his great literary work.

As for the rest, I loved the tactile nature of the horrors in James' work, the sense that they can be touched, and can touch one in turn. And I couldn't love someone who didn't love Wodehouse's Jeeves & Wooster books. People are sometimes surprised by the level of humour in my work, but without it some of my novels would be very bleak—and untrue to human beings, and their capacity to imbue even the darkest of situations with a certain wit.

MOR: You started out in journalism; at what point did you know you wanted to write fiction?

JC: I actually wrote very little fiction for a long time. I worked in local journalism before going to college and moving on to national newspapers. I suppose I saw journalism as a way to be paid to write, but I never really started out thinking I would become a novelist. I think I just became gradually disenchanted with journalism, and there must have been a secret little part of me that actually rather hoped to follow a fiction path. Journalism was a great discipline, though, in terms of removing any preciousness from me, and treating writing as a craft, as something that had to be practised and refined. The relationship between journalism and fiction is complicated. Rather fewer journalists become novelists than one might expect, even though virtually every journalist harbours a secret, or not-so-secret, desire to write a longer work. In part, it's because they're very different disciplines, and the longer one works as a journalist, creating pieces that rarely exceed a few thousand words at most, the harder it becomes to commence work on something that may extend to 100,000 words or more. The muscle becomes trained to a different task. In that sense, I probably got out of journalism just in time. I'd spent about five years at it before *Every Dead Thing* was accepted for publication, and now I find myself in the opposite position: journalism, the succinctness of it, is quite difficult for me, and writing an article for a paper or magazine takes me much longer than writing a similar number of words as part of a novel. I'm inclined to fret, to overthink. That particular muscle has atrophied a little.

MOR: Is there any subject you'd consider too dark to write about?

JC: Perhaps the darker the subject matter, the less explicit one should be. It's all a question of balance. In theory, then, the answer is no. I'd like to think that I've learned a degree of subtlety over the last twenty years. I don't believe the reader has to have his/her nose rubbed in difficult subject matter. And there's a kind of hypocrisy to that level of sadism in a novel. I've heard writers defend some pretty appalling stuff by arguing that they have an obligation to depict the world as it is, but fiction has no such obligation. It's not a mirror to reality, it's a prism. It refracts experience. Also, I think some writers are reluctant to admit that part of their aim is to shock the reader, and that's a downward spiral. We have, as consumers, become increasingly inured to violence. Most of us are pretty hard to shock. I'm reluctant to go down that path now, although it's a lesson that took me a while to learn. *Every Dead Thing* is probably far too explicit in parts, and I wouldn't write a novel like that now. Then again, I had an elderly woman come up to me on my last promotional tour to complain that my novels were no longer bloody enough, and she still liked *Every Dead Thing* more than any of the others. Maybe it's just me: I'm getting more sensitive as I get older, and I'm destined just to disappoint my readers because of it.

MOR: How do you approach crystallizing an idea until it becomes a story or a novel? Is it immediately apparent that an idea that's bubbling is suitable for a particular form, i.e. short story or novel?

JC: I suppose there is usually one idea shouting a little louder than the others, but I never have a clear conception of what I'm going to write when I commence a book. I usually only know the first couple of pages, and maybe a scene or two later. With *he*, the Stan Laurel book, I only knew that I wanted to write about him and his world, but I didn't really figure out the form until I started writing. It's a difficult way to construct books. The voice of doubt is very clear right from the start. As for short stories, I don't write very many of them. I often think most short stories could be extended to the length of a novel, but that doesn't mean they should be. Also, I only write short stories in the supernatural form. I have no interest in writing short crime stories because I don't read them myself. The pleasure of the supernatural short story lies in not having to explain anything. They're just glimpses, a momentary lifting of the veil. Finally, I kind of have to redesign the machinery of my writing for short stories. They use a different mind space, and slightly different writing muscles. That's why I write so few of them. My concentration tends to be fixed on the longer form.

MOR: Do you plot when you write, or do you prefer to let the story develop?

JC: No. Like I said above, the experience of writing the first draft is, for me, a little like the reader's experience of reading it. It's a process of discovering the book. I'm not sure I'd want to write a book that I'd laid out beforehand. It would no longer interest me, even at that early stage. But I also suspect I live so long with some of the ideas before they're set down that some work may have been done by my subconscious, and so when I begin to write the story what emerges has been conditioned by that period of gestation. In other words, it may seem that I'm making it up as I go along, but what I'm actually doing is refining something that's been simmering away unnoticed for quite some time.

MOR: Do you ever have a problem with writers' block? If so, how do you get past it?

JC: I don't think there is any single malady called

writers' block; it's different for every writer. If I've been traveling a lot, or doing promotion, and haven't been writing regularly, I find it very had to get back into the flow. It's like going to the gym: if you fall out of the habit of going, it starts to seem like the hardest thing in the world to get back to it. My solution, when I'm growing weary, is usually to write something else: I exchange fiction for non-fiction, or vice versa. And I write in different forms—mystery, fantasy, literary— which keeps me interested. And, in the end, I may find writing difficult or frustrating at times, but I still love doing it. I'm very privileged to be able to support myself solely by writing, and I live in fear of that privilege being taken away. So I work hard, and I write pretty much every day. It's a kind of duty, in return for the opportunity I've been given.

MOR: And finally, what advice would you give to a writer starting out?

JC: Try to finish everything. You'll always find your enthusiasm for a project waning as it goes on, and you'll be tempted by a new idea, but learn to ignore the latter and continue with the former. If you start abandoning work, you set a bad precedent, and establish a pattern for the years to come. And be nice to booksellers: never let them pay for a round.

THE STORY OF A STORY

with a Number of Digressions

MORT CASTLE

That's Good!

I WROTE A good story entitled "Altenmoor, Where the Dogs Dance." Actually, I like to think I've written between 30 and 40 really good short stories (out of the hundreds I've published) but to deal with the myriad topics suggested by this book's title, *Where Nightmares Come From: The Art of Storytelling in the Horror Genre*, it's probably best I focus on only one work of fiction.

How did I come to judge the story as "good," you might ask.

Me, I usually rely on outside validation.

Yeah, yeah, I've heard all the bumper sticker philosophy:

Trust yourself.

Write to please your most important audience: You.

What do they know, anyway?

But too often I've created work on which I was hyperbolically high, convinced that heavenly angels whispered every phrase, word, and semi-colon in my ear, only to see those stories sharply criticized (often rightly, I frequently decided in hindsight with new insight) or labeled as page filling mediocrity (I often assented when I compared 'em to other stories appearing in the same anthology or magazine) or even fail to get published (usually when I most needed a goddamn check, goddamnit).

Conversely, some stories that I thought of as "not bad for a potboiler," or perhaps one scrooch better than the literary equivalent of a Tony Danza dramatic performance have gone on to win praise, reprints, and prizes.

I often tell my students that, for at least the first ten years you're writing, you are not the best judge of your own work. I seldom tell them you may never become the unerring, best judge of your own work. I haven't.

Anyway, the outside validifiers have been *tres* good to "Altenmoor: Where the Dogs Dance." The story placed sixth in the short fiction category of the annual Writer's Digest Creative Writing Contest, which that year attracted more than 10,000 entries. The story was published in 1982 in Twilight Zone magazine, and not subject to debate, Twilight Zone, then under the editorship of Ted Klein, was the best "weird fiction" magazine of the era (or maybe even ever), and "Altenmoor" has not been out of print since. It's been translated into eight or ten foreign languages, French, German, and Polish among 'em. It's a favorite for junior high and secondary school speech contests. The late editor, writer, and literary historian Bob Weinberg ranked it *Numero Uno* on his list of "Unforgettable

Stories." It's morphed into comics format for the compilation Shadow Show, a Bram Stoker award-winner for "Superior Achievement in a Graphic Novel," and it has twice been filmed. The first time was Michael Schroeder's production for the George Lucas Film Program at the University of Southern California, and then, in 2009, under the title "Elysium," director/screenwriter Nenad Arsenijevic, produced it in Serbia. In Serbian. And showed it at film festivals in Greece and Hungary.

That's "Altenmoor's" brag sheet.

Good story, okay?

How did it happen?

Ideas Come Easy

Let's start with the classic/cliché question that will no doubt be addressed in some way by half the essays in this book: *Where do you get ideas?*

The candid answer: Sometimes I steal.

Hey, no need to give myself a migraine trying to create original concepts when there are so many absolutely fine, pre-packaged and ready to go story springboards already out there, premises that have proven themselves by serving as foundations of published works.

I purloined the original "Altenmoor" story idea from the late Philip Jose Farmer, the science-fiction writer and Pundit of Peoria (Illinois). Farmer's best known for his Riverworld speculative-historical novels of sometimes dry, sometimes raunchy humor and philosophy, but he worked in the short fiction genre, too (once upon a time, darned near everybody did. See "ancient history," "real magazines and not internet BS," etc.).

In Farmer's "Father's in the Basement," a story of just under 3,000 words, we have a writer with a bad heart, desperately typing in his cellar office on *the* novel that will guarantee him a degree of literary immortality, lift him out of and high above the shabby pack of hacks where he's spent his writing career. In a shock ending, but one for which Farmer fairly plants foreshadowing clues, Millie, the writer's 11-year-old daughter, gifted with witch-like powers, helps dad finish his masterwork, even though he's dead. The discovery is made by the authorities that . . .

" . . . His fingertips are worn off, the bones are sticking out, but there wasn't any bleeding."

"I got him through," Millie said. "He finished it. That's all that counts."

I liked the idea of the child helping her father.

I liked the idea of a kid making magic (black or otherwise tinted).

There's something about your faith when you are a kid. Everyone reading this has, I am sure, your personal, vivid, unforgettable dream of flying: your feet find a certain natural rhythm, your lift your arms just so . . . and there, maybe with the magic word, or the invisible sky hook feather held between your teeth, there it is! Lift Off! Up, up, and away!

And when you woke, you had that a lingering and it feels so true sense that if you ever managed to get your feet moving just that way and raised your arms just so and remembered the magic word or recalled where you'd left your sky hook feather . . . You honest-to-God-no-kidding-kiddo could indeed fly!

You don't have to be a Wordsworthian Romantic to acknowledge that speck of belief we carry with us all our days that we do possess wondrous magical ability—if only our faith is strong and our thoughts pure and we discover the proper protocol to Make! It! Happen!

And so, I roughed out the story in my head (I never do more than a written note or two for short stories. No need for an outline as such. Even a b-b sized brain should be able to hold onto the totality of a short story—maybe even two stories).

There's this kid who knows his grandfather is not long for this world.

The kid is not a big fan of funerals. The whole idea of seeing grandpa powdered, stiff, and dead in a coffin while people mill about and say redundant, platitudinous nothings does not appeal to him. And he knows good and well his free-thinking grandfather would not dig the scene, either.

So, through sheer power of belief, the kid *wills* grandfather up from the deathbed. The kid stands at the door as Grandpa Corpse, arms before him like the Frankenstein monster, lurches out into a midnight swirling snowstorm.

The boy tells no one what he has done.

Grandfather is never found.

The End.

That was the story I planned to write.

PS: I did not plan to award a credit . . .

Based on an idea lifted from Mr. Phillip Jose Farmer.

There's little enough money in the writing biz. You don't want to split with anyone unless you have to.

Why Horror?

Time travel with me, please: I wrote "Altenmoor" some years back. As I recall, I started it in 1979. I was working then on a state of the art Smith-Corona electric portable typewriter which allowed me to correct a goof by simply a) popping out the ink ribbon cartridge, b) inserting the correction tape cartridge, c) backspacing to the goofed letter(s); d) retyping the goofed letters to cover them with white-out from the correction cartridge e) removing the correction cartridge and re-inserting the ribbon cartridge e) properly typing the word(s) that should have been there.

At the time, I was like so many (all?) writers, quite self-absorbed. I was interested in the writing process— *my* writing process.

So, as I worked on "Altenmoor," I studied my writing technique.

I learned that a quirk of my psyche demanded a page be *right* before I could go on to the next page. I was not a "throw it down beginning-to-end in a creative cyclone and then revise the whole *megillah* later."

That meant, to come up with the seven and a half typed pages that became the final draft, I typed just over 200 pages.

(Today's nostalgia for typewriters . . . Believe me, when word processing personal computers came on the scene, thanks to my wife's encouragement and a bank loan, I bought a Kaypro II computer. It had an easy to read 9-inch green screen, two 5 1/4" floppy drives, Wordstar software, and a Brother daisy wheel printer: insert a single sheet at a time to bang out the page at 16 cps with a Gatling gun soundtrack.)

As alluded to previously, it was also a time in which there were more than a few paying markets open to fiction writers. No, not *Playboy* or *Atlantic*, the chances of the average shmo selling there equaled the likelihood of flying with your magic word and feather, but plenty of mid and low pay publications did abide and abound and could be found at street corner newsstands, racks in such esoteric locales as Kroger, Jewel-Osco, and Walgreens, and even bookstores. I paid my mortgage by selling to the confessions mags ("Will He Ever Touch Me the Way He Touches Her?"), the men's magazines ("Will I Ever Touch Her and Make Her Go Ugga-woo! Oingo-Boingo-Gosharootie?"), the science-fiction, speculative fiction, and weird fantasy ("There is a Fifth Dimension beyond that which is known to man where You Might be Touched by . . . ")

Why a horror story?

I knew I could likely find a decent paying market for it.

But you could have written a story about a devoted collie who saves a little boy from drowning in the well and then the following sunshiny Sunday, the whole town celebrates with a big picnic . . . You could sell a story like that to a magazine like Aspiring Baptist Guideposts . . .

Nah.

That's not the way my brain is set up.

I've shared this before, but all horror writers are frequently asked, "Why do you write"—pause, cocking of head, perhaps some trepidation—"*horror*?"

My answer is . . .

I like it.

And, somehow, that leads to the question . . .

"But *why* do you like it?"

The answer is, "I don't know."

My friend F. Paul Wilson (we're so close I call him F), a fine writer of thrillers, mysteries, science-fiction and horror, has said he's convinced the liking for horror is hard-wired in a person. It's a matter of DNA.

Just like the roller coaster aficionado is what he is and what he is cannot be explained to the person who gets vertigo on the first step of a foot-high step stool.

I mean, Wilson ought to know. He's also a medical doctor.

Me, I always loved stories, and thus I was always drawn to the horrific, the terrifying, the dark and the scary and I've learned that most horror writers say the same.

All kids have nightmares (just like adults).

I was one of those kids who had 'em and liked 'em. When I was seven and a half, I had a dream that I remember to this day, a dream which in its own fictionally altered way, has informed ever so much of my writing.

I was the kid apprentice to the secret village poisoner. It was my job to grind up a yellow poison with the mortar and pestle and sneak into peoples' houses and dose their food and drink with the poison. Nobody suspected the village poisoner or his apprentice.

The "child with a terrible secret" theme.

I know. I was a kid. Must have been something wrong with me. I should have been dreaming about fluffy bunnies and wax lips and elves named Clippy and Dippy.

I wasn't.

I had nightmares and I loved them (I'll have more to say in a bit and what enters your head in the night when you sleep).

I loved scary movies. They weren't as all enveloping as nightmares, but you could turn them off with one button. Thank you, Chicago's Shock Theatre, hosted by a beatnik style, sardonic guy named Marvin. Shock Theater introduced me to Frankenstein's Monster and even as a kid I sensed there was something sad as well as bad about that monster.

Shock Theater introduced me to *King Kong* . . .

I could relate to that one. You know the scene in which Kong grabs the elevated train car? Well, I rode the Chicago elevated train, "the L," regularly, and it didn't take much for me to imagine a big furry apely digit smashing through the L train's window during a metal on metal screeching turn . . .

Dracula scared me. Not the Lugosi Dracula in the first filmed version but the Dracula he portrayed in *Abbott and Costello Meet Frankenstein*. I mean, if Abbot and Costello weren't safe, these guys who were on the Colgate Comedy Hour, then nobody was safe. When Dracula turned into a bat, thanks to simple animation back in those pre-CGI days, that got to me.

Anyway, by third grade, I knew I could write. I mean, I could even write cursive (not very well, which is why I learned to type in the fourth grade . . .).

I could write . . . stories!

I could write stories that scared me. We all begin as our own first audience.

But I was a munificent child.

It would have been selfish to keep my stories to myself. I wanted to share them and scare others.

So, to paraphrase and mangle a bit cranky old poet Robert Frost: "I write horror because that's the sort of thing horror writers write."

I could sell horror and I liked horror so . . .

Gangway!

I'm a'writing a horror story!

Character is What You are in the Dark— Dwight Moody

Really important writing rule: Short stories have characters.

Really important writing rule: There has to be a main character in a short story. You call him the *protagonist*, proving your literary studies progressed beyond third grade.

There are all kinds of charts to guide your character creation.

What is your character's astrological sign? Does he fit the typical pattern for Cancer the Crab, Taurus the Bull, Nemo the Clownfish?

When is your character's favorite relative?

Aunt Felicity, who gave her a roll of duct tape for her ninth birthday. This got her started on a hobby she practices to this day.

Name the last three books your character read—if your character can read. Were his lips injured by the experience?

In all seriousness, I have used and do use character charts (one of the best was developed by writer and Columbia College Chicago adjunct prof Tina Jens. It's a chapter called "Such Horrible People," in the essential horror writing guide On Writing Horror, edited by a guy I'm quite close to).

If I'm working on a novel, my character sketches for important story people can run 10-15 single-spaced pages. Even in the most far-out horror and fantasy, a well-developed protagonist is a fictional someone who is every bit as alive and just as much a unique individual as anyone we really know—really well—out here in RealityLand. That way we get to know the character so well that we like or dislike, love or hate him.

You never want a reader to feel only indifference toward a character, which is what we *do* feel toward people (fictional or real!) that we don't know well.

So that means *you* must know your characters just about as well as you know yourself.

Hmm . . . as you know yourself.

So my protagonist, he's a kid, and we'll call him *Mark!* No! Make it . . . *Marky!*

He hated being called "Marky," but she was his mom, so what could he do? Dad called him "Mark," and sometimes "Son," and that was better but it still wasn't right.

True confessions: From kindergarten to second grade, when we moved, I was called . . . *Morty.* I fear it fit my image. I wasn't skinny, I was goddamned puny, with a ribcage on which you might have played the xylophone score of "The Skeleton's Dance." I had glasses like Oldsmobile headlights when eyewear could not be classed a statement of cool. I was a *Morty*. Only way that was tolerable was if you were Mickey Mouse's nephew.

But we moved. Thank God and the loosening market for Chicago apartments, I could shed my nebbishy handle and . . . "Call me Mort, or, tah-tah, old chap, if you prefer greater formality, Morton is quite acceptable."

Uh, have you heard that fiction can be, to some degree, autobiographical?

That's because fiction, at least the fiction that has worked best for me and has proven the most successful with readers is, to some degree, autobiographical!

You bet my Mark(y) character is modeled after the guy who lived (and lives) in my mirror.

And we have another important character, included in my brief plot synopsis above: the boy's grandfather.

Grandpa.

Mark has a special relationship with his grandfather.

Grandpa knew and always called him "Boy." He felt like a "boy," not "Mark," or "Son," or (phoo!) "Marky!" Grandpa knew how to talk about things so the boy understood because Grandpa was very smart.

Grandpa sat in a straight-backed chair by the window. Grandpa didn't have a rocking chair and the boy knew why because once Grandpa had told him. "Old people are supposed to sit in rockers. Seldom in my life have I done the 'supposed to's.'"

More autobiographical insight for you. I never knew my maternal grandfather. He was a tinsmith and a sheet metal worker, I understand, and chances are I'll use that info in my writing someday. I sort of knew my dad's father. He lived in Des Moines, Iowa, so I seldom saw him. He was a vaudevillian, later a storekeeper, later a deputy sheriff. For my fifth birthday, he sent me an American Flyer electric train. Though young, I was a connoisseur of plug-in railroading, knowing American Flyer was preferable to Lionel because Lionel had a three-rail track while AF had two rails just like a real train. I liked and still have the electric train (Locomotive #282). And now you know about as much about my Iowa grandfather as I do.

But my great-grandfather! He was big and funny and he raised my dad and for a while, my parents lived with him and then, later, he came to live with us. He was my roommate. We had twin beds. He did not mind that I had a pet turtle and was careful about not knocking over the small plastic turtle tank on the dresser we shared.

Grandpa Isaac—*my zeyde*—was a good guy. No coincidence, if Mark's fictional gramps was smart, so was my Grandpa Itzy. He used to start the day reading a stack of foreign newspapers: Russian, German, Lettish, Yiddish. When he was in his 60s, he taught himself to read and write English. He used to read aloud to me and so Beatrix Potter's rabbits got Yiddishfied into "Flawpsy, Cotton-tell, and *Peh-Tear*."

Then my great grandfather lost his sight to glaucoma.

And he couldn't read anymore.

(Grandpa) was so smart that long ago, when he could still see, Grandpa even used to write books.

And then . . . A dog. Yeah, my story needed a dog. That was simply a conscious decision about plot structure. The dog would die to foreshadow the impending death of Mark's Grandpa.

Plotting advice: When in doubt, kill a dog.

Write what you know? I know dogs.

In fact, I knew one dog very, very well. He was mostly Golden Retriever, had a great attitude about the world and everything in it, and was smart enough to know when he wanted a dog biscuit, he'd bring me the box so I could open it for him.

That dog's name was Rusty. He died suddenly, heart attack, the day after Thanksgiving, 1978. And the gross unfairness of a good dog's death, well, it really rattled me.

Intelligent Design? Please, consider the dog, whose essential nature is to be your best friend, forever forgiving and never breaking your confidence, four-legged unconditional LOVE come a'walking, even if you are a despicable wretch who would be condemned to Hell by Mother Teresa. A long-lived dog might make 15 to 20 years.

Now consider a lizard-croc-agator in the Amazon. The reptile's prime life's work: It bites little village kids in half when they come down to the river. This goddamn double ugly child chomper lives 50 to 100 years.

Not fair. No intelligence in that design.

In short, dogs get a crappy Cosmic deal.

So my story gained a dog named Rusty (got some imagination don't I?). And Rusty dies.

Mom said Rusty was very old. In a dog way, Rusty was more than a hundred. She said Rusty had had a very good life because everyone loved him a lot, and now Rusty's life was over.

The way Mom talked made the boy think she was trying not to frighten him. Then she hugged him so hard all his air rushed out and he thought Mom was trying not to be frightened, too.

How do you create story characters? Where do you find them?

My life is full of characters.

So is yours.

Voices in the Night

You know it when you hear it.

It's that voice that yanks you out of sleep.

It's portentous. It's prophetic. It speaks in the authoritative manner, with full reverb, that must have come directly from the burning bush when it said, "I am that I am."

And you are convinced if only you can remember the utterance that comes to you from Beyond the Beyond, it will be world changing, spiritually expanding, pretty damned terrific for you and the horse you rode in on.

But the next morning, over your Pop-Tart and French Roast, you just cannot remember what revelation snatched you from the bear hug of Morpheus.

Or worse.

You do remember!

"I've got it! This is . . . It's . . . The way to end war! NOBODY FIGHT!!!"

Or . . .

Isn't it wonderful how the tip of your index finger fits perfectly in your ear canal?

But sometimes, you get some words that do stick with you—and in some strange *nonsense* way, they *feel* like they make perfect *sense*.

Maybe that's what happened with Ms. Gertrude Stein. The Ultimato Occulto Ziggy-Zoggy ordered her to go forth and proclaim, "A rose is a rose is a rose."

And nearing death Dutch Schultz provided us with a key to the mystery of life: "French-Canadian bean soup."

Jane and I had only been married five or so years (this year, 2017, we celebrated our 46th anniversary). It's about three-thirty in the morning, and the Flashing Roar of Indisputable Wisdom fills my head. I sit bolt upright and speak The Truth, the Real Deal, the Stone Emmis:

Gone where the dogs dance, say I.

And now Jane is sitting up alongside me and she is obviously awestruck by, lo! What has been revealed by *moi!*

She says, in the tone of one righteously confirmed in the faith, "What are you talking?"

I say, "Gone where the dogs dance!"

She says, "I was asleep."

Oh, my dear, once we were all sleepers, but now we are AWAKE. I am here to say . . . *Gone where the dogs dance!*

Jane says, "That doesn't mean a thing. Forget it. Go back to sleep."

I think she also said something about writers and their not always fathomable natures. I don't really remember.

But I could not forget . . . *Gone where the dogs dance!*

I'd be stopped at a red light, tapping my fingers on the steering wheel and realize I was tapping them to my chronic ear worm: *Gone where the dogs dance.* Or I would ask a person, "Where'd you go on vacation this past summer?" and before his lips could move in reply, I'd sort of hear him say, "Gone where the dogs dance . . . "

Writers, if there's a phrase that takes up residence in your head like it's paid property tax for the past six decades, you know you've got to use it in something you write.

If you do not, someday you will be lying on your deathbed and the family will gather round to hear your last words and . . .

"Gone where the dogs dance."

What did the old goof mean by that, anyway?

Writers . . . Sheesh.

\<Insert Title Here\>

I'm not good at titles. I've never had a novel appear under the title I originally gave it. Titles for over half of my short stories and articles have been wisely changed by editors.

You know about the dancing dogs.

And "Altenmoor?"

I live 15 minutes from a nice suburb called Flossmoor.

Alten . . . That's German for Old People.

Alten + ~~Floss~~moor = Altenmoor.
"Altenmoor, Where the Dogs Dance."
I had my title.

Final Draft

I wrote the story. Wrote it in my slow, pound it out way. No "word count goal" for the day. No date circled on the calendar to give me a self-inflicted deadline. Cranking paper into Mr. Smith-Corona. Getting sometimes three sentences written before . . . *Yeah, I should keep the opening word of the dependent clause in the second sentence!* Roll paper out of typewriter and . . . One! More! Time! Leading to One! More! Time! Leading to One! More! Time! Leading to . . . Etc., etc., etc., said the King of Siam. And so it goes, said Kurt Vonnegut. Just keep pushing, said Sisyphus.

And then, one day, O frabjous day! Callooh! Callay! I chortled in my joy. 'Twas brillig!" Or at least it was as brillig as it was going to get. I had a final draft.

Well, a *nearly* final draft. Now that I had a beginning, middle, and an end (still more literary terms the aspiring writer would be well advised to learn), I could give it the last polish and then . . . Submit it!

So, let's take out the polish-it-up guidelines and . . .

Was I following the *needed* rule? That is, every paragraph, sentence, phrase, and word in a good piece of writing must be needed. So that means every paragraph, sentence, phrase, and word that is not needed gets cut. (The Prime Rule of Self-Editing: Cut, cut, cut!) And when you've finished cutting, you'll be sure that every word in your work contributes to the piece's overall effect. The yardstick to measure *needed*: If you can do the job in a sentence, don't write a paragraph. If you can do the job in a phrase, don't write a sentence. If you can do the job in a word, don't write a phrase. If you don't need a word to do the job, don't write it.

Yeah, the story was . . .

No! No, no, and O Sisyphus! I have failed!

There was the opening of the story, in which Mark went to school, was bored to borderline comatose (which is how your humble scribe regarded most of his time spent in mandatory elementary education) and thought about getting home and goofing with Rusty, his good dog, and hanging with Grandpa and . . .

The writing was smoothly functional.

But I was ignoring yet another rule. It's simple sounding and hard to follow:

Begin at the beginning

Too many stories in this age of internet word bloat begin way before the beginning. I don't think that was the case when publications had to lay out honest to God *mazuma* to put together pages and not pixels.

I discovered my story really began right there at the bottom of page six, the point at which the theme of the story is first hinted at. Prior to that, all prologue. Needless prologue. Damned few short stories and not many novels need a prologue.

So, scrap the prologue (a writer's literal or virtual wastebasket is a good working partner). First line at bottom of page six becomes the beginning of the story.

Thus "Altenmoor" opens:

> One day in spring, when the boy came home from school, he did not find Rusty in the backyard, on the screened-in porch, or anywhere downstairs in the house. He knew Rusty could not be up with Grandpa. Last winter, when the weather had gone so cold, Rusty's back legs had gone cold, too, so cold he could no longer climb stairs.

Okay, now we have it.

Final Draft Redux

We are off to the races!

Except . . . The ending.

There goes dead Grandpa, ambling, shambling, staggering off to nobody knows where and that is that . . .

And it was pat and facile and contrived and . . .

This was intended to be a horror story!

I am *not* horrified.

See, here's how it works: If I am to horrify *you*, I must first horrify *me*.

Maybe this gives me the quick grin, the "Ah ha!" tick of satisfaction that comes from a classic "the biter bit" conclusion that wrapped most of the EC comics stories in Tales from the Crypt and The Vault of Horror, but there wasn't that bone chill, the unforgettable, the . . . Quoting Kurtz, who speaks directly from personal knowledge of "the heart of darkness," "The horror! . . . The horror!"

So, how could I revise "Altenmoor," transform it . . .

It was then the story itself spoke to me.
It said, "No."

Let It Be

"No," the story says.

"No? Hold on here. You are *my* story. You must do what I . . . "

"Listen, sometimes stories start to live; they claim their independence. They must be true to their essence. You have launched the story. Now you must hear it. It will reveal what it wants to be."

"But I . . . This is my horror story."

"No. If you set out with your oil paints and brushes to create a painting of a covered bridge in New England and you wind up with "Girl with a Pearl Earring" on the canvas does that mean that girl and her headscarf and her earring and her enigmatic gaze are really meant to be a covered bridge?"

"I . . . "

"A rose is a rose is a rose."

The story was right of course. It wasn't a horror story. It wasn't about a kid with a mysterious reanimating power.

It was a story of faith and our need for belief and above all, above all, it was a story of love.

Winter moonlight seeped through the window. Grandpa was in bed, lying on his back, the blankets drawn halfway up his chest. His hands were outside the blankets, fingers of the right over those of the left.

"Grandpa?" The boy . . . thought about what

he would miss about Grandpa, things he wanted to keep in his memory. There were a lot of things, and once he was sure he had them all, the boy touched the back of Grandpa's hand, then took hold of three of Grandpa's fingers and squeezed.

Grandpa's eyes opened. Beneath the milky glaze his eyes looked right at the boy, and this time the boy was almost certain Grandpa could see him.

"Yes? What is it, Boy?"

"Are you going to Altenmoor now?" the boy said.

Slowly Grandpa sat up. "Yes, I believe I am."

"Then I have to help you."

"Yes." Grandpa nodded. "Keep hold of my hand, Boy."

The boy did. It took a long time, but he could feel himself giving all the strength he could give to Grandpa.

Then Grandpa said, "Thank you," and took away his hand.

(The boy) went to the door, then stopped and looked back. " . . . Goodbye, Grandpa."

The next morning the boy was up early because his mother and father came to his room and woke him and told him he wouldn't be going to school.

Mom held the boy close to her. She was crying.

She said, "Grandpa is gone, Marky."

"Yes," the boy said. He wished he could

explain but he knew she would never understand.

That's the conclusion of "Altenmoor, Where the Dogs Dance."
It's not a horror story.
It is what it is.
And I think it is a good story.

NOVEL ROUNDTABLE INTERVIEWS

with Kevin J. Anderson, Silvia Moreno-Garcia, and Christopher Golden

EUGENE JOHNSON AND JOHN PALISANO

What drew you to wanting to be a storyteller?

Christopher Golden: It's all I ever really wanted to be. In high school, I wanted to go to film school—become a filmmaker. My plan was to get the best education I could get, and then go to film school for graduate school. All through college I took creative writing classes, and by my senior year, I had started writing my first novel, *Of Saints and Shadows*. By then, I knew film school was not in my future.

Kevin J. Anderson: From watching monster movies as a kid, even before I could read. I would make up my own stories.

Silvia Moreno-Garcia: My great-grandmother used to tell stories, I tell stories too. The format doesn't matter, whether it's oral or written. You either want to tell stories or you don't. If you want to, you'll find a way to do it.

What is so appealing about writing a novel?

CG: I just like to tell stories. I did theater as a kid, and even then it was just about helping to tell the story. Writing a novel lets you tell the whole story, lets you pull all the strings. You get to decide every detail. Words on paper is the only medium that allows that kind of freedom and control.

KJA: Right now, I really enjoy the process. It's very satisfying to build the world, craft the storylines, get to know the characters, and then take them through the journey. Writing a book is even more satisfying than reading one. (On the same note, I prefer to cook a fine meal instead of eating in a restaurant . . .)

SMG: There is no appeal. It's just that you need more words to tell the story, so it becomes a novel. Of course, you might get paid something semi-decent if you sell a novel and someone might even read you, whereas with short stories you essentially exist in obscurity.

Can you please break down your process when setting out to tell a story with a novel?

CG: That's a huge question. I do workshops on the subject. It would be impossible to answer it effectively here. I will say that I do prefer to have at least somewhat of an outline, some idea of where I'm going . . . but I diverge from it whenever the story decides to go off on a tangent. For me, being too loose with where the story is headed—or too strict about following an outline—are both recipes for disaster.

KJA: I develop the story, jot down many storylines, write up character biographies, which usually spark other chapter ideas, other stories, other connections. It's like a snowball effect, and most of my novels are pretty substantial, 100 chapters or so, ranging from 150,000-200,000 words, and even those are usually part of a trilogy or a series. Once I have sketched out the framework, a "skeleton" outline with about one line per chapter, then I flesh that out into a full-blown outline, a paragraph or two describing the action and arc in each chapter. Then I start writing, usually two-three chapters per day, every day, until it's finished.

SMG: I don't have outlines for stories. I tend to write a rough outline with a novel. That's pretty much it.

How do you decide if a great idea is right for a novel and not a short story, or novella?

CG: I do think you can sense it. There are times when an idea that really ought to be a novella becomes a novel, or when an idea that really could be a full-length novel is a short story, but even then, you ought to have a sense of the size the story wants to be.

KJA: A novel has to be a big idea, a whole world or universe, with a cast of characters, a complex story arc—a feast, rather than an appetizer. Sometimes an idea is best served in a smaller portion, and story ideas are great too, but I really prefer to get down and dirty in a big, big project.

SMG: Gut feeling. Some ideas are only good enough for a quick snapshot view while others necessitate a longer treatment. But I don't write novellas. You can't sell them. I'm stuck with one right now.

What is different about current horror vs the horror novels of twenty years ago? Thirty?

CG: Again, we could do an entire book on the subject. Times have changed and fiction has changed to reflect the world. Beyond that, I'd say the biggest change is the difficulty finding good horror. There's plenty to be found, but gone are the days when you could walk into any bookstore and find a horror section. Some still have them, but I truly miss the ability to browse all the latest horror releases, to hold the books in my hands, read the first couple of pages. Now it's largely word of mouth, and it doesn't matter who published it or whether it was self-published. Also, so much horror is published under a different genre umbrella that often you have to really seek it out.

SMG: In the 80s and until the beginning of the 90s horror existed briefly as a category. Then the category imploded. The horror of nowadays went the way of the Western in terms of bookshelf space. You can still find horror, but it's likely not labeled that. There was also a brief period of mega thick books (Stephen King probably popularized that), but novels are no longer likely to be that long. The end of horror as a major category also gave way to a lot of tiny presses. That's the environment we live in.

How does one sustain horror through a novel-length story?

CG: Through character, always. The situation might be terrifying, but the reader isn't going to feel it unless the characters feel it, and unless you can make the reader afraid FOR the characters.

KJA: Several techniques. You can build and sustain a brooding, ominous sense of suspense through atmospherics, and that permeates the story. You can make sure the reader cares about your characters, so that when they are in danger, the sense of horror is greater (when a random security guard gets eaten by the monster, it's entertaining but not usually gut-wrenching). You can add suspenseful, pulse-pounding action scenes—a scary chase through the woods, for instance. And you can even use violence and gore for the shock value.

What does a horror novel offer a reader that a short story doesn't?

CG: I love both, but a novel gives the author much more opportunity to build a world, to bring the reader inside that world, to a place where imagination creates texture and atmosphere. It's harder to do that in depth if you're writing five thousand words. Not at all impossible. Just harder.

KJA: A story can be a quick scare, a twist ending, something to shock and disturb the reader. But it's one strike and you're out if it doesn't work. A novel, like

The Shining, can build and build, ratcheting up the horror, riveting the reader as things get progressively worse.

What does horror bring as a genre that others don't? What does it do well?

CG: Horror is the most human genre. It has no real boundaries. In horror you can write about anything, any theme. Fear is universal.

KJA: It has a way of showcasing our fears, our sins, our mortality in ways that other genres don't (many genres deal with those questions, but horror makes them front and center). I remember when *Silence of the Lambs* was up for the Bram Stoker Award for best horror novel, the author or the publisher disputed that it was a horror novel, saying instead, "No, it's a visceral exploration of the darkest side of human nature." Umm, that's what horror IS.

SMG: All genres can do all things. Except maybe romance, since romance is understood to have a happy ending. Hence romance can't really do tragedy, at least our contemporary romances with their contract of a Happily Ever After. I don't know why horror appeals to others, but growing up, I liked it because it allowed me to escape. A werewolf's lair or a scary haunted mansion were more appealing than some of my daily interactions. I couldn't quite escape the same way with other genres. Perhaps it just makes you feel better that at least you are not being chased by homicidal children in a cornfield. I also like the feeling of the uncanny. Unheimlich.

Is there a future for horror in mainstream literature? It's been re-branded, its sections taken away from chains, even as the top-rated television shows are horror. Why does horror literature seem to take a backseat in literary circles and retail?

CG: Too many people still think horror as a genre means gore or ultra-violence for its own sake. I hope that changes someday, but I've been saying that for more than twenty years.

KJA: There's always a future for horror, and I've never been a fan of labels anyway, because I write all over the place in whatever genre interests me, whatever story needs to be told. The whole publishing and book industry is undergoing dramatic shifts; there may be a fine renaissance, so long as readers can find it.

SMG: Because it doesn't sell anymore, not in the numbers it needs to. If something sells, it'll get a section. I also doubt the top-rated TV shows are all horror. *Game of Thrones* is not horror. Do we have horror shows on the air, movies? Sure. But you shouldn't confuse what works on screen with what works in print. The biggest selling book category is romance. If our TV shows reflected that, then most shows would have to be soap operas and most top-earning movies would be romances. But that's not the case.

Are there any lines you won't cross? Are there lines even horror shouldn't cross?

SMG: No, but I find 'extreme' horror to be extremely dull.

Are extreme subjects and situations tainting horror? Or are they making it more appealing than ever?

KJA: I don't like portraying the violent misogynist or child molester as a good guy. I don't like showing torture as a fun activity. There are too many nuts out there who might be inspired.

How are horror novels reflecting the current world climate? Or are they? Are they instead becoming retro comfort zones for their readers and fans like *Stranger Things*?

CG: Both things are happening, no question. And I definitely think you'll see more and more of both, particularly as the climate continues to unravel.

KJA: I certainly enjoy fun nostalgic horror, like *Stranger Things*, but also really intense psychological stories. Can a horror writer really concoct something worse than what ISIS has done to real prisoners? People read for various reasons. One size doesn't fit all.

SMG: I suppose all fiction reflects our current situation. There's a bit of a retro vibe in some quarters right now, but I don't think it's an overwhelming trend.

Who are some horror authors that we should all be reading?

SMG: Nadia Bulkin has her first collection out now. She is one of the more interesting writers to pop up in recent years.

Do you have any advice for writers reading this book and for writers out there wanting to write a horror novel?

CG: Keep your day job. I'd say this to any writer, not just horror writers. I've been a full-time writer for twenty-five years—I just turned fifty—but if I were starting out now, I'd wait and be damned sure I could support myself as a writer before going all in. As for writing advice—write what you love. Life is too short and publishing is too unpredictable to worry about what's popular.

KA: Read a lot, write a lot, learn a lot, get better each time, and don't give up. Nobody ever said this was an easy profession. Oh, and don't quit your day job!

SMG: Read Shirley Jackson. Read things that are not horror. Read authors you wouldn't expect to classify as 'horror' writers, like Patricia Highsmith, who never the less wrote some very nice horror stories, including one of the best snail horror tales ("The Snail-Watcher"). Check out current writers who are successful in the mainstream with horror books. Paul Tremblay, Joe Hill. Be aware of the publishing environment. It's not 1975.

HOW I SPENT MY CHILDHOOD LOOKING FOR MONSTERS AND FOUND POETRY

For Mom and Dad

STEPHANIE M. WYTOVICH

WHEN I WAS LITTLE, my father used to create treasure hunts for me in our basement by building these huge, sweeping blanket forts that he'd fill with whatever odds and ends were lying around the house— baskets, flashlights, costumes, and one time, even a giant stuffed cow head—and in each separate world he'd create, he'd tell me a story, a haunting tale of death and mystery, destruction and twice-lost riches. These stories were often about giant monsters that lived in our crawl space, or pirates who had buried dark secrets underneath the foundation of our house. I spent my childhood looking under my bed and creeping around corners, and for years, I ran around dressed as a spy or an archaeologist, a doctor or a storm chaser, ever trying to find clues, or dig up fossils, or track tornados as a way to keep the characters and pictures of my father's stories alive.

I had a [plastic] skeleton that I built bone by bone, only to then beg my parents for plastic organs to stick inside him so I could see how the body worked and structured itself against other mammals.

I drew pictures of faraway worlds where everything was topsy-turvy or inside out because I was hesitant to take everything around me at face value.

I sat outside for hours at night looking at the sky and consulting it against my constellation book so I could learn to read the stars.

Needless to say, I had a wild imagination, not to mention a voracious drive to learn.

My dad then started to write short poems on scraps of paper in our junk drawer and leave them for me all throughout the house. My mom and I would find all these ridiculous little riddles that we would have to solve in order to find the treasure, or our lunch, or whatever else my dad had decided to hide from us that day. Even now, all these years later, when one of us has to communicate something to the other, we still leave limericks and brainteasers for the other to find as a way to keep our old blanket-fort worlds alive.

That was my first introduction to storytelling, but as I got older, my dad only got more creative.

You see, Halloween is my family's Christmas, always has been, and it was non-negotiable that my brother and I harbor an intense love of the holiday, much like my mom and dad who tried to make our first words 'trick or treat.' Needless to say, soon enough my treasure hunts turned into nightmare machines and it wasn't long before the Wytovich Scare War (WSW) was born.

I can vividly remember the first time I saw M.

Night Shyamalan's *Signs* (2002), because it created my intense fear of aliens and all things that lurk in space ready to probe, prick, and experiment on me. My dad, seeing my fear first hand at the drive-ins, decided that my 13-year-old self would take the dogs out when we got home, so he and my mom could start turning the wheels on that evening's trauma fest. So there I was, standing outside in the dark with my dogs, when the entire house went black. I tiptoed into the garage turning on every light as I moved, but when I got into our kitchen, my parents were gone, and the house was stone silent. My first thought was to get to my room and lock the door so wherever they were hiding, eventually they'd get bored and give up, but oh did young Stephanie have much to learn.

My dad was under my bed.

My mom was in my closet.

And down the hall in his room was my brother praying they wouldn't decide to take him to a movie next.

This kind of stuff went on for years. I've gone to leave for work in the morning only to find a stuffed clown in my backseat, and I've stepped into the shower only to see a Grim Reaper mask hanging from the faucet. My favorite WSW memory though, has to be the time when my father dressed up as the old man we used to put out on our porch every year for Halloween.

I can remember getting off the school bus and searching frantically for my house key—something that I was notorious for losing—and upon realizing that I had left it in my room that morning, went to sit on the porch to wait for my dad to get home. Little did I know, my dad was already home and he had purposefully parked his truck in our garage and swapped out the clothes with the old man on the porch. So as I sat there, daydreaming and picking my nail polish, my dad sat behind me in a mask, rocking in our chair and waiting for the perfect moment to scare the hell out of me.

Nice, right?

I vaguely recall him making a noise of some sort, maybe a mumble or two under his breath, and me turning around, anxiously searching behind me, only to find nothing, no aberration in sight. When I heard it again and chose to get up and physically walk the porch to see if something was there, my father jumped from the chair and grabbed me, sending me into a spiral of screams and kicks against his laughs.

I'm sure a lot of you are shaking your heads now and wondering who does this to their kids. I have no doubts that this seems cruel at first, but I can assure you that it was all in good fun, and that my brother and I got our revenge on more than one glorious occasion, so while I was undoubtfully crying and screaming that night on the porch, I was also impressed and terrified and proud when my dad took the mask off, and as much as I hate to admit it, even now, my dad usually wins the WSW.

I bring all of this up because playing make-believe and creating nightmares is a lot of what writing poetry is all about. It took me years to understand this because when I was first introduced to the form, I was counting syllables and drawing stress marks and trying not to get an ulcer from my many attempts at memorizing Shakespeare's Sonnet 18. This study, while important—and arguably necessary—was infuriating to me because it took all the fun away from writing. I wasn't able to escape into my nightmares because I was too caught up in the formalities and rules of the form, and because of that, my poetry ended up lacking emotion, depth, and imagery. I would often think about the ghost stories my dad would tell me and how I'd go to sleep at night with the covers pulled tight around my neck, or about how the first time I read Edgar Allan Poe's "The Tell-Tale Heart," how I checked under my bed and pressed my ear to the floor to try and hear the dead man's heart.

That feeling of terror, that striptease of suspense . . . *That* was what I wanted to bring to the form: dancing amorphous line breaks, brusque images dripping with crow's feathers and blood, a culmination of sweeping phantasmagoria soaked in an insidious tone that screeched like wolf spiders when you killed them.

So when I discovered free-verse poetry, it truly felt like being exonerated, freed from the chains holding me back, chains that later on in my career, I would actually seek out and enjoy as a challenge. But at that moment, I reveled in being able to paint pictures out of sounds, create music with images. Much like my dad, I used the world around me and collected metaphors and scents that spoke to me. I drafted lines and slept in negative space, listening to what absence had to say. It was wonderful and enlightening, but despite the leash being off, in some ways, I almost struggled more. I realized that having a lack of rules was intimidating because it became harder to find my voice, my rhythm. With everything possible and tangible, I now had to find myself in my nightmare. I experimented for years before the words started to come in a shape that worked for me, and even then, I was constantly searching for new patterns and arrangements to help grow the horror I had been nurturing since birth.

You see, writing poetry is a lot like writing fiction but without the expectation of formalities. What I mean by that, is that while there are a variety of ways to write fiction with each author having his own voice and style, the craft still requires grammatical accuracy and conventional composition techniques like complete sentences and the proper use of a sentence fragment. Poetry, however, allows you to close your eyes and jump into the ether, survive on your stream of consciousness. You're still telling stories, but you're leaving sensory images behind, creating through taste, touch, and sound. Pacing is important, so you might write the entire poem in one continual sentence to equivocate a rush, an increase in adrenaline or panic, or you might space it out using short lines and terminal punctuation to show the impact of finality. There might be scattered punctuation throughout to show your breath, or there might be none at all to show chaos or forced meditation. In poetry, you're telling the story with your words, yes, but you're always whispering the narrative in the shape of your stanzas and the length of your lines.

Periods can be death notes.

Commas can be a surge of fresh air.

In a lot of ways, being a poet is being a visual artist.

Each key stroke, every space, helps paint the picture, tell the story.

Now despite my upbringing in a Nosferatu-loving

home, I grew up in a small town with small resources, and I had little idea of what was really out there in the world when it came to art that wasn't mainstream and being shoved down my throat. Our town's library was small and arguably not to my tastes—*did people actually not like the idea of a masked axe-wielding maniac chasing after teenagers?*—so when I got to college, I was amazed at the wealth of possibilities that I was now able to access and study.

When I decided I wanted to write poetry on a professional level, I made a lot of decisions that probably would seem counterintuitive at first. As a freshmen undergraduate student, I made the choice to double major in English Literature and Art History, rather than focus my studies on Creative Writing. I did this because: 1) I wanted to study literature to find out how and why it worked, as well as fine-tune my tastes and influences, 2) I wanted to look at visual art and understand its roots and influences on contemporary culture, and 3) I needed to read as much as possible. Now this isn't a plug for higher education, but it is a rally cry stating that if you want to write, you have to read, and more importantly, you have to read as much outside of your chosen genre as within.

In fact, immerse yourself in art completely: music, art, performance, drama, literature, film.

It will open your eyes to new techniques and philosophies, and your writing will be thankful for the sustenance later on.

Tangents aside, the more I studied literature, the more I started to understand the way stories worked and the better able I was to find my voice. I tracked allegories and allusions, sifted through themes and anachronisms, and this all became paramount to my poetry, because in a lot of ways, I was learning how to tell a story, and better yet, how to tell it well. I needed to see how the structure of a story worked, how the denouement was delivered against a background of rising and falling tension. I became fascinated in all the different ways stories were delivered, whether classically, or through epistolary or stream-of-conscious verse. It was fascinating to me and it opened my eyes to different ways I could format my poems and deliver stories with variations on line break, white space, and punctuation. Couple that with what I learned from studying art, i.e. the importance of light and shadow, how to blend color, the importance of history and movement, body image and medium, and I was almost overwhelmed.

I stared at Francis Bacon's paintings for hours and marveled at Salvador Dali's films and visions. Frida Kahlo gave me strength and confidence, showed me how to turn my art inward and embrace the notion of identity and reflection, and Georgia O'Keefe taught me about the representation of female sexuality. I walked through Dublin and Florence, New Orleans and Los Angeles and I devoured architecture and took photographs, spent the nights in abandoned buildings and visited Death Museums throughout the country. I couldn't stop watching David Cronenberg films, and when I first saw *Alice in Wonderland* played out as a ballet, I couldn't have stopped smiling if you cut off my lips with a chainsaw.

Inspiration was (and is) everywhere, and it became obvious to me about halfway through college that I thrived on finding horror in the seemingly safe and innocuous, in addition to the otherworldly and vaguely threatening. I would walk around campus and take pictures of wooden chairs and flower gardens, vegetable patches and baseball fields, and then I'd look for the doors, the subtle nuances that allowed me to take the harmless and give it a knife.

I kept a notebook under my bed and wrote my nightmares in it.

I made collages of art that inspired my fears and phobias.

I kept a running note on my phone filled with odd couplings and strange title ideas.

When I started writing and submitting poetry to professional markets, I knew who I was as a person, and I continued to work on whom I was as a poet. While leafing through poetry collection after chapbook, biography after memoir, I began to understand my morals and soapbox lectures, my dislikes as well as my obsessions. Plath spoke to me in a way that Anne Sexton screamed. Ted Hughes had a brilliant accent but he had nothing on Charles Simic who left me breathless page after page. I wanted to comb through the spirit world with W. B. Yeats and contemplate the human soul with Rumi.

I watched YouTube clips of Bukowski doing live readings, and I downloaded audio clips of contemporary poets performing poetry slams. I wanted to see the line breaks in their breathing and hear the inflections of their tones as they spat or paused. Ginsberg taught me how to be blunt, and Neruda taught me how to be soft. I started following magazines and reading literary journals, holding myself accountable to reading a least one poem a day.

By graduate school, I realized that my love affair with horror had sent me searching for monsters in my childhood, but as an adult, I'd found them and collected them in poetry instead. I wrote raw, vulnerable lines about mental illness. I talked with psychopaths in stanzas crafted from untreated traumas. I took what I learned from art and from literature, from years of solving riddles and crawling out of blanket forts, and I focused and honed it in a way that let readers see how horror, to me, has always been a game of survival, a trial run to confront what's waiting for you beneath the covers, around the corner, or deep inside your head.

It was important to me in my writing to take my fears and paranoia, my weaknesses and vulnerabilities, and give them teeth. I'd spent years watching movies and reading books where women were used as vessels, as toys, as stock characters made up and presented for marriage, sex, or enjoyment. I wanted my poetry, my stories, to reflect the strength that was in the female psyche, body, and soul, and further bring out the concept of the final girl, the last girl standing, the one who solves the mystery, kills the bad guy, and survives the nightmare.

But you know, with her clothes on.

So needless to say, when I take out my journal, or sift through photographs and collages, highlighted books and collections of quotes, it's hard not to think of those first moments of terror standing outside my house in the dark while my parents lurked in the shadows of my bedroom, laughing and waiting for me to wander on in so they could start that night's version of the scare war. For me, it's impossible to imagine myself as a horror writer without my dad's blanket forts and made-up excavations, without my mom handing me *Pet Sematary* and making me watch *The Lost Boys*. My parents were the ones who taught me about mysteries and curiosities, oddities and suspension of disbelief. And trust me, when you grow up in a household where Dracula teaches you to count, and a copy of *Christine* is your 16th birthday present, it's hard not to see the world covered in cobwebs and fog.

But truthfully, I wouldn't have it any other way.

I love being able to sit down at night with a cup of coffee or a glass of wine and call my mom to read her my latest poem, or have my dad look at a story to tell me if it scares him or not. It's fun to hear my mother tell me the pause in my poem reminds her of the static on the phone in *Black Christmas,* just like it will never get old hearing my father say "Stephanie, is the eroticism really necessary in this poem?" and then having to have yet another conversation with him about the shadow self according to Carl Jung. It's a small joy being able to share that kind of enjoyment and conversation with my parents, and oftentimes, when I'm staring out at the same stars I tracked as a child, I like to think that my parents, too, are watching the moon shift into an eye, or hearing the trees as they start to laugh, ever encouraging me to open my mind to the possibilities around me and set all my nightmares free.

Thankfully these days, I won't be hiding behind the flower bush, or lurking in the dining room dressed as Ghostface when I do it.

BITS AND PIECES:

Storytelling And Creating An Anthology

An Interview with Jonathan Maberry

EUGENE JOHNSON

JONATHAN MABERRY is a New York Times best-selling and award-winning author and editor. He has edited numerous best-selling anthologies including, *Out of Tune Vol 1 and Vol 2* (2014, 2016, JournalStone Publishing), *X-Files: Trust No One* (2015, IDW Publishing), *X-Files: The Truth is Out There* (2016, IDW Publishing), *X-Files: Secret Agenda* (2016, IDW Publishing) and *Scary Out There* (2016, Simon & Schuster). As well as co-edited anthologies Joe Ledger: Unstoppable with Bryan Thomas Schmidt (2017, Simon & Schuster), and *Alternate Sherlocks Vol 1*, with Michael Ventrella (2016, Diversion Press). His latest anthology *Nights of the Living Dead*, co-edited with Legendary filmmaker George Romero (2017, St. Martin's Griffin) has released to fantastic reviews. In the following interview, Jonathan Maberry discusses storytelling, horror, and editing anthologies.

Eugene: You have some amazing work as a writer of adult fiction, young adult fiction, comic books, and even an editor of anthologies, etc. How do you develop an idea for a project? What inspires you?

Jonathan Maberry: Pretty much everything has a kernel of inspiration in it. That's how writers see the world. If, for example, a non-writer sees a bird on a windowsill then it's just a bird on a windowsill. A writer sees the bird and wonders what drew it to that window. Is it hiding from a bigger bird? Is it lost? Is it looking for a place to build a nest because it's ready to lay an egg? Is it trying to get in? Does it see a juicy bug inside that the people living there do not? Is the bird a spirit in bird form? And so on. It's a what if game that never really stops. And that not only makes for a rich creative life but it also makes life itself a lot more entertaining. Writers are seldom bored. There's always something to see and something to wonder about.

When thinking of a specific project, you look for the doorway that lets you in. Or you climb in through a side window. With something like my latest novel, *Deep Silence*, I was at a lecture at a movie producer's house where the speaker was the admiral of the Pacific submarine force. All the way through his talk on modern submarine technology I was making notes for a novel that would incorporate that data. After the talk I spoke with the admiral and the Force master chief, and hit them with some questions that were tied to the new story idea, and their answers helped me expand the idea into what will be the 10th in my Joe Ledger thriller series.

I also read a lot of nonfiction—articles in trade journals, books on science, technology, politics, etc., and I play the 'what if' game with every interesting tidbit I find.

Eugene: Can you talk a little bit about why you decided to start creating your own anthologies? What's an editor's role in the storytelling process?

Jonathan Maberry: Anthologies usually start with an idea an editor has and brings to a publisher. Often there are themes—zombie stories, Sherlock Holmes, creepy dolls, end of the world, etc.; or sometimes the theme is more general, like 'horror' and 'mystery.' I like themed anthologies, as a reader, writer and editor. Typically the editor roughs out a projected word count and budget, and then reaches out to a handful of notable writers to see if they might be interested in contributing should a deal be reached. Then the editor takes that list of notable writers and adds them to a formal pitch that he sends to a publisher. There's always a bit of haggling over money, delivery date, word count, etc. If the deal is closed, the editor tells the writers the basics of the deal and secures their commitment. Often there are some open slots that are either filled by an open call or by invitation. I prefer to do invitation-only anthologies because I simply don't have the time to read a few hundred submissions. And I like to hand-pick my writers. I tend to work in what I call a 'no prima-donna zone,' meaning I prefer to work with writers who are talented, professional, and easy to get along with. I don't have time to handhold or stroke egos. Luckily there are a lot of people who fit that bill, so I always have a lot of great writers to draw on.

Eugene: What made you want to be an editor, creating great anthologies?

Jonathan Maberry: I've always been a fan of short fiction. More as a reader than a writer, though that changed in the late-2000s when I started writing short fiction. I read a ton of anthologies because they give me a chance to discover new writers and to see some of my favorite writers taking creative risks. Some years back I was invited by Max Brooks (*World War Z*) to write a novella for a GI JOE anthology he was editing for IDW Publishing. When that wrapped, the publisher asked if I might be interested in doing their next anthology as editor, and if so—what would I want to do? It was the first time I'd thought about editing an anthology, and I thought it would be fun to do a shared-world project. So, I cooked up an idea for a viral outbreak that kicks off a vampire apocalypse. I wrote the framing story and invited a bunch of writers to do stories that fit into the same world. That was the first *V-WARS* antho, and the success of that led to additional volumes in that series, and from there I expanded out to do other anthologies of different kinds. My next project was *Out of Tune*, for JournalStone, which were stories inspired by old folk songs and murder ballads. Each year I deepened my footprint in the anthology world, and have done books for several different publishers, and at the same time I continue to write 10-20 shorts for other editors' anthologies.

Eugene: What's the storytelling process in being an editor and creating a great anthology?

Jonathan Maberry: With theme anthologies, you need to take pitches so that you don't get eight stories that hit the same thematic note. And you want to have a wide range of styles. As the stories come in, you begin prioritizing them as to where they'll fall in the table of contents. You want a strong opener, a solid anchor in the middle and a killer closer. If you do your job right there are no weak spots anywhere. And, with themed anthos you want to make sure there are stories that present and explore the theme early on and some that twist the model and deepen the theme midway and later in the book.

Eugene: What draws you to the horror genre?

Jonathan Maberry: My grandmother was very much into what she called the 'larger world.' Imagine Luna Lovegood from the Harry Potter books as an old lady, and that's her. She was a little witchy in some ways. She read tea leaves and taught me about ghosts and vampires and all sorts of supernatural critters when I was a kid. And my brother gave me his stack of EC comics when he went into the air force in the sixties. I grew up watching old Universal horror flicks and the newer (at the time) Hammer films. And on TV we had *Twilight Zone* reruns and the first runs of *Outer Limits* and *Night Gallery*. So . . . I was born into it. Plus, when I was in middle school, my school librarian was the secretary for a club of professional writers, so she introduced me to guys like Richard Matheson, Ray

Bradbury, Harlan Ellison, Robert Bloch, and others. Matheson and Bradbury, in particular, mentored me and gave me a lot of books to read. Some science fiction, some fantasy and a lot of horror.

Eugene: You have an amazing new anthology coming out soon, *Nights of the Living Dead*, co-edited with George Romero. Can you talk a little bit about how that project came about?

Jonathan Maberry: When I was ten years old my buddy and I snuck into a movie theater to see the world premiere of *Night of the Living Dead*. He was freaked out; I was dazzled. From that point—at the very beginning of what would become the zombie craze—I was already thinking about how I might survive if the dead rose. My fourth novel, *Patient Zero*, dealt with zombies, and it was a hit. I was invited to write zombie stories for anthologies. One of those stories, "Family Business," for Christopher Golden's excellent *The New Dead*, became the seed for my first young adult novels, the Rot & Ruin series. But then I wrote *Dead of Night*, which was my homage to George A. Romero. I wanted to tell a story that explained how the zombie apocalypse might start, and I worked with top scientists to come up with a frighteningly plausible cause based on parasites that exist in nature. I told the story from the first zombie, the first bite, and I dedicated the book to George Romero. Around that time, I started thinking about how much fun it would be to do an anthology of stories that explored the very beginnings of the rise of the living dead. The idea cooked for a while and then I said, what the heck, let me pitch it. St. Martin's Griffin loved the idea, especially when I said that I would try to get Romero involved in some way. So, I reached out to Romero through his agent and bam, we were on the phone together! He was familiar with my writing and said that he considered *Dead of Night* to be the official prequel to *Night of the Living Dead*. Talk about a jaw-dropping thing for him to say!

We talked it out for a while on the phone and I asked if he would give his blessing to the anthology. He said he would, but on three conditions. The first was that he wanted to co-edit it. That was an easy and enthusiastic yes. The second was that he wanted to write a story for it. Um . . . yeah. That would work. And the third blew me away. He said that he wanted me to write a story that officially connected *Dead of Night* to *Night of the Living Dead*.

Eugene: You have had a very versatile career, having worked as a writer, and most recently a collaborator with one of the most famous masters in horror, George Romero. Can you talk a little bit about the process?

Jonathan Maberry: Versatility is very useful to a working writer. As a young teen, I had advice from smart people to avoid being trapped in a box. My middle school librarian insisted that for every book I checked out that was in my comfort zone I also take and read one book in a genre outside of that space. I resisted at first, but over time I realized how much it was broadening my understanding of the world, of storytelling, and of the craft of writing. Around the same time Richard Matheson advised me to think beyond what I believed was my 'writing sweet spot' and try new things. After all, his novels are all over the place—*The Shrinking Man, I Am Legend, Somewhere in Time, Stir of Echoes, What Dreams May Come, Duel.* So, over my career as a writer I've tried a lot of different things—feature articles, reviews, columns, how-to pieces, college textbooks, mass-market nonfiction, folklore, pop culture analysis, poetry, song lyrics, greeting cards, advertising copy, plays, novels, short stories, flash fiction, and comics. Some of those things resulted in good career advancement, some were less useful to me. And even within fiction I enjoy writing different kinds of stories for different markets. I write horror, urban fantasy, epic fantasy, suspense, thrillers, science fiction, mystery, dark fantasy, comedy, westerns, steampunk, post-apocalyptic, contemporary drama, and more. And I write for adults, teens, and middle grade. Some of my greatest successes have come from stretching myself and trying new things.

Eugene: What was it like collaborating on your anthology with George?

Jonathan Maberry: George is a hoot. He's wise, funny, kind, good-natured, and deeply knowledgeable about storytelling in its various forms. We had a blast.

Eugene: How did you work together on the anthology?

Jonathan Maberry: We compiled a wish-list of writers

we thought would work well in this project, including John Russo, who co-wrote *Night of the Living Dead*. We both wrote introductions and each of us—at the other's request—wrote short stories. As the stories came in, I handled the initial editing and he read through to give his seal of approval. There was a lot of back-and-forth, and we're both happy with the result. We still have a little editorial work to do, but we're nearing the end on that and are about to turn the project over to the good folks at SkyBoat Media, who are producing the audio version.

Eugene: You have an amazing lineup for the anthology, including Brian Keene, Carrie Ryan, Chuck Wendig, Craig E. Engler, David J. Schow, David Wellington, Isaac Marion, Jay Bonansinga, Joe R. Lansdale, John A. Russo, John Skipp, Keith R.A. DeCandido, Max Brallier, Mike Carey, Mira Grant, Neal and Brenda Shusterman, and Ryan Brown. Can you talk a little bit about putting that lineup together?

Jonathan Maberry: George and I both spend a lot of time at conventions around the world. After a while you tend to get to know the other key players. You do panels and events together. A lot of these folks become friends and some of them have logged frequent flyer miles in my anthologies. So I built my wish list and gave it to George. He added some names and once we had a lineup that we thought would bring real game to the book, I started sending emails and making calls. I think it took me an hour to get everyone we wanted to say yes. A couple of people could not participate because of schedule conflicts—notably Robert Kirkman and Max Brooks—but they gave us resounding support and encouragement. Everyone wants to see this book happen. And there are a lot of folks—a whole lot—who have expressed interest should we do a second volume.

Eugene: You're a big fan of the zombie genre. What was it like working on this project compared to your other zombie projects?

Jonathan Maberry: This is a dream project nearly fifty years in the making for me. It's surreal that I'm actually working on a project that is officially part of the Romero universe. And it's delightful that among my friends these days are Max Brooks (*World War Z*), Robert Kirkman (*The Walking Dead*), Seth Graeme Smith (*Pride & Prejudice & Zombies*), Carrie Ryan (*Forest of Hands and Teeth*), Mike Carey (*The Girl with all the Gifts*), Craig Engler (*Z Nation*), and so many others. The zombie community is tight, mutually supportive and fun. And the fans are glorious! They are my people.

Eugene: How cool was it to work in George's universe?

Jonathan Maberry: Writing a story for *Nights of the Living Dead* was unexpected. Typically editors don't also contribute, but George made it a condition of his being involved. He wanted me to connect *Dead of Night* and its sequels to *Night of the Living Dead*. That is still hard to process. And it makes me want to do the Snoopy dance.

Eugene: Any plans for a sequel to the *Night of the Living Dead* anthology?

Jonathan Maberry: We're discussing it. But with all anthologies it's a matter of seeing how the first volume does. However . . . I'm very optimistic.

Eugene: This is not your first collaboration on a project. You have collaborated with a few people before, such as Bryan Thomas Schmidt, and more. What draws you to collaborating on projects?

Jonathan Maberry: I'm insanely busy. This will be the third year where I'll have written in excess of a million words for publication. In order to do anthologies, I often have to share the load. Bryan Thomas Schmidt and I did the upcoming *Joe Ledger: Unstoppable* antho, which debuts on Halloween. We each bring certain skills to the game. I'm very good at structural editing; Bryan is better at proofing. We share the other tasks of contracts, building contributor lists, chasing revisions, and so one. That way neither of us has to carry all the freight. I also worked with Michael Ventrella on *Baker Street Irregulars*, and we just wrapped a second volume and are in discussions for a third, unrelated book. That process was fun, too, and it involved sharing the workload.

Eugene: How do you pick your collaborator, and the project?

Jonathan Maberry: With Romero, the choice was obvious. Though at first I planned it as a solo editing gig and reached out to him for his blessing. He asked to co-edit and I was absolutely fine with that arrangement. I am not actually insane! For *Joe Ledger: Unstoppable*, Bryan cooked up the idea and reached out to me. Same with Mike Ventrella.

Eugene: Do you have any advice for people that want to get into writing and become a storyteller?

Jonathan Maberry: There are several important things to know about becoming successful as a novelist. Things I wish I'd know earlier in my career.

First—be very good at what you do. Having a natural gift for storytelling is great, but you need to learn the elements of craft. That includes figurative and descriptive language, pace, voice, tense, plot and structure, good dialogue, and many other skills. Good writers are always learning, always improving.

Second—learn the difference between 'writing' and 'publishing.' Writing is an art, it's a conversation between the writer and the reader. Publishing is a business whose sole concern is to sell copies of art. Publishing looks for those books that are likely to sell well. There is absolutely no obligation for anyone in publishing to buy and publish a book totally on the basis of it being well written. It has to be something they can sell. A smart writer learns how to take their best writing and find the best way to present it to the publishing world, and then to support it via social media once it's out.

Third—you are more important than what you write. A writer is a 'brand.' That brand will, ideally, generate many works—books, short stories, etc. Each work should be written with as much passion, skill, love, and intelligence as possible, but when it's done, the writer moves on to the next project. And the next.

Fourth—finish everything you start. Most writers fail because they don't finish things. Be different.

Fifth—don't try to be perfect. First drafts, in particular, are often terrible. Clunky, badly-written, awkward, filled with plot holes and wooden dialogue. Who cares? All a first draft needs to have in order to be perfect is completeness. It is revision that makes it better, and makes it good enough to sell. So, don't beat up on yourself if your early drafts are bad. Everyone's early drafts are bad. Everyone.

THE REAL CREEPS, OR HOW TO CREATE HORROR NON-FICTION SHORTS

LISA MORTON

ONE OF MY favorite pieces of advice for new writers looking to make more sales is to consider trying some non-fiction. As an author who is known for both fiction and non-fiction, I periodically get requests for articles from editors who tell me that for every 300 short story submissions they receive, they get . . . well, zero non-fiction submissions.

I think many writers have this notion that non-fiction requires a different skill set, or doesn't provide the emotional satisfactions they get from fiction. My answer to that: Then you're doing it wrong. Certainly some non-fiction is intended to be first and foremost educational. Interviews should aim to reveal the person answering the questions; reviews are there to help consumers gain insight into possible purchases. But we've probably all read magazine articles that have angered us, amused us, or (for purposes of this genre) unnerved us. Moved us emotionally, in other words . . . like fiction.

Magazine articles can be a perfect way for writers

to break into tough markets, and I'm going to suggest here that articles should be approached in much the same way that short fiction is. First, decide on your subject; it will be easier for you, the author, to choose something that you either have experience with or an emotional connection to. Have you ever had, for example, a paranormal encounter that left you shaken? Perhaps you witnessed a terrifying accident or even a crime. Maybe you saw a movie that scared the heck out of you, and you've always wondered why it was so effective.

Now you've got the heart of your piece. What would you think about next if this were a short story? A plot. Characters. Style. Ways to disturb your readers. Well, surprise, surprise: you should apply all of those elements to your non-fiction piece, too. A sequence of events will unfold around an unsuspecting person or persons; if the writing is solid and the pacing good, it'll build to a finale that will affect both those within the story and those reading it. See? That can describe either a short story or an article.

The biggest difference between a short fiction and a short non-fiction work might be in the research (and the amount of it you use). I just finished writing a story that involved interstellar travel; for the story, I researched space travel theories at some length, but then threw out most of my research and kept only what served to advance the plot. Had I been writing a non-fiction piece, however, I would've included more of that material in an article. I would have structured that research in a way that would build to the most dramatic conclusion possible. Whoever you've chosen to be the central "character" in your non-fiction piece would play into that climax, too. If that protagonist is you, don't be afraid to get up close and personal. Level with your readers about how you felt, about how this experience marked you or impacted you. Be honest. Use the same powerful language you would employ in a short story. Aim to leave your readers trembling, gasping, and still thinking about the piece days later.

Writing an entire non-fiction book can be a considerably daunting experience. Even if you're writing about a subject you already know very well, research could take years, and there are a whole bunch of extra tasks with a non-fiction book, ranging from obtaining rights to use illustrations to preparing an index of your book. I would only recommend a full non-fiction book to someone who is aware of the time investment involved and prepared to make the commitment. But writing non-fiction short pieces doesn't have to be any more time-consuming or labor-intensive than writing short fiction . . . and the end goals of selling a compelling piece that will entertain readers should be the same in both fiction and non-fiction.

THE MONSTER SQUAD

Or, How I Learned to Stop Worrying and Love the Publisher

JESS LANDRY

EVERY AUTHOR NEEDS a champion: Someone to stand behind you and your work, someone to hold your hand and guide you down the publishing path, someone to be the Merricat to your Constance, or, better yet, the machete to your Jason Voorhees. That champ, in the wonderful world o'books, is the publisher. And much like Leatherface, the role they play in getting an author's work from slush-pile-hopeful to real-life-awesome-smelling-book is one that requires many faces.

I can only speak for myself and the processes I go through with JournalStone and Trepidatio Publishing, but in a nutshell, the main focus of anyone working on a piece of fiction (from the publisher to the author, and everyone in between) is the story. It's what draws us in and keeps us there, like a warm blanket in front of a roaring fire on a cold night, or a Chestburster nestling comfortably in your ribcage. From the very first line, the story must engage its audience, and the publisher's role in maintaining your voice, your style, and your story, is their *raison d'être.*

Depending on the size of the press (in this case, let's zero in on smaller ones), one of the first faces the publisher wears is slush pile reader (and what a pretty face it is, all young and smooth, full of hope and enthusiasm).

To go at it alone is tough, so the publisher may recruit a team to assist sorting through the pile. This team, the Readers of the Slush, are the (un)fortunate souls who give their time and effort to scour through endless mounds of rape-revenge stories and plots about space velociraptors from the planet Goldblum who abide by the tyrannical laws enforced by their leader, the Clever Girl (can someone actually write this, please? Thanks.)—yes, they are a publisher's best defense, a writer's only hope, and the unsung heroes of any press, big or small. And it just so happens that every once in a while, their patience is rewarded.

I used to imagine, back in the days of paper, the Readers of the Slush wading through a sea of manuscripts, their exposed skin riddled with papercuts, their mouths dry from excessive use of saliva to wet their sandpapered fingertips. They'd rifle through hundreds upon thousands of sheets of paper, the words on the page eventually blurring together, some seemingly becoming infected à la *Pontypool* ("kill is kiss," isn't it?). Then, when all hope seemed lost, they'd come across a manuscript unlike any other, one that they continued reading past the first ten, twenty, two-hundred pages. With shaking hands, they'd pull the MS from the sea like King Arthur pulling Excalibur from the stone, presenting it to the publisher with shaking hands. Finding that special manuscript in the day and age of computers still feels that way, except instead of papercuts and dry mouths, everyone has carpal tunnel and bad posture.

There is a question that writers often ask when it comes to the slush pile: "How can I make my work stand out?" The answer, unfortunately, is not a straight-forward one, though I'd argue that luck plays a relevant role, with a dash of talent mixed in for good measure. Always include a cover letter, and try to match the tone of your work in said letter—this is the first taste the Readers of the Slush will have of you, after all. Give us a brief, yet punchy synopsis of your work, something that makes us want to throw out the rest of the pile and dive solely into your work. Tell us your accomplishments (if any)—the Readers are usually writers themselves, and are often curious to see what kind of publications you've been in. It also pays to know your market, to know who you're submitting your beloved manuscript to, and to know if they'd be a good fit or not. If you submit the aforementioned sci-fi romp "Space Raptors from Planet Goldblum" to Harlequin Romance, chances are you'll be swinging for a miss with that press. However, if you send that same manuscript over to the offices of John Hammond & Co., well, he'd probably spare no expense and send you a multi-million-dollar contract straight away.

(I know the thought of the slush pile is a horrible one. Some of us have been on both ends, and if there's one thing to take away from the idea that your manuscript may actually be one of a thousand received to your press of choice, it's this: You'll never know if you don't try. So always try.)

Once a story is deemed worthy by the Readers of the Slush, it then (in some cases) gets passed to the publisher for their approval, if the boss isn't involved in the slush process already (which is often the case with small presses). The publisher gets the final say on the work, and if your manuscript makes the grade, then slap yourself on the back, you lucky bastard—you've got yourself a book deal.

Now, I'd like to say that every press out there, big or small, is well-intentioned. I'd like to say that those presses put their authors first, that everything they do is aimed at success: success for you, success for them, one big success party with extra successiness. Unfortunately, that's not always the case. Though this could be construed as common sense, I feel it bears repeating: Never, and I mean *never*, pay someone to sell your book.

Vanity presses have been around since the 1940s, conning good people out of their hard-earned cash. The basic set-up is this: You submit your manuscript to them. They come back to you a short time later, and say, "Yes! OMG! We love your book! Here's a contract. Sign it ASAP!" You're over the moon (and who wouldn't be? You've made it, dammit! Watch out, Stephen King—I'm coming for the gargoyles on your fence!), but then they ask you to pony up for editing. *Okay*, you think, *that's fair, the book needs to be edited anyway*. But no, once that's complete, they then ask for more, "Oh, did we mention the book cover? Oh, we forgot marketing materials. Oh, darn, printing fees," until you've shelled out hundreds, maybe even thousands, for something that a publishing house is supposed to take care of themselves. The financial burden should never fall on you. Know that the vanity presses have no selection process, no slush readers. They don't care about you, about your talent, or your story. They're what the French call "*les incompétents.*"

There are also presses out there who'll not only take your cash, but lock you into a one-sided contract, tying up rights and exclusivity for insane amounts of time. I cannot stress this enough: Always read over your contract. It may not make a lick of sense with all that legal jargon, so don't be afraid to ask questions. A good publisher will answer any concerns you may have truthfully, because a good publisher wants you to succeed.

After contracts are signed (with the good guys), now the editing begins. With a smaller press, the publisher may also wear the editor face (it's not as pretty as the slush pile one: It's a bit more haggard, has some wrinkles around the eyes, and often spasms when confronted with adverbs).

Editing is, by far, the absolute most important process of the whole shebang. As an author, you know this: You've no doubt already spent months, possibly even years, editing your manuscript, polishing it the best you could before sending it off into the world. You know it's perfect, that the editor will breeze through and maybe add a comma here or there, nothing major.

Oh, you sweet, sweet thing.

I know it's rough getting back a manuscript and seeing the document marked up and redder than a tomato in Hell, but please know this: An editor has your story's best intentions in mind. They want your work to be the best it possibly can be. The changes they suggest may be hard to swallow, especially if it concerns a major re-write or re-imagining a prominent character or plot line, but their job is to varnish the shit out of your manuscript and have it come out gleaming on the other side.

Whether the publisher is also your editor, or the press has a separate in-house editor, a balance must be struck: all parties must be happy with the end result. It's up to the editor to ensure that the author's voice is clear and consistent throughout the novel, it's up to the publisher to ensure that any changes made are in line with the author, and it's up to the author to ensure that their own voice is being heard throughout the process. After all, when everything is said and done, this book is yours and yours alone. It's got your name on the cover, your words in the pages. If your voice is missing from the final product, then someone has failed you.

After the editing process is through and the final version of the manuscript has been signed, sealed, and delivered, the publisher and author then start looking for the perfect cover art. Cover art is often sorely overlooked, and I'd say it's one of the most critical factors in successfully marketing a manuscript, right behind the book itself. This is where, as a publisher, knowing the material plays a crucial role: Picking out strong imagery that ties into the story to put on the cover will get people talking. Is your story about dragons? Hell, let's make sure some fire-breathing, angrier-than-the-people-who-weren't-expecting-the-Red-Wedding-episode-of-*Game-of-Thrones* winged reptiles are on there doing bad-ass things. Is your story about space raptors? I want to see a raptor in space on your cover, flying a spaceship, eating a human in zero gravity, doing whatever it is a goddamn space raptor does best. Make it stand out—depending on your story, say, if you lean more towards a Gothic prose, a subtle-looking cover may work best. If Splatterpunk is your thing, then make it rain blood and guts.

Marketing is yet another important factor in the never-ending list of Things-To-Do. The publisher, knowing your story almost as well as you, will know the appropriate places to send your book off for review, where to run ads to promote its release, how to market it and have it appeal to its target audience, all while keeping you abreast of it all. With indie publishers, it's a two-way street, and hard work is necessary on both the publisher's side and the author's. If you've never thought about how to market your book, or consider yourself a little introverted (aren't we all?), don't be afraid to jump head-first into the shark-infested waters—you may be surprised with the end results. And always remember: No matter what the situation, the publisher has your back.

From the moment the contract is signed, the author and the publisher are a team. And though it'd be way more dramatic (and bad-ass) if contracts were still signed the old-fashioned way (with a little blood), ink does just as well. Besides, if you're ever in need of a little blood in the publishing world, just remember the person who's willing to be the machete to your Jason.

WHAT SCARES YOU!

MARV WOLFMAN

WHAT SCARES YOU, like what makes you laugh, has infinite answers. It's incrementally different for every person. What specifically digs into my mind and makes me react is probably never going to be the exact same thing that makes you fall to the floor laughing your guts out or burying your head deep into the pillows to keep out the boogeyman. Comedy and horror are, to me, the only genres that, when done well, force you to react emotionally and not intellectually.

Detective fiction, super-hero stories, soap opera writing, and others, are more intellectual exercises. What makes them work is the cleverness of the writer. The ability to set up puzzles, to lead you one way then another. But you react to the complex plotting and stories with your head and not your heart.

Of course there are moments in every well-written story that do affect you emotionally, but many of the actual stories are still basically puzzles. The satisfaction one gets from reading a well-crafted detective story is that the characters and storylines all lead to the well-conceived resolution that you either completely missed or figured it out before you're given the resolution. It's a Jenga construction, a puzzle where all the parts support the final prize.

But if something is funny to you, your laughter will be involuntary. You won't be able to control it. And if something truly scares you, you won't be able to fight that sudden cold shiver that grabs your spine and won't let go.

And that's what makes writing both horror and humor so satisfying.

Normally, people hold in their feelings. We try not to reveal emotional weaknesses to others. We put on a happy, contented face for others to see. But when you can't stop laughing or can't control the frightening tension building inside, then you're revealing a small part of your true self. The part of you that you can't prevent coming out.

So, how do you create horror for a universal audience when everyone is scared by different things?

Not an easy question to answer because there is no single answer.

But I think it's safe to say you need to write for what makes you sweat. You write allowing, perhaps encouraging, yourself to go to places that are uncomfortable. And the more uncomfortable, the better it is. When you're uncomfortable with what is going on around you, you lose the ability to control your emotions. And that is what creates the cracks that allow terror to seep in.

Yes, we are all different. A roller coaster ride scares me. If it's faster than something that would be in Disneyland, there's no way in hell I'm going on it. And, in fact, there are Disneyland coasters that I'll never be on first name terms with. Ever. But that's good.

Because if you're afraid of something, it's very likely others will be, too. So you try to find a common ground. Carnival thrill rides became the focus of a Raven comic mini-series I recently did. My fear became the stuff of horror for others. So if you are scared of spiders, maybe you'll find two more who won't go near them, either. And if there's two, there's probably hundreds if not thousands of others who feel the same way.

Of course there are people for whom spiders are pets. There are people who think jumping off a high bridge with nothing but a thin cord is the definition of a sport. I think of it as the agnostic attempt at suicide; because there's a thin rope involved, you don't want to believe you're committing suicide, but face it, you are. Nobody voluntarily jumps off bridges for fun.

That's my story and I'm sticking to it.

So how do you create tension and fear when dealing with people who don't easily frighten or aren't afraid of slow-moving zombies or even a slower moving mummy?

The answer is pacing. And lighting. And sound. And echoes. And a million different small things that separately may not touch the reader, but combined start to chip away that veneer of control we all think we possess.

In the brilliant book Hitchcock/Truffaut (although it's a discussion between two directors, I highly recommended it to everyone who wants to be a writer) Hitchcock talks about building suspense rather than stage a sudden surprise. Here's the scene: Although we don't know it, a bomb is under a table where two people are sitting. They talk and talk and talk then suddenly there's an explosion. That gives us about fifteen seconds of surprise, but prior to that it was just an ordinary scene.

But what if, as the people talk to each other, the audience is allowed to see the bomb taped under the table, and it's ticking down. We know when it's going to explode. Not knowing what's going on, they keep talking. And talking. But the seconds are ticking away and we all know something is going to happen. Any second now. Any second now. For fifteen anxious minutes, it's any second now. Then BLAM! the explosion.

Where we had an ordinary talk scene that ended with a sudden explosion, instead we have a scene that builds and keeps building. That engages the audience. That keeps us in suspense. That suspense causes our hearts to beat faster. And faster. A sudden explosion allows us to feel sudden fear but then it's over. There was shock but no personal, emotional connection. We hardly know the people, and care about them less. However, draw out those seconds to minutes, learn who the characters sitting at that table are. Shout at them to run away from the bomb they don't know is going to blow them up, then the feeling of growing dread will stay with you.

Now check out a TV show like *The Walking Dead*. That show knows how to ramp up the suspense and fear. It moves between sudden shocks and slow builds. A sudden shock allows a few seconds of horror, but what if our characters are moving through a building. No dialog. Maybe suspense music. Then we hear the familiar sounds of zombie moans. They start soft. They're not close. But then they grow louder. Then softer again. Then louder. And louder. And louder. Where are they coming from? Louder.

And then nothing. Silence. We let down our guard. Then, suddenly, they're all around us and the moans seem more like screams.

Building the tension builds the horror. Even if you don't give a damn about zombies there's no way to avoid being sucked into that scene.

In comics, which is where I do most of my work, you can't actually have sound, but you can pace the material to force emotions. Instead of four to six panels on the page, you can break down the action into lots of slither-thin panels: A man and a woman sit at a table, eating. Talking. We move in close: They're laughing. Slight upshot: Pull back to show them at the table; one drinks from a coffee cup. It's so ordinary. Continuing the upshot: the bomb is under the table. Closer on the bomb. The seconds are ticking away. They are laughing. Having a great time. Tick Tock. Tick Tock.

And so on and so forth. We break down the action into multiple panels to force the reader to take more time looking at the page. Ten panels on the page takes the reader longer to read. The longer they take, the more they get involved with what's pictured. We are ratcheting up the suspense.

In comics we can affect the lighting of a panel. We can show the underside of that table and highlight the bomb so it's clearly seen. And if we want, to keep reminding the readers what's going on, we can do long shots of the scene and have a glow coming from under the table where the bomb is. Later on we don't even have to see it to know it's there.

Our readers or viewers don't have to fear the same things in order to be engaged with the scenes we write. We can force their emotions by playing with the pace of the story and by making them fear the normal, ordinary scenes even more than the outright shocks of monsters and other such evils.

I never went to horror movies as a kid. Didn't like them. Not even when I was in my early 20s. I loved writing them. Just didn't like watching them. But I went to see *The Exorcist* with a number of friends. The movie was disturbing me. It was making me feel queasy. But the event that forced me to get up and run out of the theater was not Regan's 360-degree head turn or the pea-soup vomiting, but the very real and very ordinary spinal tap scene.

Using music, pacing, sound effects and more, they drew me into their story, but it was reality, not Satan, that forced me to react.

Because we react best to what we know best, creating scenes that make every day moments terrify an audience is one of the ways you build horror.

And that's what scares me.

PLAYING IN SOMEONE ELSE'S HAUNTED HOUSE

Writing Horror-Based Media Tie-Ins

ELIZABETH MASSIE

CREATING HORROR FICTION is a blast. Are you kidding me? Of course it is! There are so many unsettling and terrifying locations in which we can place our tales—haunted houses, craggy forests, cemeteries, attics, cellars, and sheds, as well as those more ordinary locations that become frightening thanks to the dark magic of the writer—a park, a school, a brightly-lit mall, an ordinary apartment building. And then there are the characters who populate our horror stories—men, women, teens, children, ghosts, vampires, werewolves, shape-shifters, aliens, monsters and ghouls (both human and non) of every shape, size, color, origin, and inclination. Writers are the creators, the gods of their universe, the masters of their world.

But then, some horror is written within someone else's universe, someone else's world. It directs characters someone else has already imagined and made real.

Media tie-ins are works of fiction based on a

previously existing property such as a film, television series, game, website, or literary property. For decades now, movies and television shows have spawned original novels, novelizations, and short stories based on them. As a kid and teen in the 1960s, I devoured novels based on *The Man From U.N.C.L.E.* (I had a major crush on Illya!), *Get Smart*, and, of course my all-time favorite, *Dark Shadows* (I had an ultimate crush on Quentin!). In the 1970s more media tie-in novels were published, based on properties such as *Starsky and Hutch* and *Star Trek*. These books gave what dyed-in-the-wool fans were after—more, more, MORE! Media tie-ins continue to do that to this day.

Now, as far as I know, not all movies or television shows have successfully marketed themselves beyond their original incarnation. I mean, seriously, have you ever seen a *Manimal* novel or collection of original *My Mother the Car* short stories (though my husband, Cortney, found a *My Mother the Car* coloring book!)? To qualify as media tie-in worthy, a property must have a strong following or the potential for a strong following. Which brings me to horror. True horror fans are incredibly loyal to that which they like. When they find a television show or movie that catches their imaginations, scares the crap out of them, and moves them emotionally, they're hooked. And for the creators of that television show or that movie, this means it's time to expand. It's time for more! It's time to launch media tie-ins!

Now, before I go any further, let me mention fan fiction, or "fanfic." Fanfic is fiction created much like any media tie-in; the stories are based in a popular fictional universe and it is written by fans. However, unlike media tie-ins, fanfic has not been commissioned by nor given official approval by the creator of the universe. There is a ton of fanfic these days, from *Star Wars* to *Fifty Shades of Grey* to *Friday the 13th* to *A Nightmare on Elm Street*. The legalities of fanfic depend on what is considered "fair use" in a particular case, and if the work has a transformative status (enough variation from the original to have become original in itself). I've never written fanfic but can imagine it is a great deal of fun, not only crafting the stories but sharing the stories with other fans.

Back to media tie-ins. After having created my own horror novels and short stories for fifteen years, I was given my first opportunity to write a media tie-in novel. The universe was *Buffy the Vampire Slayer*. Asked by an editor at Pocket Books to craft an original Buffy novel, I was thrilled, but also a bit uneasy. First, everything I'd written to that point was my own. I'd made up my own settings, my own characters, my own plot lines and themes. Being asked to write a story with Buffy and her buddies was like being asked to create a brand new room in someone else's haunted house, but having to be damned sure the room fit the mood and aura of the house as a whole, that the creepy furniture and peculiar paintings purchased for the room not only looked right but were placed just right, the lighting and shadows spot on, and then to invite the previously-created characters into the room and give them something intriguing and scary to deal with. Second, I was not your basic Buffy fan. I'd seen a few episodes, but with the way my life was going at the time, I had little time for television; I didn't know many of the intricacies of the characters' lives as true fans would.

But I was very lucky. To help me out, the network sent me two huge boxes in the mail. One was packed full of videotapes (yes, this was back in the days of videotapes!) containing all the episodes of the first several seasons. The second box was packed full of scripts from the first several seasons. And so, I dove in. Over a period of three days I had a marathon viewing session (thank goodness my old VCR player was still in working condition . . . it died soon thereafter) and I read the scripts. All this was more critical to the creation of my novel. I had to immerse myself. I had to really, really get to know Buffy, Willow, Xander, Giles, and Oz. I needed to be familiar enough with Sunnydale that I knew where my characters could go and not go. Watching the show and reading the scripts gave me a solid sense of supernatural horrors that Buffy and her entourage had faced and might face. Most importantly, though, I had a deeper understanding of the characters. Not just how they looked or spoke, but how they felt about certain things, how they reacted to certain things, their strengths and weaknesses. Because in any good piece of fiction, a character must be fleshed out and believable, no matter how unbelievable they might initially seem (even a vampire or ghoul needs some depth, something that gives the reader or viewer some idea of his or her inner workings). After viewing, reading, and a great deal of pondering, I came up with the idea of a powerful Greek muse (Calli) wreaking havoc and terror in Sunnydale with her own extreme version of feminism. My editor gave me the green light and the original novel, *Buffy the Vampire Slayer: Power of Persuasion*, was born.

My second foray into horror media tie-ins came right on the heels of the Buffy book. I was approached by an editor at Harper to see if I might be interested in writing a novel based in the *Dark Shadows* universe. Are you kidding me?!! I thought. Unlike Buffy, this was a universe I knew well. As a teenager, I never missed an episode of this horror-themed soap opera. I knew Barnabas, Quentin, Elizabeth, Carolyn, Willie, Victoria, Angelique, David (the little brat!), Roger, Maggie, Julia, Rev. Trask, and the rest. I was certain I could find my way around most of Collinwood blindfolded—both inside the mansion itself and the vast grounds around it, including the ominous "Old House" and the cliff at Widows' Hill. I knew the town of Collinsport and the dark, moody dive, the Blue Whale.

There were no boxes of videos or scripts sent to me. But I didn't need or want them. What I did want, though, was a fellow *Dark Shadows* fan to get on board with me for both the fun of the writing and the additional knowledge he would bring to the story. And so I contacted Mark Rainey, a friend from way back. He drove up from North Carolina to my home in Virginia. I "borrowed" a long piece of bulletin board paper from the local elementary school and, with the paper stretched out on the floor, we mapped out the storyline. Mark agreed to write all the chapters that were set in Thomas Rathburn's (our original vampire) POV and I agreed to write all the chapters set in Victoria Winters' POV. Then he went home and we exchanged chapters via e-mail. Thus was born the original novel, *Dark Shadows: Dreams of the Dark* (our original title was *Dark Shadows: Dreams of the Damned*, but Dan Curtis Productions, owners of the Dark Shadows property, nixed that, proving that media tie-ins are actually collaborations between owners and writers). And we were able to convince the Dan Curtis folks to let us reveal something important that was never revealed in the television show! That was a major kick! Knowing the personalities, quirks, fears, and strengths of the characters, being familiar with the setting and the dark, spooky tone of the television show, we had fashioned what we felt (and what *Dark Shadows* fans felt) was a terrifying and satisfying tale.

In addition to original novels, I've also had the opportunity to write novelizations, which are media tie-ins based on prewritten scripts, television episodes, or movies. Though the Showtime television series *The Tudors* and the 2015 French mini-series *Versailles* are billed as historical fiction, some of the world's worst horrors are historically based. Seriously. Think back for a moment. Drawing and quartering. Burning at the stake. Public beheadings. The terrors of the rack and the garrotte. Ultimate powers in the hands of those who may or may not be sane. In fact, there are quite a few realistically-crafted historical novels that could easily be classified as historical horror.

It was an honor to be offered the task of writing works based on the second and third seasons of *The Tudors* and the whole mini-series, *Versailles*. However, instead of creating unique storylines as was done with *Buffy the Vampire Slayer* and *Dark Shadows*, it was my job to flesh out the plots provided each set of twelve scripts (one set for season two, one set for season three) and fashion what was there into a fully formed novel. This may seem easier than creating original novels based on someone else's property, but trust me, it's very challenging in its own way. There are countless scenes in any one script, short scenes that go back and forth between settings, between characters. Even within one scene there can be various points of views. This is easy to do with a television or movie camera, panning around from face to face; much harder to do with the written word. As often as I could, I drew scenes together to keep the work from coming across as choppy. I had to decide whose point of view I would use in a particular scene to move the story forward, describing the facial expressions and body movements of other characters to help provide other necessary plot points. As any fiction writer knows, internal dialogue can be crucial. In the scripts, no such dialogue was provided, so it was up to me to put myself in the minds and souls of the characters and provide those thoughts. In addition, there was extensive historical research. How long would it take to ride a horse from London to Wales? What did people wear? What did various castles, roads, forests look like at that time? And, of course, details on the dreadful demise of some of the most likable characters. One poor man, in trying to earn money for his daughters, was bribed to poison some of Henry VIII's entourage. For his trouble, he was bound, lifted by a crane, and slowly lowered into a vat of boiling oil. Another man, suspected of infidelity with the King's wife, had his eyes crushed with a knotted rope. Then he was slowly torn on the rack as he begged for mercy, forced to crawl up to his place of execution, and then, was mercifully beheaded. If that isn't horror, I don't know what is.

As to short fiction and comics, I have works out based in the universes of the Phantom, Kolchak: The Night Stalker, and even Zorro. Again, great fun. Again, requiring an ability to work within specific, solid parameters while drawing on the well of creativity and craft.

And so, for anyone venturing into the world of writing horror-based media tie-ins (or any genre, for that matter), let me offer these bits of advice. Know that you must please the original creator of the universe. Know that you must give the fans/readers what they are clamoring for. Get into the characters hearts and minds, and in doing so whatever horrors they face will be all the more real—and therefore more satisfying—to the readers. Know that you can be just as creative within given boundaries as you can in a wide, open field. Accept the challenge. Enjoy your time setting up the details in the room of that haunted house. And have a blast!

CREATING MAGIC FROM A BLANK PIECE OF PAPER

An Imaginary Roundtable

INTERVIEWS BY DEL HOWISON

ONE OF THE most gratifying things in my business is to sit down and listen to talented individuals who are willing to share a portion of their knowledge with you concerning the operation of their craft. When there are several of them sharing their viewpoints on the same questions we call that a roundtable, and a rare occurrence. But gathering a group of working, hard-driving, busy talent in one place for a discussion like this is akin to corralling spiders.

To make things easier on everybody involved I asked several extremely talented writer/directors the same questions individually and then weaved together their answers to create a simulated roundtable discussion. None of them were allowed to hear what the others had to say, so their viewpoints are completely original and untainted either by a steady glare or laughter from the other participants. What we wanted to get to was the heart of their creative process. Where did the ideas come from and how did they feel at different stages of the creative process? Well, they offered up their hearts . . . and the guts, too.

As a group, the participants have quite an impressive collective resume and make up a good deal of Hollywood horror royalty behind the camera. Individually it rolls out this way—**Kevin Tenney** made his debut (not counting those early 8mm films as a kid) as the writer/director of the cult film *Witchboard*. He has 11 writing credits and 15 directing credits, mostly dominated by such horror classics as *Night of the Demons*, *Witchtrap*, and *Brain Dead*. **Fred Dekker** arrived on the doorstep of horror fans by writing the classic horror comedy *House*. Since that time he has written and directed both for film and television predominately in the horror/science fiction world, including *Night of the Creeps*, *The Monster Squad*, and *Robocop 3*. **Amber Benson** may never fully get out from under her memorable acting gigs such as playing *Tara Maclay* on the television hit show *Buffy the Vampire Slayer* or *Lenore* in a couple of episodes of the long-running series *Supernatural*. But she has also written best-selling novels and been able to turn her literary series *Ghosts of Albion* into film by both, writing and directing the movies. **Tom Holland** broke things open as a writer with *The Beast Within*, *Class of 1984*, and *Psycho 2*. That should be enough for any resume, but he was just getting started. Now add *Fright Night*, *Child's Play*, and *Thinner*. Those last three he also directed. We now have a roundtable group that deserves merit badges and your undivided attention.

Del Howison: For an original idea do you sit at a computer and just grind things out until there is a spark, or do you pull ideas from anywhere with the writing for your own project being at the whim of the muse?

Amber Benson: As a writer/director, I'm always looking around for inspiration. Often, I'll read an article or see something online that sparks my interest and then I'll start researching. This can lead to a completed project but more often than not it just leads to a little folder in my Dropbox that I may or may not come back to at a later date. I have so many possible ideas sitting on my hard drive and in the cloud and in notebooks that it's not even funny. But sometimes I'll just be inspired by a dream or a piece of music or meeting someone interesting and I'll sit down and start writing. I appreciate it when the muse strikes but I know I can't rely on her. She's a fickle creature. So I'm always on the hunt for things that pique my curiosity.

Fred Dekker: I worked with a writer once who said, "If you don't know where you're going, any road will take you there." Which is another way of saying I can't sit down to start writing until I have a game plan—a *shape*.

The first ideas are usually fairly random. Notions, snippets. But eventually I figure out how to weave them into some kind of story shape. That becomes the outline, which usually starts as note cards for each scene. Eventually I do sit down and the outline becomes a fully written treatment—with a lot more detail, even some dialogue. The treatment is a kind of dry run for the script. That's my process, anyway. **Aaron Sorkin** supposedly writes without any outline, just from his head (but, I'm sure, TONS of research). There's no right way, if the work is good.

Once I have an idea where I'm going . . . *then* I can let the muse help the writing of the actual scenes. It's like a jazz pianist riffing on a melody; I have to have the melody first.

Tom Holland: Both. I've had stories comes from nowhere. I've had them come while I was working on other projects. I've had them come from writing short stories. I have thought of story fragments and been unable to make them work, only to have the answer drop in months later. And I've had them not come no matter how hard I try. It's a total mystery to me. I have also found the act of writing can force me to work out plotting problems that remain opaque to me when I am trying to outline. OTOH, if you free-write without any idea of where you were headed, you can put in a lot of work only to find you don't know what the end is—or how to get there.

Del Howison: Does the idea or the financing come first? In other words, do you maybe outline but stall out on a fleshed out script idea until the green light is given in terms of financing?

Kevin Tenney: It depends on whether it's a work for hire or spec. If it's a spec the idea comes first. I think of something I think would be a cool idea that would make an interesting story. If I don't know anything about the subject, like with the Ouija Board when I did *Witchboard* I researched Ouija Boards, I read about them. There were a lot of people telling different stories that happened to them so I took some of the better ones and kind of incorporated them into the script.

Tom Holland: At this point, I won't write without a deal in place—unless it's my own idea, but I am not going to write yours for free.

Amber Benson: I'm just a maker of things. It kinda doesn't matter if they never get made. I don't think about financing or casting or anything that would take me out of the creative process. I find that I can't make stuff to please other people (unless it's a paid gig and those parameters are very different), I make things to please myself. If I'm not engaged with the subject matter then there is no point. I make things because I have to. It's in my DNA and there is a real joy in the servicing of that part of myself. Plus, I suck at raising money. That's a skill set I don't have. Give me a notebook or a laptop and I'm happy, but don't ask me to harass people for dough. I am the worst at that.

Fred Dekker: Everything starts with the script. On *Robocop 3*, there was an existing script by **Frank Miller** that I rewrote for production. On *The Predator*, **Shane Black** and I were paid to come up with a story and write a screenplay. But the green light for production almost never comes until the script is finished in some form. I've certainly started things that the promise of a green light would motivate me to finish . . . but the idea always comes first.

Del Howison: Do you approach the script writing differently if you are writing/directing as opposed to just writing or just directing?

Amber Benson: No, the approach is the same because (and don't spread this around wink, wink) I'm directing the movie in my head as I'm writing. Whether I take a project all the way through production, or just do the heavy-lifting of writing, I know what it will look like. There will be changes here and there, obviously, if someone else directs, but my DNA will always be there just under the surface.

Tom Holland: No. I have to answer so many questions in order to write it in the first place, it makes no difference what my role is.

Kevin Tenney: I write like a director in that I probably put in a lot more description, visual description, than the average writer does. For me it's not just the story, it's how I'm going to tell the story. I'm known for my visual style as a director. So for someone who can't visualize this stuff I try to help them see what I am seeing, how I'm going to shoot it.

Fred Dekker: If I'm directing, I definitely feel free to write in more of shorthand. This is because the movie is in my head and a lot of the details will come to the surface during prep and production. I don't have to write these details because I know I'll be collaborating with the various department heads and telling them my intentions.

Writing for others requires a lot more specificity; really describing the action and the sets and the mood in a way that's not open to interpretation. On *Star Trek: Enterprise*, for instance, I learned from **Rick Berman** and **Brannon Braga** to make the stage directions very literal and clear, so that nobody's confused about the intention.

Del Howison: Wearing which hats do you figure you get more opportunity—writer, director, or writer/director?

Kevin Tenny: I think I get more as a writer/director. Honestly, I get more respect for being a director than I get for being a writer. But I think writing is harder. I think, if I had my choice, I would be the kind of director where people brought me scripts . . . and they do. But they usually suck. I'm hoping someday to be at the point where people bring me scripts that are actually as good as I can write for myself.

Del Howison: *Whether you are creating a short or a feature-length film as a writer, director, or both, how does the creative energy differ if you are given an idea to write and direct for a producer as opposed to getting your own original idea out there?*

Tom Holland: I don't know, but depending on the relationship I have found a director and/or creative producer to be both a help and a hindrance, depending on the relationship. I could do an hour on this question, but brevity being the soul of wit, won't.

Amber Benson: Creating for other people or for money is a totally different beast than creating for yourself. I liken it to being a puzzle maker. You have all these parameters that you have to stick to and people that you have to satisfy. It's a very intense way to work with someone always looking over your shoulder. I like the challenge. I like moving pieces around and retrofitting other people's ideas onto my own so that they subscribe to what's being asked of me creatively. And if, in the end, you end up with a project that everyone loves, well, then you've done the job to the best of your ability. Which is super satisfying.

Del Howison: How much does budget restrict your original writing or do you write big and pare down to the budget?

Fred Dekker: It's never good to go into something creative thinking about the limitations, but oddly, it can also be helpful to focus you. On the projects I've done with Shane Black, I've found that he thinks very big and the final film will inevitably have to be trimmed or re-thought to make it practical to actually produce. Every filmmaker wants to have the whole candy store, but knowing the budget parameters ahead of time allows you to pick and choose where to spend; to know what the big, expensive set pieces are, but also when to pull back a little and do things smaller and more simply.

Kevin Tenney: You always pare down to the budget. You almost always have to. But, in general, budget always affects you. Any film I've ever done, after you have your cast and crew screening, somebody comes up to me and asks, "So did it turn out the way you wanted?" No! Because when I wrote it was going to have a 120-day shooting schedule, **Meryl Streep** was going to star in it and I was going to have $25,000,000 to make it. I ended up with $800,000, a bunch of no names and 3 weeks to shoot it. No, it did not turn out like I wanted. It turned out as well as it could have. I have not had anything that I was fully satisfied with.

The people I know who are always satisfied with their stuff or the ones who talk about "I'm writing something and it's going to blow your mind. It's the greatest thing ever." They're usually the ones who are really bad, bad writers, bad directors. When they have to tout their own horn about how great it is. It is usually because no one else is touting that horn for them.

I think that if you are truly competent you always see what you could have done better. You're always dissatisfied with the final product. I say I am ready to shoot a film the day I wrap. If I could shoot the whole thing first, cheap and easy on videotape with just stand-ins and then cut that together, and then go shoot the movie I'd be happier. Because you find out so much while you are shooting the film of things that won't work, will work, this could've worked, etc. Or later you look at it in the editing room and think if I had put the camera just three feet to the left that shot would have been so much better. That's me. I'm always looking at my stuff like that.

My stuff always looks like home movies to me. As a matter of fact, I was flipping through channels once and I saw a movie with **Todd Allen** in it. I thought oh look it's Todd. He's an actor I worked with on *Witchboard*. I stopped to watch it and thought what is this? Almost instantaneously I realized it WAS *Witchboard*. But for those two seconds that I didn't know it was *Witchboard,* it looked like a real movie. I was so excited by that. Oh my God, when I didn't know it was mine it looked like an actual movie! It was nice to see that when I saw it through other people's eyes I didn't think this looks like a piece of crap. But otherwise, when I'm seeing it through my own eyes it looks like a home movie. A good home movie, maybe, but still a home movie.

Tom Holland: Yes, always. Even when you have a decent budget, I find myself paring, usually after production had begun and the true cash flow had been seen. The producers will especially come after you toward the end of production to cut. Also, anything that requires a company move will be in danger of being cut as production continues.

Amber Benson: Oh, I write what I see and then I make budget changes accordingly when I do revisions or notes. I don't like to limit myself, it makes the process boring. I go big because it's entertaining to do so, but I also find that it's way easier to pare things back than to add stuff.

Del Howison: Have you ever written something to see it ruined by another director or producer?

Amber Benson: I've been relatively lucky so far, but who knows what the future holds. Nothing that I was super passionate about has ever been butchered. I've had some stuff that I didn't love and it got beaten up a little, but I've never had a baby killed. Sadly, it's part of the price of doing business in Hollywood, it happens to everyone

Tom Holland: Yes. It's why I directed *Fright Night*. Self-defense. I wrote a movie called *Scream for Help*, directed by a delightful fellow, **Michael Winner**, which was so badly directed it could not be cut together. Michael was a noir action director without any feel for psychological suspense. The only reason I am talking this way is because he is gone. He was a delightful luncheon companion and a true wit and gourmand. Hitchcock he was not. He had a big success with *Death Wish* and thought the secret of film success was to cut dialogue. Didn't work with my script.

Fred Dekker: "Ruined" is a pretty strong word. I think it's more charitable to call it an occasional "difference in creative vision."
And sure, I've written things that turned out differently than I'd hoped—but I'm sure the writers whose work *I've* rewritten and directed feel the same way about me.

Kevin Tenney: If I was the director I've never had a producer ruin it. They might have ruined one sequence which is more frustrating than having it ruined by budget. Budget you accept as, "We couldn't afford to do it the way I wanted so we just couldn't do it." But when you could afford to do it and you had the time to do it right and the producer forced a bad decision on you or in the final cut made you change something, that's frustrating. I've had that on almost every film to a degree. It could be something minor or it could be something major.

Del Howison: So sometimes you rewrite on the spot to get around a problem?

Kevin Tenney: Yes. I've done that before. We've had a film I did not technically write although I did a massive rewrite but I didn't get a writer's credit on it. But the script was not that great. They had an issue and we had to add a day on. It was right before the holidays and one of the actors already booked his flight. Basically, he's gone. They said, "If we have to pay him to stay it will cost us this much. But we're willing to do it if we have to." They called me on the set and I said wait a minute. I ran through the script, everything we shot and what was left, and I said, "We can give his line to this other guy and we don't need him so let him go." It worked.

Del Howison: What about a director ruining something you've written?

Kevin Tenney: I had a director completely destroy one of my pictures, trashed it. It's funny, as it wasn't a script I was in love with anyway but what he did with it was like . . . But that wasn't just my opinion, that was the production company's, too. They took it away from him, gave me all the dailies, and had Dan and I recut the film. Then any place where we said we needed a pickup shot of this or that would help they gave us money to go out and shoot pickup shots to help. It was a band-aid on a gunshot wound. So it was something. I don't think that I'm high-maintenance super control freaky and the fact that the production company that was financing the film said something I knew it wasn't just me. After taking it away and giving me the dailies and having me and my editor recut, they had me hire my brother to redo the soundtrack because they didn't like the original composer's soundtrack. That says something. They didn't like too much.

Del Howison: Do you prefer directing your own script?

Fred Dekker: Honestly, I'd be happy to never write at all. Unfortunately, I can't afford the writers I'd most like to work with (also many of them are dead or retired)—and for better or worse, I do have very specific ideas of what I want to do. So, until cloning is perfected, I'm kind of stuck with myself as the writer.

Tom Holland: Yes. Underline that. Here: Yes. You have to make many of the same decisions writing that you do directing, so there is overlap. And why do more work than you have to?

Amber Benson: No, I actually prefer directing other people's work and having other people direct my stuff. Isn't that funny? Like I said, I direct in my head when I write, so it's not as exciting to do my own stuff, in fact, it's like directing twice. For me, getting a virgin script that I didn't write is way more fun to direct. It's like having a fresh white canvas to paint on.

Kevin Tenney: Well here's the thing and I'll admit this as a writer myself. The nice thing about being given a script is that whether it is good or bad you're still a fresh pair of eyes and you're going to see stuff that the writer didn't see. You'll think, "This doesn't make sense where this guy does this here and that there." It might be because three drafts ago there was a scene that explained that but it was excised and they forgot to make this change because they know it so well they didn't notice that this doesn't make sense now.

I know that has happened to me, too. I know it because in *Witchboard* we had a scene, in the finished film where Jim and Linda are getting ready for the party. It's actually like Scene 13 in the script. We showed a boat explosion and the kid dying and then we thought that might be giving everyone too much information and it's better if they find it out through the Board. Then they don't know whether David's real or not, but if we show them the boat accident then they know he is. But we show that the boat accident takes place in Big Bear and it says *Big Bear 20 Years Ago* or whatever it is. So later in the script when Brandon says "Yeah, I believe it is David and he's doing stuff. That's why I'm going to Big Bear." It got a big laugh in theaters because it sounds to the audience like he's running. "The ghost is killing people so I'm headed to Big Bear." But that's because they didn't have the benefit of knowing that's where he died. Because we forgot you're never told where he died. You're told he was killed in a boating accident but you're never told where. You were shown in the scene that got cut. So because of that when he says that line it gets a big laugh. He says right after that, "That's where David died." But it comes after the laugh. It would have been very easy to fix but we didn't realize that people would laugh. We knew David dies in Big Bear and everyone working on it knew David died in Big Bear so the line didn't stick out to us.

Del Howison: In the beginning, if you are writing your own script, what is the most important aspect of it—the characters, the story, the catchy horror twist or something else? Why and does that focus of importance shift for you further into the process?

Fred Dekker: It varies. It's like asking what makes you fall in love with somebody; it could be their spirit or sense of humor, their smile, how they make you feel. A script is the same thing . . . but there's usually one thing that compels you.

For me, I love movies like *Jaws* and *The Exorcist* where ordinary people are caught up in extraordinary events, and have to survive (or not). Any variation of that will usually compel me, but from there it's vital that I *believe* the characters—that they seem, and act, like actual people.

You can work on the elements separately (concept, story, character) but by the end, you want everything to work together seamlessly.

Tom Holland: Gawd, these are good questions.

Character, cause no matter the genre, the audience has to be emotionally involved with your characters, hate or love 'em, for the movie to succeed. Your questions above go to the question of whether or not the story is character or plot driven. For me, both. For critics, character, but what do critics know?

Amber Benson: I love plot. I like coming up with the plot and the atmosphere (the vibe/tone) of the piece first. The characters and their psychological back-story come next. The twist often comes last, which seems like I'm putting the cart before the horse, but when you put everything together and know what the end point of the story is only after doing all that other work, can I start building the narrative trap that leads us to our ending. I liken it to writing a detective story, you have to reverse engineer the whole thing, like I know who was murdered and how, but the why only comes after much thought and study.

Del Howison: Kevin, you are quoted as saying, "What works for any genre is a good story. Bottom line. Your audience will forgive everything else. They will forgive you if the acting isn't up to par, if the lighting isn't up to snuff. But the worse your story is the better everything has to be to make up for it." Do you still feel that way?

Kevin Tenney: Yes and here's a perfect example. Watch something like *Jurassic Park*, not a bad story but a pretty simple story, and then watch *Dinosaur Island* or something or one of the Sci-fi channel horror films. Their scripts really aren't much worse, they are, but not so much so. It's all in the monsters. The monster looks better.

A perfect example is **Mike Mendez**'s *Big Ass Spider*. Not really that bigger a budget than most like *Sharknado*. *Sharknado* is popular because it is so bad. People enjoy laughing at it. *Big Ass Spider* is actually a really well-structured, well-written, good story with likable characters that are funny because it is supposed to be funny. You're not laughing at *Big Ass Spider*, you're laughing with it. The effects are good. But I've seen some Sci-Fi channel movies where the effects are really bad, and others where the effects are pretty good. But the story doesn't hold up the way Mike's story does. So yeah, I think first and foremost it's story.

Del Howison: If somebody hires you to direct your script, do you have footnotes or asides in the margins of your script that might be just silly words but they are clues for you, like shorthand that only you understand?

Tom Holland: Yes, but that better describes my hen scratches that I call storyboards.

Kevin Tenney: No. you know why? It's because even if I'm directing the script, now it's getting made, they make 100 copies and give it to everyone in the crew. I don't want each crew person come up to me and ask what does this mean? Another reason I like to be very visual in my description is because a lot of times on a small budget you don't have the money to get a storyboard artist to help visualize and storyboard out the film. But if you can describe it well enough people can see it in their heads just as if they are looking at a picture, then they know what you want.

Amber Benson: Ha, no one has ever asked me to direct something that I wrote. If I wrote it and directed it, I was the producer, too. That's how you get yourself the job, create the job in the first place. I don't have silly worlds or clues in the margins. I actually storyboard the whole film and I use that as my shorthand. I've used an artist—which was amazing— and I've just done the stick-figuring myself, but I find the process to be very elucidating. Taking my words and putting them into picture form is a necessary part of directing for it's when I take off the writer hat and put on the director beret.

Del Howison: Kevin, I read somewhere that you mentioned you would like to direct in every genre. Do you approach horror differently than you approach writing and directing in any other genre?

Kevin Tenney: No, because a good story is what it is all about. For me, no matter the genre, it has to start with a good story and interesting characters. That's true of any genre. In a lot of ways horror and comedy are similar because it's all about timing. I've seen horror films where they show the girl walking alone, she looks over her shoulder, the music swells and the guy attacks her and you don't jump. Then you see someone else shoot that exact same sequence a different way and you come out of your seat. It's because one guy knew how to time it and stretch it and the other guy didn't. It's the same way with a joke. If the punchline comes too soon or too late, if the set-up isn't just right it doesn't take much to throw it off.

Del Howison: How much of that original creation is in the shooting and the writing and how much is in the editing or is it usually drastically different?

Fred Dekker: Somebody smarter than me once said that you write a movie three times. The first time is when you write the script. The second is when you shoot it. And the third is in the editing and post-production process.

This is absolutely true, and what it means is this: not that you re-write during each phase, but that each phase informs the story and the movie that you're making. You cast an actor, and they make the role their own. They may add lines or nuances, but the character definitely changes based on their input and personality. Then in the editing, you trim or cut or re-arrange, you make it work as best you can, but inevitably, organically, it's changed from what it was originally on the page. That's just the process.

Kevin Tenney: Oh, shooting is everything. That's the problem with writing horror or comedy. I've written two horror films I did not direct with scenes I knew would get a good jump, if I had directed it, fall flat because this guy didn't know how to direct it. Even in the script I really described it. All he had to do was to direct it the way I described it and it would have worked. He didn't. You've got an instruction manual and a blueprint, dumbass.

Tom Holland: I shoot the script, especially when I write it. Editing is a matter of making work what I have already written and laid out in storyboards. I know just what I want in most scenes, and get it probably 75-80 percent of the time. But that means 15-20% of the movie I shot doesn't work the way I expected.

Your question is two-fold. The script isn't the thing itself. The movie is. It won't reveal itself until it is edited together. Test screenings will tell you more, especially where to trim. You tighten up the film in the process, trimming the scenes. I very seldom drop entire scenes, but it does happen. Also, the suits always want you to cut the comedy, which is unfortunate, but then so few of them have a sense of humor.

The only protection in the editing process is to have a successful preview from the very beginning. Otherwise, the money is on you like the fearful jackals they are.

Del Howison: You have written sequels. Outside of the fact that you are working with characters who have already been established and a storyline from the past, is there any way to really put your mark on a sequel to make it your own and rise from the series? It seems one might be tempted to just write for the money and not have a real focus on creativity.

Tom Holland: See *Psycho 2*. I wasn't messing around there. Money had nothing to do with it. I wrote that carefully and put a huge amount of work (and love) into it, out of respect for Mr. Hitchcock (the world's greatest director, along with **John Ford**).

Fred Dekker: If I'm not compelled, I generally steer clear of doing it, money or no. On *Robocop 3*, I just loved that character. He's a lot like Frankenstein's monster; a mishmash, resurrected person who just wants to be human again but sadly, never can. With *The Predator*, I actually got excited about addressing some of my misgivings about the first movie. I thought there were some elements of the *Predator* mythology that didn't make sense, so I asked Shane Black and 20th Century-Fox if we could explore those questions . . . and that's what we did!

So yes, it's imperative you put your own stamp on it. But sequels are tricky tightrope walks. The audience wants another helping of the same thing but they also want to be surprised, so the challenge is what to change and what not to. If the audience feels you got the balance wrong, they're very unforgiving.

Del Howison: Finally, ignoring the fact that money makes the world go 'round, in the early process of story creation, what have you learned that you didn't even think about back in the days when you were starting out?

Tom Holland: Budget. Casting. The other thing that I have always done, or tried to do, is make the structure so tight they (the money, the suits, whatever you want to call them) can't rewrite you to the extent that it will hurt the script. If you are working only as the writer, they will always believe in doing a "dialogue polish" once they get rid of you.

As illuminating as this discussion was there is no doubt that every artist paints their canvases with their own technique. Neither right nor wrong in their individual approach and style, the things they share is a love for what they create and a desire to put the best product they possibly can up on the screen—be it a big or small one—despite all the obstacles inherent in each project. No two endeavors are identical and no two artists work the same. The drive they each carry inside is the key to the fear mechanism they share with us, the audience.

Z NATION:

How Syfy's Hit Undead Show Came to Life

CRAIG ENGLER

Z NATION IS a television series that didn't start out as a TV show. It started out as a made-for-TV movie on Syfy called *Zombie Apocalypse* that I co-wrote with a friend. The movie was notable for two reasons. First, it featured Ving Rhames killing Zs with a sledgehammer, which is always a crowd pleaser. Second, it ended with an attack by what is probably the first zombie tiger ever put on the small screen.

Zombie Apocalypse turned out to be a hit. It wasn't just Syfy's highest-rated film of 2011, it was their highest-rated film in years, by a huge margin.

Fast forward to 2013 and Syfy was interested in developing some of its successful movies into TV series. I told my friend at the network that I'd always thought of *Zombie Apocalypse* as the last episode of a five-year TV series. He was intrigued, so I pitched him the show concept.

In the movie, a group of survivors have walked from New York to Los Angeles to reach the last surviving human safe haven on Catalina Island. The movie was set in LA, and the cross-country trek from the East Coast was referenced only as backstory.

The TV show would focus on the backstory, starting out in New York and following the group as it made the year's long journey across an apocalyptic landscape filled with the undead. And to amp up the drama, the show would have higher stakes than the movie.

The impetus for our hero's journey wouldn't just be getting to a safe haven. In the expanded TV version, they were setting out on a quest to find a cure for the zombie plague. So it wasn't just their lives hanging in the balance, it was the fate of the entire human species. Without the cure, humanity would cease to exist.

The characters also changed substantially. Part of that was because the show wasn't going to be *Zombie Apocalypse* the TV series, it was going to be a new series loosely based on the concept of the movie. And practically speaking we probably couldn't get most of the actors back. Some of them wouldn't sign up for a TV show even if they were available. So I started from scratch, although we kept a character named "Mack" in both as an homage. And the show would have strong female leads, just like the movie. The initial round of characters morphed further as we brought on a showrunner and the writers' room started weighing in.

The series also needed a new name, since Zombie Apocalypse is fine for a one-off movie but probably too generic for a show. I wanted to keep the "Z" in there so people would get the fact that it was a zombie show, and added "Nation" to convey the scope of the series. We were going across the entire U.S., not just California. *Z Nation* seemed like it hit all the right notes (later on in the writers' room the network asked us to come up with alternate titles, but after going through a few dozen alternates, everyone agreed *Z Nation* worked best).

Another big difference between film and TV is that television shows need a premise that can sustain not just for two hours, but week in and week out for years. That's why sometimes movies that get made into TV shows fail horribly. Often it's because they ran out of story to tell. In fact, the weekly driver for a TV series is called its "story engine" because you need an engine to power something as long-lasting as a weekly series.

Interestingly, one reason you see a lot of cop shows, medical dramas and lawyer series on TV is because they all have self-sustaining story engines. In a cop show, every week there's a new crime to solve. In medical dramas, there is a never-ending supply of patients to save. And in a lawyer series, there's always a new case to litigate.

For *Z Nation*, the story engine was built into the premise of the show: Every week our heroes had to take one step forward on their journey to California, but every step they took put them further in peril. The drama is inherent in their mission. And it's not just the characters' lives that are at stake. The fate of the world hangs in the balance.

Z Nation also contained another key element of a good genre show: world building. People like horror, science fiction and fantasy shows in part because those shows give them a glimpse into other worlds. In *Game of Thrones*, every week we're taken to a medieval world where magic and dragons exist. In *The Expanse*, we get to travel through the solar system.

In *Z Nation*, every week we take viewers into a zombie wasteland. Because it's a travel show, we also see how other people are coping with the apocalypse. So far our heroes have come across religious cults, cannibals, a safe haven where only women are allowed, and many others. Part of the fun of *Z Nation* is seeing what crazy group of survivors our heroes will encounter next.

We also wanted to expand on the mythology of zombies by introducing many types of the undead. That was again something carried over from the movie. In *Z Nation*, our team has fought off radioactive zombies, plant zombies, fungus zombies, fast zombies, slow zombies and dozens of others. The world of *Z Nation* is vast and diverse, and viewers know every time they tune in for the next episode they'll see something new.

That expansive world lets us give our characters plenty of things to do every week. While they're always focused on their core mission of saving the world, they usually find themselves in some kind of peril each episode. One week they'll need to find gas to keep their vehicles moving, and the next week they'll have to survive a tornado filled with writhing zombies.

Another story driver of *Z Nation* is the sheer danger of the zombie apocalypse. No one is safe in our show. In the first episode, we killed the character you thought was going to be the leader of the series. Then we did it again six episodes later, killing our next lead. All of that was by design. The reason wasn't to shock viewers or to get people to tweet about the show, but because our show is dangerous. Viewers need to feel this is a place where anyone can die at any moment.

And that in turn ups the drama of the show. When we put main characters in jeopardy, you know we mean it. Which also gives us a continual reason to add new characters and introduce new storylines to the show.

Even small details about world building can have a big impact. Early on I decided our characters would use the word "zombie" in the series. That seemingly trivial choice has non-trivial implications for heroes. It pre-supposes they know what zombies are and how to combat them, so they don't have to spend forever figuring out that you have to destroy the brain to kill a Z. Our characters know just as much about zombies as viewers do, so we don't have to bother explaining it all or having our heroes go over well-trod ground.

Another big ingredient of the show is humor. I'm a big fan of "road" stories like *Band of Brothers* or *Lord of the Rings*, because in those settings the characters bond and develop a deep camaraderie. And one of the way people bond is through humor. Especially in dire circumstance. Gallows humor is a way we have of coping with horrible situations. So our characters crack jokes and have fun in between fighting for their lives and saving the world.

That unique combination of horror, humor and heart really resonated with viewers. *Z Nation* debuted as Syfy's highest-rated acquired show in the network's history. And our ratings grew during the season, something that rarely happens with TV shows. Usually the first episode is the most watched as people sample it, then the ratings drop a bit and settle into a pattern. Our first season of 13 episodes did so well that Syfy increased our order to 15 episodes the next season.

We're now working on season four of the show

thanks to the support of viewers and a story engine
that keeps us moving along. That, in turn, lets us tell
fun stories and create more zombie mayhem.

LIFE IMITATING ART IMITATING LIFE

Film and Its Influence on Reality

JASON V BROCK

WITHOUT AN IDEA, there is no tale; without a tale, there may be something to say, but no way to say it.

In other words: Humans, as natural storytellers, are tapping into more than simply strings of ideas randomly put together when they write a short story or make a film. There are other considerations after the idea which comprise the tale itself: point-of-view, structure, purpose, characters, meaning, and so on. As well, the "teller" (be it a writer or director) and/or the medium (novel, film, play, comic book, or something else) are considerations...but the story is the thing.

This is especially true of horror-based narratives, which frequently rely (ofttimes to their detriment, which is another point) on a simple idea told in a straight-forward manner utilizing strong (or at least memorable) characters in a story arc that culminates in a cathartic pay-off (though not always, granted). Terror tales are stereotypically driven by an emotional, not cerebral, connection with intended audiences— though the greatest of them transcend this limitation.

For centuries, likely since the dawn of humanity, these types of stories have served various roles: as entertainments, morality plays, cautionary tales, even as a way of confirming the best and worst aspects of human tribality ("we are this way, which is righteous; they are this other way, which is taboo"). It is natural that this idiom would be used not only in written accounts, but in visual art, musical works (to include ballads, opera, ballet, folk, and popular songs), and, of course (much later), in radio, movies, and television.

Film, as the dominant mode of mass media expression in the modern and post-modern era (only recently supplanted by the Internet), has created new ways of understanding the world during its tenure by not only isolating and examining what it means to be alive, but also by providing intentional and accidental insights into the larger culture we inhabit. The way this is accomplished is by turns complex and simple; additionally, much can be gleaned from longitudinal studies of popular trends in cinematic articulation (such as which genres are popular during certain decades, as well as shifts in editing techniques or directorial styles, et cetera). Before we get too far into this examination with respect to the field of horror films, however, let's step back and examine something less dynamic from a collaborative viewpoint (film, after all, is more than just the work of a single entity), and consider the foundation of cinema: Writing. Before a film can be made, it must have a screenplay; the leap from idea to the cinematic visualization of it on the silver screen is a huge one, with many phases (and art forms) as intermediary steps before final effectuation. The catalyst, of course, is the idea, as written by an author (the screenwriter in this instance). Screenwriting, like poetry, is different in form and function than prose, and by necessity; there are limitations the writer must endure in order to keep the process running smoothly, and a screenplay is never really "completed" until the film itself is shot, edited, scored, and distributed (promotion is another enterprise).

Roughly, filmmaking is divided into four sections: Pre-production (producers secure financing, then gather a script [writer], production team [for example the cinematographer and director] and a crew [makeup artists, grips, set designers, et al], which comprise "below-the-line" costs, before hiring actors and other "above-the-line" talent), production (rehearsals and filming), post-production (editing, scoring, and so on), and finally distribution and promotion. A screenwriter, as part of the core team, must understand their role (as both the creator of the structure, and as a support to the director, actors, and producers, not as an egotist), and therefore be easy to work with, flexible, disciplined, and an anchor to the inherent chaos of the filmmaking venture. As a result, they must (similar to comic book writers) put aside their literary aspirations and focus on helping the director (and producers) obtain the best possible end-product considering the investment entailed. To that end, there are rules that a screenwriter will understand in the process of writing a screenplay (or teleplay): 1) There can be no "interior" in a script, only dialogue and action; 2) if there is interior, it can only be voiceover, and is best avoided; 3) not to get into too much detail on the script—let the director have the leeway to make decisions about the way things are shot, how characters dress, and so on, sketch out only the bare minimum with respect to shots; 4) the first thing to do with adapting a work (after learning script format) is to break the original source into scenes, and decide which elements can be made physical, or that need to be combined, or jettisoned altogether. Another thing to understand is that a page of script is roughly a minute of screen time. A TV show (half-hour) is about 22 pages (this allows for commercials). A novel adaptation should be around 90-120 pages. These are the strict (mostly physical/logical) limitations; in attempting to understand the process more fully (of idea to screen), let us consider a few things and agree on general guidelines of how humans interact with one another with respect to exchanging such ideas.

It has been noted that people largely have three working vocabularies, though there is overlap between them: what they are able to understand when reading, how they communicate in writing, and what they comprehend within the framework of a spoken conversation (dialogue). Utilizing this observation as a starting point, one can begin to parse the attributes of an author's written output—knowledge of which exploits, consciously or unconsciously, all three of these vocabularies. Therefore, through the prism of various modes of expression available to us for critique, we can come to certain conclusions about the "how and why" specific works (and thus their creators) resonate throughout time and experience with consumers (the audience). In one sense, this is quite a feat, as writing is explicit, and is reliant upon individual hard realities of linguistic syntax, cultural references, and even alphabet—something that makes the written milieu less universal than other art forms which are not dependent on literacy, but perhaps more powerful as a result (to include film).

What I mean by that is there are several non-language forms of communication that cut across all times, all cultures, all social strata, and all mores. Among them are the strictly visual art realms of painting, photography, or sculpture; the auditory experience of music; olfaction (the impact of which is expressed so elegantly in Proust's *Remembrance of Things Past*); kinesthetics (such as dance or theatre); cinema (which combines aspects of many art forms in a synergistic fashion); and calculation—the latter capable of examining and explaining ideas due to the universal acceptance of common numerical symbols and principles within the architecture of mathematics (this, in turn, forming the backbone of disciplines such as astronomy, computer science, physics, and others). Each of these, in various ways, can captivate the observer/experiencer in concrete as well as emotional terms. For example, an equation may be deemed "beautiful" (Einstein's famous $E=mc^2$), a ballet may be passionately moving, a painting could incite feelings of revulsion, and so on. This phenomenon is due to individual interpretation (subjectivity) filtering the universal fundamentals of these modes (images, sounds, movement, smell, touch) into something so transcendent and simple that they require no clarification to be comprehended. Instead, these elements drive straight into the heart of the human experience: We've all felt these basic sensations, and can immediately relate to their appeal or repugnance, as these ways of communicating (with the possible exception of calculation, and even there not in every instance) are open-ended (at times even ambiguous, conceptual, or representational—not rooted in the physical or "real"), inviting aesthetic appraisal and understanding. We grasp unconsciously the meanings on display; we intuit what we are experiencing as a commentary of reality itself (though distanced by the vehicle in use, such as a stage, canvas, or book)— namely an imitation of life presented as an explanation of what life is "about."

These scenarios are an entirely different situation than what is presented by "pure" literature, which, as noted previously, is quite specific; in fact, it is so specific as to require literal translation from one language to another. That specificity is the primary characteristic (and strength) of this art form as opposed to all others, however; it is a form of mind-to-mind communication and direct thought transference. Even as "language" (to include all variations of dialect) itself has evolved—starting with sound and the oral storytelling tradition; shifting to drawings which became miniaturized symbols (an alphabet); later codified by print; now returning (by way of the visually-based Internet) to an oral/visual mode—this has remained a consistent feature of sharing stories and dispersing information, whether fictionally or as nonfiction.

As this is the case, why do the works of some literary practitioners seem to capture the collective imagination while other efforts—of equal or even greater merit—never seem to find an audience? It cannot be solely due to language. Instead, I feel strongly it is due to the influence of the individual's personal considerations—meaning what they decide to pursue, omit, condense, or expand. This is mostly what we deem the editorial notion of "personal style" or stylistics. The message might be quite similar from writer to writer (this is the creation of a "genre" for example), but the way that message is expressed is also part of the consideration of the value of a work (the "shell" which includes its contents).

To that end, when analyzing a literary work, the primary attribute (for good or ill) of any author is directly on the page (the "text"), followed by—and more important, arguably—what is conveyed but not written (the "subtext"); the circumstances that it is being presented under (the "context"); also, how and what that means to the world more broadly (the "intertextuality," including the "meta-" aspects and so on). When we read and ingest (this is crucial: that we not just "grasp" meaning, but also internalize what is being shared) the works of authors such as Homer, Edgar Allan Poe, H. P. Lovecraft, Ray Bradbury, Franz Kafka, Jorge Luis Borges, Gabriel García Márquez, and so many others, we are, on the one hand, adopting what they are describing to us, relating it to the personal and identifiable (making it "real" to us, and relevant to daily life); but we are also looking for novelty (by way of vicarious living)—for how this experience or circumstance is new to us and what we can learn from it. The result is that—when a writer has learned to master their approach and honed what we can eventually (over their corpus) identify as a "voice"—their unique take on the world aids us as readers to delineate and focus our own take on same.

Stylistics are key here; they engender in us a feeling that we are in a "conversation" or "dialogue" with the creator, and not just a bored spectator. The true masters transcend consumerism and commerciality—if they even attain it, which is not always the case—allowing a suspension of disbelief that promotes not simply diversion, but also leaves us awed, and thinking in ways we never have before. It touches us; we are changed, transformed. We leave the experience improved and wiser than the person we were before we began the journey—and all for the better.

These observations duly noted, within the sphere of motion pictures, there are multiple forces at work, in contrast to the sole voice of an author of a novel, as film is a collaborative art form. Cinema has evolved faster than perhaps any other mode of expression except television, with which it shares common technological DNA, and both formats boast the unique aspect of cannibalizing all other art forms (music/sound, visual art/design, writing, performance) to achieve their collective aims—a cohesive vision/narrative synthesizing technology, creativity, and multiple points of view. With respect to accomplishing these goals, there has been a gradual concentration of power and influence away from studios, writers, and producers and toward the director as the author of the final product, with the dual implications of taking the hit for terrible failure, or reaping the rewards of great success. This idea—known as the "auteur theory"—has generated much controversy among filmmaking scholars, and has likely produced greater (and more terrible) works as an operating strategy than previous structures it replaced (the studio system, et cetera). As a microcosmic mirror for the rise of the individual in Western conceptions of the mind, auteur theory takes the notion of a deterministic self as the most significant aspect of an endeavor—in this case the creation of a film as opposed to the establishment of a social fabric—and elevates this principle to the highest position achievable within the enterprise, even though the outcome is still ultimately contingent on mutual collaboration and large-scale cooperation inside the context of the effort. This is a misdirection of reality, however; although a director may be described as an "auteur," they are still indebted to producers, writers, score composers, actors, artists, designers, effects people, and editors to bring their vision to the masses. Also, just as in the world of written works (often an inspirational starting point for filmic efforts), there are major descriptive staples worthy of note which shape a given project—mob films, romantic comedies, Westerns, science fiction, horror, and so on—which most students and casual observers would identify as genres. Consequently, since the creation of a movie is such an elaborate task involving such a wide gamut of talents and perspectives, it is not an enterprise that, at its most effective, can purely be quantified as a collection of tropes or stereotypes from the mind of a single person—just as a novel is more than the sum of its chapters, or a play is more than actors wandering around on a stage.

Roughly speaking, as an institution, auteur theory (especially in the realm of horror films, in my estimation) reached its zenith in both popularity and influence in the groundbreaking works of the late

1960s to the early-1990s. This period owed much to pioneers from the 1950s French New Wave movement (members of *Cahiers du cinéma*, including filmmakers and critics such as François Truffaut, Jean-Luc Godard, Éric Rohmer, Claude Chabrol, and Jacques Rivette), as well as vocabularies developed during that era still in use today: extensive use of jump cutting, cinéma-vérité, and other techniques which consciously draw attention to the artifice of filmmaking (as opposed to trying to mask it, though traditional movie making principles are still utilized as well). Auteurs also admired the control and dominance of vision (as contrasted with creation via committee) exercised by directors such as Alfred Hitchcock, and, especially, Orson Welles in his seminal *Citizen Kane* (1941).

As the 1960s wore on, film schools largely embraced the auteur conception of creating films, leading to greater exposure of the aesthetics and ideals of this methodology in a structured classroom environment, which encouraged not only experimentation, but also critical analysis of the techniques and psychological dynamics involved in the creation of movies (and their visceral impact in the long term). This would eventually result in greater filmic realism and much more emotionally raw experiences (and resonances) for filmgoers. Much as the cinematic art form was swamped by a sea change with regard to what was able to be accomplished (technologically, artistically, and performance-wise), society was also in the midst of convulsive tumult: Assassinations of political and religious figures became commonplace; the reportage of the horrors occurring in Vietnam was unrelenting; drug use and sexual liberation was reflected in a counterculture fed by various youth movements, feminist theory, and the disintegration of the Old Guard and their (suddenly) outmoded philosophies.

After this, a brief social relaxation occurred in the 1970s as the world economy slowed due to myriad issues in the United States and abroad (the Vietnam war, and the widespread use of drugs, to name but two items on the agenda). Still, it was a fertile time for the creation of films and the arts generally. The envelope was continually pushed in increasingly more eye-opening ways (pornographic movies, documentaries, cinematic realism) than it had been in previous periods, where movies (and TV) bordered on basic efforts to capture tightly-scripted performances by well-clothed actors. The "stagey," more formal aspects began to fall away, inviting audiences to directly experience what the filmmakers were attempting to show—less in voyeuristic terms, and more as active participants in the proceedings unfolding on the screen, large or small. As the veil lifted with respect to techniques and technology, it afforded cineastes greater latitude with regard to what stories they chose to tell, and how they could tell them.

As the '70s slipped away into the 1980s, a new sobriety gripped the world. It has been observed that in times of economic privation (and/or in epochs of a more conservative bent), the literature and art of cultures become more inward—focused on the immediate vicissitudes of life and its hardships. This can be reflected in turn with a preoccupation of the self as existential flotsam in an ocean of uncertainty, which, in real terms, often translates into reactionary self-examinations of one's circumstances that may lead to a need for expressions of care-free escapism, or violent explorations of victimhood, even inversions of what the broken social order should have done differently. All of these can be seen in cataloging films of the 1980s: reactions to the looming AIDS crisis, cosmetically ameliorated by numerous vapid teen sex comedies (*Porky's* [1981], *Fast Times at Ridgemont High* [1982], et cetera, which, in retrospect can also be read as callbacks to perceived "simpler times" in the 1950s and '60s with respect to sexual liberation); the rise of *First Blood* (a 1982 movie [later franchise] based on the eponymous 1972 novel by David Morrell) in answer to the "defeat" of Vietnam; responses to the presidency of conservative Ronald Reagan in efforts such as Brian De Palma's *Scarface* (1983), scripted by Oliver Stone, and, later, Stone's own *Wall Street* (1987); and, famously, the advent of slasher films such as *Friday the 13th* and *Maniac* (both 1980), and innumerable others, with their gory preoccupations and pseudo-conservative leanings (teenage sex was often "punished" with brutal death; the [usually] deformed [either psychologically and/or physically] male killer was invariably undone by a neo-feminist [albeit chaste] "final girl," and so on).

Of course, it must be noted that the context for the popularity of the slasher film was embedded in a wider tableau, normally referenced as "the 1980s Horror Boom." During this boom-time, largely brought about in publishing by the phenomenal success of authors Stephen King (*The Dead Zone*), Clive Barker (*Books of Blood*), Peter Straub (*Ghost Story*), and Anne Rice (*Interview with the Vampire*), whose collective coattails would provide mainstream access in mall-chain retail bookstores (in the "Horror" section, no less) such as B. Dalton and Barnes & Noble, and large advances for a wide coterie of authors of varying quality (though several of the best are still producing good works), horror was "in." There was even a short-lived transgressive subgenre of note, so-called "Splatterpunk," and the go-to publication of record, outside of occasional fiction in men's magazines, was *Twilight Zone*, published by the widow of Rod Serling, Carol—which was fitting, as Serling and The Group (Charles Beaumont, Richard Matheson, William F. Nolan, Ray Bradbury, George Clayton Johnson, John Tomerlin, Jerry Sohl, et al) provided a bridge in print and on TV and film between tales and techniques of the Gothic (pre-Modernist) type (Poe, Lovecraft) and the modern/post-modern output of Dean Koontz, Dennis Etchison, and others.

This was additionally, as previously touched upon, a significant and influential period for terror in cinema (lavishly chronicled in glorious color by *Fangoria* magazine; there was even coverage by major outlets such as *Playboy* and *Penthouse*), as many of the efforts in the literary world were adapted into films from A-list to Z-grade, most settling comfortably in the Roger Corman-inspired B-movie plateau, and a few gems going on to become genuine classics in the horror genre. Even the nascent world of cable TV was put on the map by the debut of Michael Jackson's epic music video *Thriller* on M-TV (the mini-film was co-written [with Jackson] and directed by John Landis in 1983, based on the hit song; the special effects were supplied by longtime Landis collaborator Rick Baker who—

along with Tom Savini—was a superstar of the makeup world, known even to the general public of the era). Such was the populace's appetite for all things scary and gruesome at this time that, for a while, the rising tide lifted all boats in a wine-dark sea. In the end, a few became very wealthy indeed, while others are still able to eke out a living, and the rest, if not outright consigned to the depths of literary and cinematic history, have become little more than half-recalled phantoms, the crew of a foundered Flying Dutchman age, apparently never to be duplicated.

In the world of movies, as the bubble collapsed in the publishing industry, and the public interest in horror waned with the dawn of the 1990s tech explosion during the presidency of Democrat Bill Clinton, the money and exposure dried up, and the popularity of the horror genre was displaced by a renewed interest in other modes and approaches to storytelling, to include science fiction. The age of realism gave way to the tent-pole style blockbuster (B-films with A-list budgets) in the wake of the Spielberg/Lucas effect, as Computer-Generated Imagery (CGI) took a larger and larger role away from traditional filmmaking techniques. As a result, actors are increasingly instructed to react to green screen environments without any physical elements, and the rest is filled in later during post-production. The trend has only accelerated in recent years, and shows no real signs of abating as practical effects and human interactions are replaced with digital methods of shooting and virtualization. This has, in my estimation, created a blurring of lines (and a flattening of effect) in the ways that audiences not only experience modern films, but also with respect to emotional heft, as movies progressively drift into the arena of video game flatness and irreality (the Uncanny Valley Effect, in part), and video games continue to mine the methodologies of traditional cinematic syntax and execution (such as shot mapping and scoring). We do live in interesting times, it appears. Despite this situation, there is reason to have hope: As always, people can surprise, and old may yet become new. Simple things and ways are sometimes best, or at least the start of greatness to come.

But first, someone must have an idea, and then write it.

WHERE DO NIGHTMARES COME FROM

A Look at Storytelling and Screenwriting

PAUL MOORE

WHERE DO NIGHTMARES come from . . . ?

To get the complete answer to that question, I suspect it will take years of therapy and far more money than you shelled out for this book. However as far as in regard to that question of the origins of screenplays is concerned, I might be able to shed a little light in that particularly dark corner. Or at the very least, hopefully entertain you with my attempts.

So who am I and what qualifies me to answer that question?

The short answer is that I am an independent writer and director whose features have been distributed by Lions Gate Home Entertainment, appeared on the Syfy channel and played at major genre festivals worldwide. In addition, I am also an author who has been published in a variety of genre anthologies, the co-owner of fully outfitted motion picture production studio and a lifelong fan of the horror genre on the page and the screen.

What I am not; is a household name. I am certain

that many of you are not familiar with my work and many of you are Googling my name in an attempt to determine whether or not you should skip to the next chapter. Completely understandable (especially if you've seen my first film), but if you will overlook that and read further, I think you might find few things of interest.

Still with me? Good. Let's start.

Sometime in the early part of this century, I was invited to the wedding of a college friend in Charlottesville, Virginia. At the time, I was living just outside Washington, DC and it was roughly a four-hour drive. Fancying myself a filmmaker/writer/artist, I had adopted a late night schedule as I needed to cultivate an appropriately dark and brooding persona. Fifteen years ago, it was not only important that one wrote and created, but that they did it publicly with a scotch in one hand and a Lucky Strike in the other.

For the sake of full disclosure, it is one o'clock in the morning and I am sipping scotch in a dive bar as I type this. I really don't know if it helps with the writing, but I do know it doesn't hurt with the ladies. And at my age, I need all the help I can get. But, I digress . . .

So, I accepted the invitation and the night before (or morning of, depending on how you count your days) I began my drive from Oxon Hill, MD to Charlottesville. The drive went as expected until I hit highway 64, about forty minutes from my destination. Around that time, my car died. No fanfare, no sparks, smoke from beneath the hood, clunking noises, etc . . . It simply died.

For those of you who are familiar with the highway

64 between Richmond and Charlottesville, I share your pain. For those of you who are not, I will simply describe it as 21st-century wasteland. Most of the service stations close when the sun goes down and the truck stops don't begin until you've passed the city, over Afton mountain and into the collection of cheap motels and fast food joints that comprise the sleepy burg of Waynesboro.

Now that I type this, I realize the name of that town pretty much sums it up.

However, though my car was mysteriously inert, it was under warranty and I had recently purchased a cell phone. Even more miraculous in a story directly related to horror films, my cell phone actually received a signal. Excited about escaping being a complete cliché, I called Hyundai Roadside Assistance and reported my situation. The kind lady at the other end of the line assured me that a tow truck driver had been dispatched and he would join me shortly.

Two hours later, my tow truck arrived. The driver's name was Earl and Earl was not just a simple redneck. He was a full-blown, Confederate flag waving, gun toting, tobacco chewing, dyed-in-the-wool-of-the-last-sheep-he-fucked, Virginia good-old-boy hillbilly redneck. One other thing about Earl, he liked to talk.

Once my car was hooked up and I was in the cab next to him, we began our trek over Afton mountain to Waynesboro; where Earl assured me he knew an honest mechanic who could fix my car for a fair price (stop me if you've heard this one). My Roadside Assistance was good for five years, but my physical warranty ended at one hundred thousand miles. I had burned up those miles in the first two years of owning the car and I was on year three. So, I agreed.

As we drove along the empty highway in the dead of the night, Earl regaled me with tales of his youth and his opinions on politics, religion and what was generally wrong with society at that time.

SPOILER ALERT: Democrats, women, homosexuals, Catholics, Jews and racial minorities were not cast in a particularly favorable light during Earl's proclamations.

For me, the entire ride was an exercise in discomfort and most of my responses consisted of statements akin to "Is that so?" and monosyllabic grunts. However, having been a lifelong resident of the South, I was accustomed to these situations and knew how to navigate such social interactions without sacrificing my (questionable) integrity. It was when Earl asked me if we could take a detour that I should have asserted myself and insisted we stay on course, but I didn't. After all, he was the only tow truck that responded, the sun was coming up in an hour, I had a wedding to attend and I was exhausted.

My spirit beaten and my mind weary, I agreed to allow him to turn off the highway before we had reached the pinnacle of the mountain. What followed was a personal tour of Earl's world. And it is here that I want to be very explicit . . .

If a tow truck driver named Earl wants to take you into the backwoods of Virginia at four o'clock in the morning, say NO!

Sadly, I didn't.

The tour started with him pointing down certain side roads and at particular houses (I'm being generous with the use of the word "houses") and telling me about all the women he hooked up with in those locations. One of his tales had a very "Dear Penthouse" vibe to it as it involved a woman and her friend and later the same woman and her sister. I won't go into the lurid details here, but sufficed to say, these experiences were not relayed with the subtle turns of phrase or poetic language usually attributed to Shakespeare. In fact, the vulgarity of Earl's limited vocabulary only served to make the situation even more uncomfortable than it already was.

It was also about that time in the trip that I had a belated revelation.

I'm 6'3" tall, 240 pounds, broad-shouldered and bald. I was also both a private investigator and bounty hunter before I turned my attention to filmmaking and writing. Needless to say, most people think twice about engaging me in a physical altercation or criminal endeavor. When I leave a bar at 2:00 in the morning, I don't give much thought to the idea of being assaulted, mugged, etc . . . But this was not that situation. My earlier choices were limited to a binary option; get in the truck or rot on the side of the road.

Being who I am, I chose the truck. But what if I wasn't me? What if I had been a woman who stood 5'4", weighed a 118 pounds and the worst altercation of my lifetime involved an upside down, skinny, low fat, Caramel Macchiato and a snarky barista?

How vulnerable, helpless and downright terrified would I feel riding through the seedy underbelly of rural Virginia? And what could this man do with me considering the flimsy trail of actual facts I had left.

One call to Roadside Assistance. No calls to home, friends or anyone for that matter.

Other than Earl, only one other person knew my situation and there was a good chance they were oceans away working at a call center in one of those countries that did not concern themselves with detailed records of anything.

I was still pondering that question when Earl informed me he had to make a quick stop. I was already in for the long haul, so I just nodded. He made his stop and I waited in the truck. Five to ten minutes later, he emerged from some rundown house and climbed into the truck. We did not discuss the nature of business, but I did notice him slip a wadded baggy beneath his seat.

I will let you, the reader, fill in the blanks.

Eventually, my vehicle was dropped off a local garage and I was dropped off at the motel across the street. One of those places that still had a physical key and you had to leave a deposit to receive the remote controller which would activate your bolted-to-the-dresser television.

The remainder of the story is inconsequential for our purposes here, but I will summarize it for the completists out there.

It turned out the alternator was the issue with the car and I paid an unreasonable amount of money to get it replaced that day. However, I had already made peace with the fact that I was going to get ripped off, so that took away some of the sting. I also made the wedding on time. It took place in a backyard and I'm pretty sure the marriage license was printed on a cocktail napkin. Two years later, my friend was a "widow" as her husband took his own life due a string of long fermenting mental issues.

An entirely different kind of nightmare that we won't be discussing here.

What we will discuss is that moment on the back roads. That moment I posited an alternate scenario to the situation that had gone far beyond my control. And why discuss that? Because . . .

That is where nightmares come from. At least for screenwriters.

Most horror scripts begin with the question "What if . . . ?"

What if the undead wiped most of the human race from the Earth? What would the survivors do? How would they behave? What would be the reason to stay alive at all?

What if a local legend told the story of a wronged man who stalks and kills teens, but it turns out to be his mother? What if an escaped mental patient returned to exact revenge on his sister?

What if a group of teens ran afoul a family of cannibals? What if vampires ruled the world?

What if an unhinged doctor attempted to create life from a collection of cadavers or alien DNA? What if not everything around you was what it seemed to be?

Do not get me wrong as it is not a linear process. Writers develop characters, backstories and individual scenes as their minds chew over that central question of "What if . . . ?" Often one idea reveals another as one piece of the puzzle slips into place or replaces a previous puzzle piece. Each new decision or addition changes the landscape of the story, but the central question always remains . . . What if . . . ?

I used my experiences that night to ultimately develop the movie *Keepsake*. *Keepsake* was the story of a mute tow truck driver (he was mute because on my best day I could never accurately reproduce what came out of old Earl's mouth) who picks up a young woman stranded on a back road.

She inadvertently discovers he is impersonating the actual tow truck driver; whom he has killed (for the record, that driver was named Earl, but I don't think we need Sigmund Freud to explain why I wrote that into the script) and the rest of the movie plays out as a captivity/serial killer/cat-and-mouse horror thriller.

Keepsake became my most well-received film and has flourished overseas. In the States, it fell victim (as did many other fine films) to the collapse of the DVD and home video market in 2008. I do encourage you to seek it out after reading this. Not because I make any money from its sale or rental (I don't), but mostly because it's a great film and I believe it would serve as an interesting coda to this chapter.

Horror screenwriters are charged with a particularly difficult task. They have to ask that "What if" question (that's the easy part) and come up with an answer that genuinely frightens people. On the surface it sounds easy. What are people afraid of? Monsters? Yes. Ghosts? Yes. Psychotic killers? You bet.

But . . . Wait . . .

Haven't we seen these things again and again? Over and over? Different scenarios and circumstances, but the same boogeymen? And the answer to those questions is also a resounding; Yes! I can think of no genre that has recycled more conventions, situations, character archetypes and even specific shots more than the genre of Horror. Endless parades of tired sequels and pale imitations have haunted the history of horror films far more than any ghost who happened to stumble across a group of Japanese schoolgirls. Horror is the haven for Hollywood hacks looking to exploit low budgets for quick cash returns.

But it also the launching pad for some of the most fascinating and terrifying writers and directors of our time. Even Steven Spielberg, arguably one of the greatest living filmmakers, got his start in the world of horror with films like *Duel* and *Jaws*. And why is that? Because the great writers know how to tap into our primal reactions.

The reaction may be laughter, sorrow, thrills or fear, but an innate understanding of how those emotions affect us and how to instill them in others is an essential skill of any successful screenwriter.

The responsibility of that task does not rest solely on the shoulders of the screenwriter, however, it begins with him or her. They are the architects of the foundation for any film and no amount of additional talent whether it be producers, directors, actors, cinematographers, editors, etc. can save a bad script. If they are truly talented, they might be able to raise a poor script to the level of mediocrity, but never greatness.

And that leads to an age-old argument of whether a script is a blueprint or a bible. Is it a diagram for a successful construct that grows and evolves as the builders, painters, electricians and plumbers take hold of it, or is it an immutable document that must be executed word-for-word and scene-by-scene?

Any who fancies themselves an auteur will tell you

that the answer is the latter, but any experienced filmmaker will say that it is definitely the former. There are exceptions like Kubrick, Tarantino and Malick, but most screenwriters are not also directors, producers, etc. Most are simply talented individuals who know how to spin an entertaining yarn in a format suitable for cinema. They write their scripts, receive notes from the appropriate parties, revise, receive more notes, more revisions and then finally they turn in their masterpieces and hope that at least fifty percent survives the journey from the page to the screen.

It is a process that is equal parts joy, frustration, satisfaction, pain and ecstasy. Inspiration strikes and a scene suddenly blossoms from functional to great. However, the reality of shooting strikes back and the scene goes from great to nonessential. So as a storyteller, how do you navigate the Rube Goldbergesque mechanics of bringing a story from the page to the screen? The answer is simple . . . Write the story you want to write. If you subscribe to the concept I addressed earlier, you have asked a question. A theoretical question that almost anyone can answer with their own thoughts and ideas. Those answers can range from the musings of dullards to the fantastic ravings of a true visionary, but those answers aren't your answer. And that is the only one that matters.

And why is that? Another simple answer . . .

Because until the point that it is taken from your hands, you have lived with it the longest. You are the one who spent countless hours ruminating on the questions. You are the one who spent all of their waking time (and some of their slumber) creating and developing scenarios both large and small.

You are the one who toiled for days on a scene only to determine that as exciting as it was, it was not meant for that story.

The same goes for the characters. You created them. Their appearance, behavior, words and actions all came directly from the answer you gave to that initial question. No matter how invested the actors or directors become in these figments of imagination, those figments and every effect they have on your story and on each other came from you and you, alone.

These are people and creatures that you have interacted with for every moment you spent in front of your computer, thinking in the shower, wondering while driving and even when watching other creations by other writers unfold on the big screen. You know what these characters will say before they say it. You know what they would say or do if thrust into other storylines with other characters. Even the greatest method actor will never understand these characters with the intimacy and intensity that you will for one simple reason . . .

They are a part of you. You gave birth to them and their DNA comes directly from you. From the very first moment you gave them a name and typed that name on the paper, you injected them with purpose and presence that came from you. Not just your imagination, but from your experiences, your hopes, wishes, desires and fears. Other people will take that basic DNA and alter it, change it and in the best cases improve upon it. But in the end . . .

It was little pieces of you that were used to stitch together the final edit.

There are a countless number of very good books

on style, format, technique, etc. when it comes to the craft of screenwriting. I invite you to seek them out, read them and use those that speak to you on a personal level. For the record, the two I usually recommend are Viki King's *How to Write a Movie in 21 Days: The Inner Movie Method* and Stephen King's *On Writing*.

Both of those books spoke to me on different levels and I have found many of their themes and concepts very useful, but that's me. You might find that many of the others speak to you on a more personal, intimate level or just simply make more plain sense to you. That's great. Use what works and disregard the rest; regardless of how often people tell you, you have to do this or do that. Their intentions may be good, but the only person who knows what's best for you and your writing is you.

Speaking of intentions, mine are well intended, but I have wandered somewhat astray of the central question; where do nightmares come from?

I stand by my answer that they come from an interesting question posited by a darkly imaginative individual with an even darker story lurking beneath the surface.

Nightmares are the product of our subconscious working through our experiences, fears and anxieties while we sleep, so that we can better function while we are awake. Try to resolve them into a story and see where it takes you. My guess is that it won't be too far. There's an old saying that academics are fond of using, which is, generality is the enemy of art. The example being that attempting to paste together fragments of a dream will not usually bring a truly cohesive narrative that will frighten anyone other than yourself. I can agree with that.

However, I do not agree with the above statement as a hard and fast rule. In fact, I think it's just more circular, academic bullshit. Art has no enemies because no one can actually define what art is.

When does something pass from being a consumer product or actual, literal garbage into being art?

For the answer to that question, borrow $60,000, party away four years of your life and then come work on one of my sets for a free hotel room, decent craft services, credit and copy. And if you'll do me a favor when you get to set, fill me in on the answer in between shots.

Nightmares start with that question; what if . . . ? They end when after hours, days, months or years of thought, work, perseverance, revision, speculation and revelation someone provides a ninety-five-page answer in the form of an honest, uncompromised script.

However, if that doesn't work for you, just run your car off the road in southern Virginia and call for a tow truck. And if you happen to run into Earl . . . Say for "Hi" from me.

STEPHEN KING AND RICHARD CHIZMAR DISCUSS COLLABORATING

INTERVIEW BY BEV VINCENT

STEPHEN KING HAS collaborated with a number of authors over the years. He has written two books with Peter Straub (*The Talisman* and *Black House*), and intends someday to co-write a third novel featuring Jack Sawyer. He has published two stories co-written with son Joe Hill ("Throttle" and "In the Tall Grass") and another with Stewart O'Nan ("A Face in The Crowd"). Recently, he and his son Owen King published a long near-future fantasy novel called *Sleeping Beauties*.

In 2016, he started a story that he couldn't figure out how to finish. *Gwendy's Button Box* is the novella that resulted after he and Richard Chizmar of Cemetery Dance Publications decided to work on the tale together. Chizmar is no stranger to collaborations, having co-written stories with Brian Keene, Ray Garton, Barry Hoffman, Norman Partridge, Brian Freeman and Ed Gorman.

One issue with collaborations is whether the story will sound like one author or the other, or whether a new, third voice will emerge. In the following interview, the two authors discuss the origins of the story, how the collaboration came about and how they worked together to produce a seamless tale that is part King, part Chizmar and part something else altogether.

Bev Vincent: Steve, what can you tell us about the genesis of "Gwendy's Button Box"?

Stephen King: I had the idea for the story last July [2016], and thought it was a little like Richard Matheson's "Button, Button," but could be its own special thing. I liked it because it basically postulates putting the fate of the world in the hands of a child (like Trump).

BV: At what point in the writing process did you seek out a collaborator?

SK: I didn't know how to finish it. So it just sat there until this January. I didn't seek out a collaborator; one kind of fell into my lap. I've corresponded via email with Rich Chizmar for years. I sent him *Gwendy*," and basically said, "Do what you want, or it will stay unfinished."

BV: So, set the stage for us, Rich. You're sitting at your computer one day and you get an email from Stephen King asking if you'd like to work on a story with him?

Richard Chizmar: Steve and I email and text pretty regularly about a wide variety of subjects. On that particular day, we started talking about round-robins (multi-author projects) and collaborations. He mentioned that he had a short story he couldn't finish and I told him I'd love to read it if he ever wanted to send it over. The next evening, I remember it was a Friday and I was on my way to my son's hockey game, *Gwendy's Button Box* showed up with a note that read: "Do what you want with it."

BV: When you picked yourself up off the floor, how did you respond?

RC: I sat in the parking lot and read the manuscript, and emailed Steve back right away. My response that Friday night was "Absolutely! Yes! I'd love to finish it!"—but I was also moderately terrified. I let the idea settle over the weekend and when I sat down to write my story notes on Monday morning, moderate fear blossomed into full-blown terror for about an hour or so. How in the hell was I going to collaborate with Stephen King? Right?! Thankfully, the feeling didn't last, and the story just sort of took over and stole me away. The nerves disappeared, and before I knew it, I found myself in Castle Rock.

BV: Given that he's been rereading all of your books and stories for his Stephen King Revisited project, Rich seems like an obvious choice—he'd be familiar with Castle Rock and its history and geography. What was it like working with him?

SK: Working with Rich was very easy. For one thing, he knows my stuff, backward and forward—probably better than I do. I didn't give him any direction (that I remember), just let him run with the ball. He did a terrific job of bringing it home. My confidence in him came from reading his short fiction. And he's good with suburban family life. Terrific, actually; very loving, which gives the scary stuff extra bite. He wrote the middle and the end. I did some work on the end, expanding it, and there it was. Tout finis.

BV: Did you discuss story possibilities externally or did you just write and see where the story took you?

RC: The unfinished story that Steve initially sent clocked in at just over 7,000 words. I sat down and blazed through a lot of pages in the next three or four days and quickly sent them to Steve before I had a chance to chicken out. He did a pass of his own, and sent it back to me for another run at it. Then, we did the whole thing all over again—one more draft each. We did discuss some possibilities via email, but mostly we just ran with it. We each tweaked things the other had written and went off in our own directions. The whole process was fascinating and so much damn fun. That's what I kept telling Steve: This is fun!

BV: I was impressed by how seamless the writing was in the finished product. I couldn't tell who wrote what.

SK: If it seems seamless . . . well, that's always the goal, isn't it? You don't want the reader to be jarred by one voice giving way to another (it may have helped that we were men writing from a girl's POV). The secret ingredient is that we both went over the story, giving it additional layers—you'll see the same thing, I think, in *Sleeping Beauties*, the collaboration with Owen.

BV: There must be a temptation to try to imitate Steve, but nothing in the story felt like imitation. How did you approach this?

RC: I truly never gave it a moment's consideration. I just sat down and started writing and let the story take me where it wanted to take me. I didn't try to do anything different stylistically than I would have had the entire story been my own. And, somehow, it worked. When we were finished and I read over the completed story, I was astonished to find that there were times when I couldn't immediately recall who wrote what.

BV: What was it like to work in someone else's well-established universe? How did you make sure you were "playing by the rules"? Is this something you've done before with another writer—working in an established setting?

RC: I've collaborated a handful of times before, but never in someone else's specific universe. Fortunately, I know Steve's work very well, and I also have some good friends walking around with a wealth of King-related knowledge in their heads (Bev Vincent and Brian Freeman are two that come to mind), so playing by the rules wasn't an issue at all. I didn't find working within an established universe the least bit confining or restrictive either. I honestly just kept thinking "I'm in Castle Rock," and tried my best to honor the ground I was walking on. I felt a very real responsibility to that.

BV: Steve, why did you decide to return to Castle Rock? And does *Gwendy* tie in to the newly announced Castle Rock series on Hulu?

SK: I went back to Castle Rock with this one before JJ [Abrams] sold the series to Hulu, so that didn't play a part. Mostly, I just . . . well . . . missed the place!

BV: When commenting about your recent collection, A Long December, Steve said that you set your tales "in no-nonsense, middle class neighborhoods I can relate to." How do you envision Castle Rock? Is it a bad place, a place that attracts bad people, or is it just an ordinary town with a history?

RC: I think Castle Rock is a pretty ordinary town with a colorful history, like a lot of small towns tucked away in New England. Now, Derry . . . there's a bad place that attracts an awful lot of bad people. I think Castle Rock makes perfect sense for the story of *Gwendy's Button Box*. It fits.

BV: You've had a long and productive writing career, not to mention an illustrious publishing career where you continue to publish many terrific authors. How does this experience rank in terms of your career to date? Do you have future collaboration plans?

RC: It's the cherry on top, no question. I've always been a big dreamer, but I never dreamed this big. Not even close. As for future collaboration plans, I'm actually writing a story right now with my 18-year-old son, Billy. It's about a haunted lighthouse in Canada and will appear this summer in an anthology called "Fearful Fathoms." We're having a wonderful time with it.

BV: Steve, do you plan to work with Rich again, or with other writers in the future?

SK: I don't have any plans to collaborate again, but no plans NOT to, if you dig.

CHARLAINE HARRIS DISCUSSES STORYTELLING

INTERVIEW BY EUGENE JOHNSON

EUGENE'S INTERVIEW WITH author Charlaine Harris is a perfect example of what happens if you work on your craft every day. The fact that you're reading this book means you're ready to get it done. You are a storyteller.

Here's the great part. Writing is a lot like storytelling in the sense that, the more you do it, the better you become. The more you write, learn and practice new skills, and work toward improving your craft, the more natural it becomes. Eventually writing becomes an instinctive reflex of sort, something you are able to do without thinking too much about it. It takes a lot of time, yes, but during that time you also grow your platform, contacts, and general life experience—the fuel for your literary fire.

If you've already been doing this for a while now, you'll know what I'm about. Writing becomes a natural part of who we are. If someone later on dissects your work, they'll point out the techniques and skills you so expertly used, but you won't even remember applying them at the time, because they came naturally. Like Stephen King said, the first million words is just practice.

This advice has been given several times in this book, and you'll read it again in the next piece: finish what you start. Being an author is not an overnight success. It's not a race, it's a marathon. The loneliness of the long distance marathon—be ready for it.

On a daily basis you should take a step toward improving your craft, platform, and standing among your peers. Keep writing, reading and learning. Growing. Expressing your thoughts and feelings. If you have to, see a psychologist to help you open up.

This experience clearly comes across in the words of Charlaine Harris . . .

Eugene: Ms. Harris, you have some amazing work as a storyteller, having written novels, short stories, and graphic novels. You've even edited anthologies. Your work has even gone on to become a popular television show. What draws you to writing and storytelling?

Charlaine: A writer is all I've ever wanted to be. I was thrilled when I first realized actual people wrote books, and it was possible I could become one of them. I love reading, and the desire to write became a natural extension of my ambition.

Eugene: Can you talk a little bit about what inspires you? What type of plots, genre and ideas are you drawn to as a storyteller and writer?

Charlaine: I'm up for anything that transports me to another reality, in my reading time. I resent any jarring element that knocks me out of that happy experience. That's what I look to achieve in my own storytelling. I enjoy any plot, in any genre, that delivers that essential element of sucking me into another world.

Eugene: What is it about the storytelling process that you enjoy? Is there anything you do not like about it?

Charlaine: It never gets easier! You would think after thirty-plus books that I'd have the process down pat, but it's always a battle with the page. And sometimes with my own brain. At the same time, that's the fun part, wrenching the story out of your brain and out through your fingers onto the computer screen.

Eugene: Can you talk a little bit about how you breathe life into an idea, developing it into a full story?

Charlaine: Thanks for assuming I do that. I try to anchor my characters into a real life, with all the elements and dimensions that pertain. People have friends and families, they have pasts, they have moral and religious issues, they have to make their livings . . . and if they don't have some of these constants, it's interesting to find out why.

Eugene: How do you go about developing the different main elements of a story? Plot, characters, point of view, tone, etc.

Charlaine: Hmmm. I'm what I like to think of as an

'organic' writer, which is to say, I don't plan much. I have a natural feel for the rhythm of the story, when it should rise or fall, when something dramatic should happen, when something mundane should remind the reader that my character is a person who must deal with the same elements in her/his daily life as anyone else. I guess sometimes that decreases the impetus of the story, but it's important to me.

Eugene: Do you follow a blueprint or outline when building a suspenseful story: How do you know if you're giving away too much? When do you choose to drop clues and why?

Charlaine: That's where experience and a good editor are important to your work. Even if you're writing a first novel, keep on going. It's very hard to plant clues and yet keep them invisible until the readers reflects. It's so helpful to be an avid reader, and one who really studies a successful book (which doesn't mean a bestseller, but a book you've loved to read). Go over a book that's knocked your socks off, and discern how the writer achieved such an effect on you. You can learn so much that way. And a good editor can help you understand if you've reached your goals, and if you haven't, how to fix that.

Eugene: Do you use any devices (red herrings, etc.) to maintain suspense throughout?

Charlaine: Sure. That's a mystery tradition, and one I adhere to. You have to give the reader a surprise, or at least some compelling reason to stick with the book to the end.

Eugene Johnson

Eugene: You have written in different genres such as mystery and horror. What draws you to the horror genre? What do you think makes a good horror story?

Charlaine: I wish I had some magic phrase I could repeat to tell you that! I write urban fantasy, science fiction, conventional mysteries, and you're kind enough to say I write horror. Thanks. I believe horror has to contain dread, and dread is a hard thing to write, to build up. You can't do better than read Stephen King or Dean Koontz and learn from the masters about building up the dread level. Shirley Jackson, too. She could get your nerves humming, even in her short stories.

Eugene: You have written novels such as *Night Shift* and *Dead Until Dark*, as well as short stories such as "Crossroads Bargain." You've even turned some ideas into anthologies you edited: *Crimes by Moonlight*, *An Apple for the Creature* and many more. How do you decide an idea is going to work better as a novel, short story, anthology, etc?

Charlaine: Sometimes it's just what I'm invited to write. If you have to contribute a short story, that's the way you think. If you have a book due, that's what's on your mind. Short stories are very hard to write, for me. Every word counts. So you don't want a plot line that relies on a lot of explication. The reader has to understand the world very quickly.

Eugene: You have had your novel series The Southern Vampire Mysteries, and the Midnight, Texas trilogy developed into television shows. How much involvement, if any, do you have in that process? What is it like to work toward developing your stories in a different mode of storytelling such as television?

Charlaine: Also, I have to point out that I have the Aurora Teagarden mysteries in two-hour presentations on Hallmark Movies and Mysteries. I have almost no involvement in the process. That's the way I get to still enjoy my life. I make deals with people I think I can trust, they do what they do best, and hopefully, it all turns out. What's on the screen is never going to match what's in the books, and I don't expect that. My hope is that seeing the stories on the screen will compel the watchers to buy the books.

Eugene: Do you have any advice for people who want to get into writing and become a storyteller?

Charlaine: Read, read, read. Write, write, write. Don't stop until you reach the end of the book. If you can't complete a work, you are never going to achieve your goal.

WHAT NOW?

JOHN PALISANO

WHAT NOW? You've gotten this far. You've read the articles in this book. You've made up your mind that, darn it, you're going to write. That story inside you is just dying to be born. You've got stacks of paperbacks and you just know that one day your name is going to grace the cover of one, too. It's now time to put everything you've learned together. Are you ready? Bursting at the seams? Your story just dying to be born?

But wait: how do you get there from here?

We've covered a lot of theory. We've heard a lot of methods. We've read about other writer's adventures in the maze of modern publishing. We've come at this writing thing from so many perspectives.

What about you? How are you going to bridge the gap from talking about . . . theory . . . and put it all into practice?

It's the easiest and hardest next step.

Write.

But how?

Pen and paper. Computer keyboard. An app on your phone.

Do the work. Figure out a method to focus. If you

have ten minutes during lunch, do it. If you have an hour when you wake up, do it. If you have five minutes with your phone before you conk out after putting the kids to bed, use that time. I know one thing for sure: if someone really, really, really wants to do something . . . if it's just making them crazy with passion . . . they sure as heck will find the time. Turn off the television for an hour. You can watch that second hour of 'The Bachelor' when you're done for the day. You're going to have to sacrifice a little of your leisure time. It'll be worth it, though.

Here's a truth.

There are no shortcuts. Like learning a musical instrument or working out, the time you put in directly reflects in the finished product. You cannot fake it. Someone else can't do the work for you. Only you can tell your story. Just like only you can get in shape. Or learn another language. Or learn how to cook a killer new dish. We can't download stuff right out of our brain and onto the page. Maybe one day there will be a cord that we can stick in our ear and it will write down what we are thinking, but that tech hasn't been invented yet. Until then?

Get to it. Write.

Writing can be a challenge for even the most disciplined person. Again? It's a lot like working out. Lots of people develop a mental block toward writing. It seems hard. It seems like climbing a mountain. It can be overwhelming.

Don't let it be.

One of the best tools you can have is to take it all in bite-sized chunks. There's no reason you need to scale Mount Everest on your very first hike on your very first day. And that's what it often feels like to folks. Even veterans. Remember that your word count is your own. Do what you feel comfortable doing. Don't worry about what other writers are doing per day. You may have friends that are stating they're hitting 3,000 words a day. Maybe they are. Maybe, in the end, they are editing out a lot of what they write out in later drafts. Maybe someone is only producing a third of that, but it needs less editing. Maybe it doesn't! The point being that word counts aren't necessarily the only factor in your daily writing regime.

Writing is unique in that a number is assigned. When learning an instrument, do music teachers want you to play 500 notes a day? 3,000? No. They ask you to practice a piece until you know it. Maybe we as writers can worry more about getting our stories right than getting attached to word count goals.

That being said, word counts are important in professional writing. When submitting short stories and books and articles, you are told the length of the piece the market is looking for. It's important to get a feel for how much storytelling makes up those different works.

Being a writer, or any creative person, takes using the practical business side of your head half the time, and the dreaming, creative part the other time.

The Pluses and Minuses of Using an Outline

Here's where an outline can save your hide. If you use a structured outline, you can break down your story into parts, and then break those parts down into chapters. Then, if you divide the overall amount needed to fulfill a book, you can get an idea of how long each chapter should be. There is certainly some give and take there. If you need 1,500 words per chapter to make the goal, for example, it's common for some chapters to be shorter, and for others to be longer. That's okay, and normal.

The other great thing about an outline is that you now have a road map. You can write one chapter a day, for example. Or one chapter every two days. It helps to take away the 'blank page' syndrome where a writer will look at a blank page and feel they don't know where to write, or where to start. If you have an outline, you'll know, for example, "I'm on chapter three. This is the part where Jim meets Mary for the first time." You'll know what to do.

Here's the other big not-so-secret truth about outlines: writers rarely stick to them a hundred percent. As the story is written, you will see other avenues you'll want to explore. Characters will come to life, and will make choices that you couldn't foresee. Often this will change your original outcome. Great! So you can always go back and adjust your outline to reflect the change. You're not married to it. It's just a map. Be open. Again, on the flip side? Sometimes the outline works out just fine, and that's great, too. Listen to your story.

How Will I Know When I'm Done?

This is a question I receive often. When is the story done? How do you know when you've hit the end of your story? For me? There comes a point where the ending sneaks up on me, and I write a line and then I get chills up and down my spine and I know . . . I just feel . . . the end of the story has come. It feels natural. There's a closure. It's like the old cliche: I don't know how to describe it, but I'll know it when I see it!

There have been cases where writing a few different endings has been a good exercise to find the real ending. Often exploring different possibilities makes clear the right possibility.

Opening Scene

Another great exercise is to look at your opening once you get to the end of your story. By the time you've made it to the end of your journey, sometimes that opening can be tweaked. Don't get hung up on your opening line or scene or chapter. You can re-do it later. The same goes for chapters and sections later on.

Writer's Block

Just as with your opening scene, you may find yourself somewhere in the middle of writing your story when you will find yourself stuck. It will seem like you've hit a huge wall. Don't panic. One of the tricks I use when I hit that place is to write a scene from later in the book. That's right. I know it goes against popular belief, but sometimes doing so breaks that wall. I can backtrack later. My first drafts sometimes have places where I'll put a parenthetical to come back to later.

Example:
[writer at wall. Scales it with ropes and a pick axe.}

And then I will come back. I find the mind will work on that scene while I've gone off and taken care of other scenes ahead that were more fully formed. And that's okay to do. I don't recommend doing this often, as things can get confusing quickly, but it's a great way to break writer's block.

Other tools I use to combat writer's block include:

Freewriting in another document. It could be something unrelated. It could be a scene from a character's past I'll into use in the book, but it can help me know them better.

Drawing can be useful. Sometimes it's easy to sketch a scene, even primitively, to help jog the imagination or to block a scene like a movie director in order to see it better in the mind's eye.

Changing the medium you write in can also help. If you're staring at the same document for months, sometimes using a new writing program can shake things loose. Maybe pick up a pen and a spiral notebook. Or dictate a scene out loud.

Play an instrument. Sometimes picking up a guitar or a piano can unlock the mind, and while it's in creative mode, switch back to writing!

Go for a walk or exercise! Ever hear the phrase, "move a muscle, move a thought"? It's been known to work. Many a great writer and creative has said going for a walk helps the mind to think. Albert Einstein stated he thought up many of his most famous theories while on his daily walks. He was likely on to something.

You are allowed to develop your story however feels natural for you.

And let's say you've got that first draft done. Great.

Find some trusted folks farther along than you and see if they can read it and help you usher it to the next draft. Join a writing group. Online if you're not near anyone, or can't commit to in person. Listen to the feedback openly. Then rewrite. Then rewrite it again. Make that thing perfect.

Don't rush a first draft into the world of self-publishing or traditional publishing. You've got one shot at this first impression. Make it right. Make it tight.

And most importantly?

Go write!

BIOGRAPHIES

Kevin J. Anderson has written more than 125 books, including 52 national or international bestsellers. He has over 23 million books in print worldwide in thirty languages. He has been nominated for the Nebula Award, Bram Stoker Award, Shamus Award, and Silver Falchion Award, and has won the SFX Readers' Choice Award, Golden Duck Award, Scribe Award, and New York Times Notable Book; in 2012 at San Diego Comic-Con he received the Faust Grand Master Award for Lifetime Achievement.

He has written numerous bestselling and critically acclaimed novels in the Dune universe with Brian Herbert, as well as Star Wars and X-Files novels. In his original work, he is best known for his Saga of Seven Suns series, the Terra Incognita trilogy, the Dan Shamble, Zombie PI series, and *Clockwork Angels: The Novel* with Neil Peart. Find out more about Kevin J. Anderson at wordfire.com.

A visionary, fantasist, poet and painter, **Clive Barker** has expanded the reaches of human imagination as a novelist, director, screenwriter and dramatist. An inveterate seeker who traverses between myriad styles with ease, Barker has left his indelible artistic mark on a range of projects that reflect his creative grasp of contemporary media—from familiar literary terrain to the progressive vision of his Seraphim production company. His 1998 *Gods and Monsters*, which he executive produced, garnered three Academy Award nominations and an Oscar for Best Adapted Screenplay. The following year, Barker joined the ranks of such illustrious authors as Gabriel Garcia Marquez, Annie Dillard and Aldous Huxley when his collection of literary works was inducted into the Perennial line at HarperCollins, who then published *The Essential Clive Barker*, a 700-page anthology with an introduction by Armistead Maupin.

Barker began his odyssey in the London theatre, scripting original plays for his group The Dog Company, including "The History of the Devil," "Frankenstein in Love" and "Crazyface." Soon, Barker began publishing his The Books of Blood short fiction collections; but it was his debut novel, *The Damnation Game* that widened his already growing international audience.

Barker shifted gears in 1987 when he directed *Hellraiser*, based on his novella *The Hellbound Heart*, which became a veritable cult classic spawning a slew of sequels, several lines of comic books, and an array of merchandising. In 1990, he adapted and directed *Nightbreed* from his short story "Cabal." Two years later, Barker executive produced the housing-project story *Candyman*, as well as the 1995 sequel, *Candyman 2: Farewell to the Flesh*. Also that year, he directed Scott Bakula and Famke Janssen in the noir-esque detective tale, *Lord of Illusions*.

Barker's literary works include such best-selling fantasies as *Weaveworld*, *Imajica*, and *Everville*, the children's novel *The Thief of Always*, *Sacrament*, *Galilee* and *Coldheart Canyon*. The first of his quintet of children's books, *Abarat*, was published in October

2002 to resounding critical acclaim, followed by *Abarat II: Days of Magic, Nights of War* and *Arabat III: Absolute Midnight*; Barker is currently completing the fourth in the series. As an artist, Barker frequently turns to the canvas to fuel his imagination with hugely successful exhibitions across America. His neo-expressionist paintings have been showcased in two large format books, *Clive Barker, Illustrator*, volumes I & II.

In 2012 Barker was given a Lifetime Achievement Award from the Horror Writer's Association, for his outstanding contribution to the genre.

Michael Bailey is the multi-award-winning author of *Palindrome Hannah*, *Phoenix Rose*, and *Psychotropic Dragon* (novels), *Scales and Petals*, and *Inkblots and Blood Spots* (short story/poetry collections), *Enso* (a children's book), and the editor of *Pellucid Lunacy*, *Qualia Nous*, *The Library of the Dead*, and the *Chiral Mad* anthologies published by Written Backwards. He is also an editor for Dark Regions Press, where he has created dark science fiction projects like *You, Human*. He is currently at work on a science fiction thriller, *Seen in Distant Stars*, and a new fiction collection, *The Impossible Weight of Life*.

Jason V Brock is an award-winning writer, editor, filmmaker, and artist whose work has been widely published in a variety of media (*Weird Fiction Review* print edition, S. T. Joshi's *Black Wings* series, *Fangoria*, and others). He describes his work as Dark Magical Realism. He is also the founder of a website and digest called *[NameL3ss]*; his books include *A Darke Phantastique*, *Disorders of Magnitude*, and

Simulacrum and Other Possible Realities. His filmic efforts are *Charles Beaumont: The Life of Twilight Zone's Magic Man*, *The AckerMonster Chronicles!*, and *Image, Reflection, Shadow: Artists of the Fantastic*. Popular as a speaker and panelist, he has been a special guest at numerous film fests, conventions, and educational events, and was the 2015 Editor Guest of Honor for Orycon 37. A health nut/gadget freak, he lives in the Vancouver, WA area, and loves his wife Sunni, their family of herptiles, running their technology consulting business, and practicing vegan/vegetarianism. His website is www.JaSunni.com.

S.G. Browne is the author of the novels *Breathers*, *Fated*, *Lucky Bastard*, *Big Egos*, and *Less Than Hero*, as well as the short story collection *Shooting Monkeys in a Barrel* and the heartwarming holiday novella *I Saw Zombies Eating Santa Claus*. He's an ice cream connoisseur, Guinness aficionado, animal lover, and a sucker for *It's a Wonderful Life*. He lives in San Francisco. You can learn more about his writing at www.sgbrowne.com.

The Oxford Companion to English Literature describes **Ramsey Campbell** as "Britain's most respected living horror writer." He has been given more awards than any other writer in the field, including the Grand Master Award of the World Horror Convention, the Lifetime Achievement Award of the Horror Writers Association, the Living Legend Award of the International Horror Guild and the World Fantasy Lifetime Achievement Award. In 2015 he was made an Honorary Fellow of Liverpool John Moores University for outstanding services to literature.

Mort Castle, deemed a "horror doyen" by Publishers Weekly, has won three Bram Stoker Awards®, two Black Quills, a Golden Bot, and has been nominated for an Audie, the International Horror Guild Award, the Shirley Jackson Award, and the Pushcart Prize. He's edited or authored 17 books; his recent or forthcoming titles include: *New Moon on the Water*; *Writer's Digest Annotated Classics: Dracula*; and the 2016 Leapfrog Fiction contest winner *Knowing When to Die*. More than 600 Castle authored "shorter works," stories, articles, poems, and comics have appeared in periodicals and anthologies, including Twilight Zone, Bombay Gin, Poe's Lighthouse, and Tales of the Batman. Castle teaches fiction writing at Columbia College Chicago and has presented writing workshops and seminars throughout North America.

Richard Chizmar is a *New York Times, USA Today, Wall Street Journal, Washington Post, Amazon,* and *Publishers Weekly* bestselling author.

He is the co-author (with Stephen King) of the bestselling novella, *Gwendy's Button Box* and the founder/publisher of *Cemetery Dance* magazine and the Cemetery Dance Publications book imprint. He has edited more than 35 anthologies and his fiction has appeared in dozens of publications, including *Ellery Queen's Mystery Magazine* and multiple editions of *The Year's 25 Finest Crime and Mystery Stories*. He has won two World Fantasy awards, four International Horror Guild awards, and the HWA's Board of Trustee's award.

Chizmar (in collaboration with Johnathon Schaech) has also written screenplays and teleplays for United Artists, Sony Screen Gems, Lions Gate, Showtime, NBC, and many other companies. He has adapted the works of many bestselling authors including Stephen King, Peter Straub, and Bentley Little.

Chizmar is also the creator/writer of *Stephen King Revisited*, and his third short story collection, *A Long December*, was published in 2016 by Subterranean Press. With Brian Freeman, Chizmar is co-editor of the acclaimed *Dark Screams* horror anthology series published by Random House imprint, Hydra.

Chizmar's work has been translated into many languages throughout the world, and he has appeared at numerous conferences as a writing instructor, guest speaker, panelist, and guest of honor.

Please visit the author's website at: Richardchizmar.com

Craig Engler is the co-creator and executive producer of Syfy's hit zombie series, *Z Nation*. He also co-wrote *Zombie Apocalypse*, which was one of Syfy's highest-rated original movies and the basis for *Z Nation*. Prior to his work on the series, Craig was an executive at Syfy for many years. He's the founder of Science Fiction Weekly, Sci Fi Wire and Sci Fiction, and has been nominated twice for the Hugo Award for Best Website, winning once. He also created the acclaimed comic *Lovecraft* and currently writes the Z Nation comic series.

Mexican by birth, Canadian by inclination. **Silvia Moreno-Garcia**'s debut novel, *Signal to Noise*, about music, magic and Mexico City, won the Copper Cylinder Award and was nominated for the British Fantasy, Locus, Aurora and Sunburst awards. Her second novel, *Certain Dark Things*, deals with Mexican narco vampires. She won a World Fantasy Award for co-editing *She Walks in Shadows*.

Ray Garton has been writing novels, novellas, short stories, and essays for more than 30 years. His work spans the genres of horror, crime, suspense, and even comedy. His titles include the classic vampire bestseller *Live Girls*, *Ravenous*, *The Loveliest Dead*, *Sex and Violence in Hollywood*, *Meds*, and the novellas *Crawlers* and *Vortex, a Moffett and Keoph Investigation*. His short stories have appeared in magazines and anthologies, and have been collected in books like *Methods of Madness*, *Pieces of Hate*, and *Wailing and Gnashing of Teeth*. He was nominated for the Bram Stoker Award for *Live Girls* and received the Grand Master of Horror Award at the 2006 World Horror Convention. He lives in northern California with his wife, where he is currently at work on a few different projects, including a new novel. Visit his website at RayGartonOnline.com.

Christopher Golden the New York Times bestselling, Bram Stoker Award-winning author of such novels as *Of Saints and Shadows*, *Tin Men*, *Strangewood* and *Snowblind*, and the editor of such anthologies as *Seize the Night*, *The New Dead*, and the upcoming *Dark Cities*. With *Hellboy* creator Mike Mignola, he is the co-creator of two cult favorite comics series, Baltimore and Joe Golem: Occult Detective. Golden was born and raised in Massachusetts, where he still lives with his family. His original novels have been published in more than fourteen languages in countries around the world. Please visit him at www.christophergolden.com

Michael Paul Gonzalez is the author of the novels *Angel Falls* and *Miss Massacre's Guide to Murder and Vengeance*. His newest creation is the audio drama podcast *Larkspur Underground*, a serialized horror story. A member of the Horror Writers Association, his short stories have appeared in print and online, including *Drive-In Creature Feature, Gothic Fantasy: Chilling Horror Stories, Lost Signals, Seven Scribes— Beyond Ourselves, 18 Wheels of Horror, the Booked Podcast Anthology*, HeavyMetal.com, and the *Appalachian Undead* Anthology. He resides in Los Angeles, a place full of wonders and monsters far stranger than any that live in the imagination. You can visit him online at MichaelPaulGonzalez.com

Taylor Grant is a Hollywood screenwriter, award-winning filmmaker and two-time Bram Stoker Award® finalist. His work has been seen on network television, the big screen, the stage, the Web, as well as in comic books, newspapers, national magazines, anthologies, and heard on the radio. His most recent short films, *The Vanished* and *Sticks and Stones*, screened at the prestigious Cannes Film Festival, and received worldwide distribution through cable channel Shorts TV and domestic distribution through Sony. *Sticks and Stones* won the Jury Prize for best Short at the NUHO Film Festival.

Grant's horror/sci-fi collection *The Dark at the End of the Tunnel* was the bestselling paperback of the year for Crystal Lake Publishing, and his co-authored comic book *Evil Jester Presents* was an Amazon #1 bestseller. He has sold, optioned and rewritten feature scripts for major Hollywood studios such as Universal, Imagine, and Lions Gate Entertainment. In addition, he created the horror-themed Fox Family animated series *Monster Farm*, had multiple scripts produced for various TV shows in children's entertainment, and wrote MTV and VH1 music videos for some of the biggest artists in the world. His most recent horror fiction appears in two Random House/Hydra Publications: *Halloween Carnival Vol. 3* and *Dark Screams Vol.9*.

Charlaine Harris is a New York Times bestselling author who has been writing for over thirty years. She was born and raised in the Mississippi River Delta area. Though her early works consisted largely of poems about ghosts and teenage angst, she began writing plays when she attended Rhodes College in Memphis, Tennessee. She switched to novels a few years later, and achieved publication in 1981 with *Sweet and Deadly*.

After publishing two stand-alone mysteries, Harris launched the lighthearted Aurora Teagarden books with *Real Murders*, a Best Novel 1990 nomination for the Agatha Awards. Harris wrote eight books in her series about a Georgia librarian. In 1996, she released the first in the much darker Shakespeare mysteries, featuring the amateur sleuth Lily Bard, a karate student who makes her living cleaning houses. *Shakespeare's Counselor*, the fifth—and final—Lily Bard novel, was printed in fall 2001.

By then, Harris was feeling the call of new territory. Starting with the premise of a young woman with a disability who wants to try inter-species dating, she created The Sookie Stackhouse urban fantasy series before there was a genre called "urban fantasy." Telepathic barmaid Sookie Stackhouse works in a bar in the fictional northern Louisiana town of Bon Temps. The first book in the series, *Dead Until Dark*, won the Anthony Award for Best Paperback Mystery in 2001. Each subsequent book follows Sookie through adventures involving vampires, werewolves, and other supernatural creatures. The series, which ended in 2013, has been released in over thirty languages.

Sookie Stackhouse has proven to be so popular that Alan Ball, creator of the HBO television series *Six Feet Under*, announced he would undertake the production of a new HBO series based upon the books he wrote and directed the pilot episode for that series, *True Blood*, which premiered in September of 2008.

In October 2005, the first of Harris's new mystery series about a young woman named Harper Connelly debuted with the release of *Grave Sight*. Harper has the ability to determine the cause of death of any body. After four novels, this series is on hiatus.

Now Harris is working on a trilogy of graphic novels with Christopher Golden and artist Don Kramer, "Cemetery Girl." On her own she is writing a new series set in the small town of Midnight, Texas.

Harris has also co-edited a series of very popular anthologies with her friend Toni L.P. Kelner, aka Leigh Perry. The anthologies feature stories with an element of the supernatural, and the submissions come from a rare mixture of mystery and urban fantasy writers.

Professionally, Harris is a member of the Mystery Writers of America, the American Crime Writers League, Sisters in Crime, and the International Crime Writers Association. She is a past member of the boards of Sisters in Crime and MWA, and she has served as president of the MWA. She is also a member of Science Fiction Writers of America, Horror Writers Association, and Romance Writers of America, just to make sure she's covered.

Personally, Harris has been married for many years. She's a mother of three wonderful children and the grandmother of two. She lives in central Texas, and when she is not writing her own books, she reads omnivorously. Her house is full of rescue dogs.

Del Howison is a journalist, writer, and the Bram Stoker Award-winning editor of the anthology *Dark Delicacies: Original Tales of Terror and the Macabre by the World's Greatest Horror Writers*. His short story "The Lost Herd" was turned into the premiere (and highest-rated) episode, "The Sacrifice," for the series *Fear Itself*. He has been nominated for over half a dozen awards. He is the co-founder and owner of Dark Delicacies, a book and gift store known as "The Home of Horror," located in Burbank, California.

Eugene Johnson is a filmmaker, author, editor, and columnist of science fiction, fantasy, horror, and supernatural thrillers. Eugene has written and edited in various genres. His anthology *Appalachian Undead*, co-edited with Jason Sizemore, was selected by FearNet, as one of the best books of 2012. Eugene's articles and stories have been published by award-winning Apex publishing, The Zombiefeed, Evil Jester Press, Warrior Sparrow Press and more. Eugene also appeared in *Dread Stare*, a political theme horror anthology from Thunder Dome press

Eugene's anthology, *Drive-in Creature Feature*, pays homage to monster movies, features New York Times best-selling authors Clive Barker, Joe R. Lansdale, Christopher Golden, Jonathan Maberry and many more.

As a filmmaker, Eugene Johnson worked on various movies, including the upcoming *Requiem*, starring Tony Todd and directed by Paul Moore. His short film *Leftovers*, a collaboration with director Paul Moore, was featured at the Screamfest film festival in Los Angeles as well as Dragoncon.

Eugene currently works at award-winning Evil Jester Press as the project and new business manager. When not developing fun projects at EJP, he spends his time working on several projects including *Brave*, a horror anthology honoring people with disabilities; the *Fantastic Tales of Terror* anthology; and his children's book series, Life lessons with Lil Monsters. Eugene is currently a member of the Horror Writers Association. He has a Masters in Mental Health Counseling, and when not writing spends his time helping others as a therapist. He resides in West Virginia with his fiancé, daughter, and two sons.

Stephen King was born in Portland, Maine in 1947, the second son of Donald and Nellie Ruth Pillsbury King. He made his first professional short story sale in 1967 to Startling Mystery Stories. In the fall of 1971, he began teaching high school English classes at Hampden Academy, the public high school in Hampden, Maine. Writing in the evenings and on the weekends, he continued to produce short stories and to work on novels. In the spring of 1973, Doubleday & Co., accepted the novel *Carrie* for publication, providing him the means to leave teaching and write full-time. He has since published over 50 books and has become one of the world's most successful writers. King is the recipient of the 2003 National Book Foundation Medal for Distinguished Contribution to the American Letters and the 2014 National Medal of Arts.

Stephen lives in Maine and Florida with his wife, novelist Tabitha King. They are regular contributors to a number of charities including many libraries and have been honored locally for their philanthropic activities.

From the day she was born, **Jess Landry** has always been attracted to the darker things in life. Her fondest childhood memories include getting nightmares from the *Goosebumps* books, watching *The Hilarious House of Frightenstein*, and reiterating to her parents that there was absolutely nothing wrong with her mental state.

Since picking up a pen a few years ago, Jess's fiction has appeared in anthologies such as the *Alligators in the Sewers*, *The Anatomy of Monsters*, *Killing It Softly*, and *Ill-Considered Expeditions*, as well as online with SpeckLit, and EGM Shorts, among others.

She currently works as Assistant Publisher for JournalStone, and as Publisher for its latest imprint, Trepidatio Publishing, where her goal is to print diverse stories from diverse writers. A current member of the HWA, Jess has volunteered as Head Compiler for the Bram Stoker® Awards since 2015, and has most recently taken on the role of Membership Coordinator.

You can visit her on the interwebs at her pitiful website, jesslandry.com, though your best bet at finding her is on Facebook and Twitter (facebook.com/jesslandry28 and twitter.com/jesslandry28), where she often posts cat memes and references *Jurassic Park* way too much.

Joe R. Lansdale is the author of 48 novels and over 20 short story collections. He has written and sold a number of screenplays, has had his Plays adapted for stage. His work has been adapted to film; *Bubba Ho-Tep* and *Cold in July* among them. His best-known novels, the Hap and Leonard series has been adapted for television with Lansdale as co-executive producer with Lowell Northrop under the title, *HAP AND LEONARD*. He has also edited or co-edited numerous anthologies.

Jonathan Maberry a NY Times bestselling novelist, five-time Bram Stoker Award-winner, and comic book writer. He writes the Joe Ledger thrillers, the Rot & Ruin series, the Nightsiders series, the Dead of Night series, as well as standalone novels in multiple genres. His new and upcoming novels include *Kill Switch*, the 8th in his best-selling Joe Ledger thriller series; *Vault of Shadows*, a middle-grade SF/fantasy mash-up; and *Mars One*, a standalone teen space travel novel. He is the editor of many anthologies including *The X-Files*, *Scary Out There*, *Out of Tune*, and *V-Wars*. His comic book works include, among others, *Captain America*, the Bram Stoker Award-winning *Bad Blood*, *Rot & Ruin*, *V-Wars*, the NY Times best-selling *Marvel Zombies Return*, and others. His books *Extinction Machine* and *V-Wars* are in development for TV. A board game version of V-Wars was released in early 2016. He is the founder of the Writers Coffeehouse, and the co-founder of The Liars Club. Prior to becoming a full-time novelist, Jonathan spent twenty-five years as a magazine feature writer, martial arts instructor and playwright. He was a featured expert on the History Channel documentary, *Zombies: A Living History* and a regular expert on the TV series, *True Monsters*. He is one third of the very popular and mildly weird Three Guys With Beards pop-culture podcast. Jonathan lives in Del Mar, California with his wife, Sara Jo. www.jonathanmaberry.com

Elizabeth Massie is a Bram Stoker Award- and Scribe Award-winning author of novels, short fiction, media-tie ins, poetry, and nonfiction. Her works include *Sineater, Hell Gate, Desper Hollow, Wire Mesh Mothers, Welcome Back to the Night, Twisted Branch* (under the pseudonym Chris Blaine), *Homeplace, Naked On the Edge, Afraid, Sundown, The Fear Report, The Tudors: King Takes Queen, The Tudors: Thy Will Be Done, Dark Shadows: Dreams of the Dark* (co-authored with Mark Rainey), *Homegrown, Night Benedictions, Versailles, Buffy the Vampire Slayer: Power of Persuasion,* the Ameri-Scares series of spooky novels for middle grade readers, the Young Founders series of historical novels for young adults, the Silver Slut superhero adventure series, and more. Massie spends her spare time knitting, geocaching, and staring mindlessly into space. She lives in the Shenandoah Valley with her husband, illustrator and theremin-player Cortney Skinner.

Mark Alan Miller has been working as a writer since 2005 when he started as a columnist for OCWeekly. It was this that landed him the position of assistant editor on Barker's novel *Abarat: Absolute Midnight*, for which he also directed the Promotional Trailer.

In 2009, Miller began shepherding the release of the director's cut of Barker's classic film *Nightbreed*. After 6 years of Miller's campaigning, tracking down the footage, and assembling the film, Barker's long-thought-lost vision was released on Blu-Ray Scream Factory and the film won best vintage release at the 41st annual Saturn Awards. Miller was there to accept the award in person. The project has garnered worldwide interest, and been featured in publications such as Entertainment Weekly, Fangoria, and Empire magazine, and was named Total Film's 14th best extended cut of all time.

His directorial efforts can be seen in the animated short "The Great Corben" as part of *Fun Size Horror Volume 2*, and in the found footage entry "Z-Volution" for the feature anthology *Virus of the Dead*.

Mark's work is not limited to horror, however, and he has produced a series of animated shorts with the comedy troupe Superego for Nerdist Channel. He can also be heard on various Nerdist channel podcasts, including The Nerdist, Bizarre States, The Dork Forest, The Nerdist Writers Panel, and The Todd Glass Show.

Currently, he is adapting the works of Clive Barker as well as Joe R. Lansdale for various projects. His work can also be seen in the bestselling Boom! Studios comic books, *Hellraiser*, the ongoing *Hellraiser: Bestiary*, the critically acclaimed *Next Testament*, the Dark Horse Title, *The Steam Man of the Prairie*, and most recently in Heavy Metal Magazine.

Paul Moore is a filmmaker who has written and directed four feature films, most recently *Keepsake* and *Requiem*. He is also the co-owner the of movie production studio Blind Tiger Filmworks and his first short story, "Spoiled," was published in the well-received anthology *Appalachian Undead*. He followed that with the story "Things" published in *Drive-In Creature Feature* earlier this year. Both were very satisfying creative endeavors which he followed by contributing the story "The War Room" to political horror anthology *Dread State*.

Lisa Morton is a screenwriter, author of non-fiction books, award-winning prose writer, and Halloween expert whose work was described by the American Library Association's Readers' Advisory Guide to Horror as "consistently dark, unsettling, and frightening." Her most recent releases include *Ghosts: A Haunted History* and the short story collection *Cemetery Dance Select: Lisa Morton*. Lisa lives in the San Fernando Valley and online at www.lisamorton.com.

Joe Mynhardt is a two-time Bram Stoker Award-nominated South African publisher, non-fiction editor, and online-business mentor.

Joe is the owner and CEO of Crystal Lake Publishing, which he founded in August, 2012. Since then he's published and edited short stories, novellas, interviews and essays by the likes of Neil Gaiman, Clive Barker, Ramsey Campbell, Jack Ketchum, Graham Masterton, Adam Nevill, Lisa Morton, Elizabeth Massie, Joe McKinney, Edward Lee, Paul Tremblay, Wes Craven, John Carpenter, George A. Romero, Mick Garris, and hundreds more.

Just like Crystal Lake Publishing, Joe believes in reaching out to all authors, new and experienced, and being a beacon of friendship and guidance in the Dark Fiction field. Crystal Lake Publishing strives to be a platform for launching author careers.

Joe's influences stretch from Poe, Doyle, and Lovecraft to King, Connolly, and Gaiman. You can read more about Joe and Crystal Lake Publishing at http://www.crystallakepub.com or find him on Facebook.

William F. Nolan writes mostly in the science fiction, fantasy, and horror genres. Though best known for coauthoring the acclaimed dystopian science fiction novel *Logan's Run* with George Clayton

Johnson, Nolan is the author of more than 2000 pieces (fiction, nonfiction, articles, and books), and has edited twenty-six anthologies in his fifty-plus year career.

Of his numerous awards, there are a few of which he is most proud: being voted a Living Legend in Dark Fantasy by the International Horror Guild in 2002; twice winning the Edgar Allan Poe Award from the Mystery Writers of America; being awarded the honorary title of Author Emeritus by the Science Fiction and Fantasy Writers of America, Inc. in 2006; receiving the Lifetime Achievement Award from the Horror Writers Association in 2010; and as recipient of the 2013 World Fantasy Convention Award along with Brian W. Aldiss. In 2015, Nolan was named a World Horror Society Grand Master.

A vegetarian, Nolan resides in Vancouver, WA.

Marie O'Regan is a British Fantasy Award-nominated author and editor, based in Derbyshire. Her first collection, *Mirror Mere*, was published in 2006; her second, *In Times of Want*, came out in September 2016, and her short fiction has appeared in a number of genre magazines and anthologies in the UK, US, Canada, Italy and Germany. She was shortlisted for the British Fantasy Society Award for Best Short Story in 2006, and Best Anthology in 2010 (*Hellbound Hearts*) and 2012 (*Mammoth Book of Ghost Stories by Women*). Her genre journalism has appeared in magazines like *The Dark Side*, *Rue Morgue* and *Fortean Times*, and her interview book with prominent figures from the horror genre, *Voices in the Dark*, was released in 2011. An essay on 'The Changeling' was published in PS Publishing's *Cinema Macabre*, edited by Mark Morris. She is co-editor of the bestselling *Hellbound Hearts, Mammoth Book of Body Horror* and *A Carnivàle of Horror—Dark Tales from the Fairground*, plus editor of bestselling *The Mammoth Book of Ghost Stories by Women* and is Co-Chair of the UK Chapter of the Horror Writers' Association. Marie is represented by Jamie Cowen of The Ampersand Agency.

Author **John Palisano** has a pair of books with Samhain Publishing, *Dust of the Dead*, and *Ghost Heart*. *Nerves* is available through Bad Moon. *Starlight Drive: Four Halloween Tales* was released in time for Halloween, and his first short fiction collection *All That Withers* is available from Cycatrix press, celebrating over a decade of short story highlights. *Night of 1,000 Beasts* is coming soon. He won the Bram Stoker Award in short fiction in 2016 for "Happy Joe's Rest Stop." More short stories have appeared in anthologies from Cemetery Dance, PS Publishing, Independent Legions, DarkFuse, Crystal Lake, Terror Tales, Lovecraft eZine, Horror Library, Bizarro Pulp, Written Backwards, Dark Continents, Big Time Books, McFarland Press, Darkscribe, Dark House, Omnium Gatherum, and more. His non-fiction pieces have appeared in Blumhouse, Fangoria and Dark Discoveries magazines.

He is currently serving as the Vice President of the Horror Writers Association. Say 'hi' to John at: www.johnpalisano.com and http://www.amazon.com /author/johnpalisano and www.facebook.com/ johnpalisano and www.twitter.com/johnpalisano

Bev Vincent is the author of some 80 short stories, including appearances in *Alfred Hitchcock's Mystery Magazine*, *Ellery Queen's Mystery Magazine* and two

MWA anthologies. His work has been nominated for the Bram Stoker Award (twice), the Edgar (for *The Stephen King Illustrated Companion*) and the ITW Thriller Award, and he was the 2010 winner of the Al Blanchard Award. He is a contributing editor of *Cemetery Dance* magazine, where his Stephen King: News from the Dead Zone column has appeared since 2001. His most recent book is *The Dark Tower Companion*. He lurks around various corners of the internet including Twitter (@BevVincent), his book review blog (OnyxReviews.com) and website (bevvincent.com). In the "real world," he lives in Texas, where he is trying to ignore the news while working on a novel.

Tim Waggoner has published close to forty novels and three collections of short stories. He writes original dark fantasy and horror, as well as media tie-ins, and his articles on writing have appeared in numerous publications. He's won a Bram Stoker Award, been a finalist for the Shirley Jackson Award and the Scribe Award, and his fiction has received numerous Honorable Mentions in volumes of Best Horror of the Year. He's also a full-time tenured professor who teaches creative writing and composition at Sinclair College in Dayton, Ohio.

Marv Wolfman is a multi-award-winning writer of comic books, animation, videogames, theme park shows and rides, children's books, novels, television, internet animation and much more. He has also created more characters that have gone onto TV, toys, games and film than anyone since Stan Lee.

Among Marv's creations are: *Blade*, *Black Cat*,

Terrax, Bullseye, Nova, Nightwing, Starfire, Raven, Cyborg, Deathstroke and dozens of others. *The New Teen Titans*, written by Marv and drawn by George Pérez, was DC's best-selling comic for more than a decade and the mini-series, Crisis On Infinite Earths, revamped the entire DC Comics line and created the concept of company-wide crossovers.

Marv was also editor-in-chief of Marvel, senior editor at DC Comics and founding Editor of Disney Adventures magazine.

Beyond comics, Marv has also been writing novels and videogames. His novelization of the movie *Superman Returns* won the industry's Scribe Award, and his 2012 script for *Epic Mickey-2*, for Disney Interactive, was nominated for a Writer's Guild of America Award and his non-fiction book *Homeland, The Illustrated History of the State of Israel* won the National Jewish book award.

Stephanie M. Wytovich is an American poet, novelist, and essayist. Her work has been showcased in numerous anthologies such as *Gutted: Beautiful Horror Stories, Shadows Over Main Street: An Anthology of Small-Town Lovecraftian Terror, Year's Best Hardcore Horror: Volume 2, The Best Horror of the Year: Volume 8*, as well as many others.

Wytovich is the Poetry Editor for Raw Dog Screaming Press, an adjunct at Western Connecticut State University and Point Park University, and a mentor to authors with Crystal Lake Publishing. She is a member of the Science Fiction Poetry Association, an active member of the Horror Writers Association, and a graduate of Seton Hill University's MFA program for Writing Popular Fiction. Her Bram Stoker Award-winning poetry collection, *Brothel*, earned a home with Raw Dog Screaming Press alongside *Hysteria: A Collection of Madness*, *Mourning Jewelry*, and *An Exorcism of Angels*. Her debut novel, *The Eighth*, is published with Dark Regions Press.

Her next poetry collection, *Sheet Music to My Acoustic Nightmare*, is scheduled to be released late 2017 from Raw Dog Screaming Press.

Follow Wytovich at http://www.stephaniewytovich.com/ and on twitter @JustAfterSunset.

Mercedes M. Yardley is a dark fantasist who wears poisonous flowers in her hair. She is the author of *Pretty Little Dead Girls*, *Nameless*, and the Bram Stoker Award-winning *Little Dead Red*. Mercedes lives in Las Vegas and can be reached at www.abrokenlaptop.com.

THE END?

Not quite . . .

Dive into more of our non-fiction books:

Horror 101: The Way Forward—A comprehensive overview of the Horror fiction genre and career opportunities available to established and aspiring authors, including Jack Ketchum, Graham Masterton, Edward Lee, Lisa Morton, Ellen Datlow, Ramsey Campbell, and many more.

Horror 201: The Silver Scream Vol.1 and *Vol.2*—A must read for anyone interested in the horror film industry. Includes interviews and essays by Wes Craven, John Carpenter, George A. Romero, Mick Garris, and dozens more. Now available in a special paperback edition.

Modern Mythmakers: 35 interviews with Horror and Science Fiction Writers and Filmmakers by Michael McCarty—Ever wanted to hang out with legends like Ray Bradbury, Richard Matheson, and Dean Koontz? *Modern Mythmakers* is your chance to hear fun anecdotes and career advice from authors and filmmakers like Forrest J. Ackerman, Ray Bradbury, Ramsey Campbell, John Carpenter, Dan Curtis, Elvira, Neil Gaiman, Mick Garris, Laurell K. Hamilton, Jack Ketchum, Dean Koontz, Graham Masterton, Richard Matheson, John Russo, William F. Nolan, John Saul, Peter Straub, and many more.

Writers On Writing: An Author's Guide—Your favorite authors share their secrets in the ultimate guide to becoming and being an author. *Writers On Writing* is an eBook series with original 'On Writing' essays by writing professionals.

Or perhaps some Tales from the Darkest Depths with our fiction books:

Tales from The Lake Vol.4: The Horror Anthology edited by Ben Eads—The Legend Continues with twenty-four heart-rending tales with elements of terror, mystery, and a nightmarish darkness that knows no end. Includes stories by Joe R. Lansdale, Damien Angelica Walters, and Kealan Patrick Burke.

Quiet Places: A Novella of Cosmic Folk Horror by Jasper Bark—The people of Dunballan, harbour a dark secret. A secret more terrible than the Beast that stalks the dense forests of Dunballan. A secret that holds David McCavendish, last in a long line of Lairds, in its unbreakable grip.

The eleven stories in *Ugly Little Things* by Todd Keisling explore the depths of **human suffering and ugliness**, charting a course to the dark, horrific heart of the human condition. The **terrors of everyday existence** are laid bare in this eerie collection of short fiction from the twisted mind of Todd Keisling, author of the critically-acclaimed novels *A Life Transparent* and *The Liminal Man*.

Behold! Oddities, Curiosities and Undefinable Wonders—Want to see something weird? Embrace the odd. Satisfy your curiosity. Surrender to wonder.

Includes short stories by Neil Gaiman, Clive Barker, Lisa Morton, Ramsey Campbell, John Langan, Kristi DeMeester and many more.

Whispered Echoes by Paul F. Olson—Journey through the Heart of Terror in this eerie short story collection. Listen. They are calling to you. Do you hear them? They are the whispered echoes of your darkest fears.

Twice Upon an Apocalypse—Lovecraftian Fairy Tales—From the darkest depths of Grimm and Anderson come the immortal mash-ups with the creations of HP Lovecraft. These aren't your mother's fairy tales.

The Third Twin—A Dark Psychological Thriller by Darren Speegle—Some things should never be bred . . . Amid tribulation, death, madness, and institutionalization, a father fights against a scientist's bloody bid to breed a theoretical third twin.

Embers: A Collection of Dark Fiction by Kenneth W. Cain—These short speculative stories are the smoldering remains of a fire, the fiery bits meant to ignite the mind with slow-burning imagery and haunting details. These are the slow burning embers of Cain's soul.

Aletheia: A Supernatural Thriller by J.S. Breukelaar—A tale of that most human of monsters—memory—Aletheia is part ghost story, part love story, a novel about the damage done, and the damage yet to come. About terror itself. Not only for what lies ahead, but also for what we think we have left behind.

Beatrice Beecham's Cryptic Crypt by Dave Jeffery— The fate of the world rests in the hands of four dysfunctional teenagers and a bunch of oddball adults. What could possibly go wrong?

Visions of the Mutant Rain Forest —the solo and collaborative stories and poems of Robert Frazier and Bruce Boston's exploration of the Mutant Rain Forest.

Where the Dead Go to Die by Mark Allan Gunnells and Aaron Dries—Post-infection Chicago. Christmas. There are monsters in this world. And they used to be us. Now it's time to euthanize to survive in a hospice where Emily, a woman haunted by her past, only wants to do her job and be the best mother possible. But it won't be long before that snow-speckled ground will be salted by blood.

Gutted: Beautiful Horror Stories—an anthology of dark fiction that explores the beauty at the very heart of darkness. Featuring horror's most celebrated voices: Clive Barker, Neil Gaiman, Ramsey Campbell, Paul Tremblay, John F.D. Taff, Lisa Mannetti, Damien Angelica Walters, Josh Malerman, Christopher Coake, Mercedes M. Yardley, Brian Kirk, Stephanie M. Wytovich, Amanda Gowin, Richard Thomas, Maria Alexander, and Kevin Lucia.

Tribulations by Richard Thomas—In the third short story collection by Richard Thomas, *Tribulations*, these stories cover a wide range of dark fiction—from fantasy, science fiction and horror, to magical realism, neo-noir, and transgressive fiction. The common thread that weaves these tragic tales together is suffering and sorrow, and the ways we emerge from such heartbreak stronger, more appreciative of what we have left—a spark of hope enough to guide us though the valley of death.

Pretty Little Dead Girls: A Novel of Murder and Whimsy by Mercedes M. Yardley—Bryony Adams is destined to be murdered, but fortunately Fate has terrible marksmanship. In order to survive, she must run as far and as fast as she can. After arriving in Seattle, Bryony befriends a tortured musician, a market fish-thrower, and a starry-eyed hero who is secretly a serial killer bent on fulfilling Bryony's dark destiny.

The Dark at the End of the Tunnel by Taylor Grant — Offered for the first time in a collected format, this selection features ten gripping and darkly imaginative stories by Taylor Grant, a Bram Stoker Award® nominated author and rising star in the suspense and horror genres. Grant exposes the terrors that hide beneath the surface of our ordinary world, behind people's masks of normalcy, and lurking in the shadows at the farthest reaches of the universe.

Or check out other Crystal Lake Publishing books for more Tales from the Darkest Depths.

Hi, readers (or should I say authors?). It makes our day to know you reached the end of our book. Thank you so much. This is why we do what we do every single day.

Whether you found the book good or great, we'd love to hear what you thought. Please take a moment to leave a review on Amazon, Goodreads, or anywhere else readers visit. Reviews go a long way to helping a book sell, and will help us to continue publishing quality books. You can also share a photo of yourself holding this book with the hashtag #IGotMyCLPBook!

Thank you again for taking the time to journey with Crystal Lake Publishing.

We are also on . . .

Website:
www.crystallakepub.com

Be sure to sign up for our newsletter and receive two free eBooks: http://eepurl.com/xfuKP

Books:
http://www.crystallakepub.com/book-table/

Twitter:
https://twitter.com/crystallakepub

Facebook:
https://www.facebook.com/Crystallakepublishing/
https://www.facebook.com/Talesfromthelake/
https://www.facebook.com/WritersOnWritingSeries/

Pinterest:
https://za.pinterest.com/crystallakepub/

Instagram:
https://www.instagram.com/crystal_lake_publishing/

Patreon:
https://www.patreon.com/CLP

YouTube:
https://www.youtube.com/c/CrystalLakePublishing

We'd love to hear from you.

Or check out other Crystal Lake Publishing books for your Dark Fiction, Horror, Suspense, and Thriller needs.

With unmatched success since 2012, Crystal Lake Publishing has quickly become one of the world's leading indie publishers of Mystery, Thriller, and Suspense books with a Dark Fiction edge.

Crystal Lake Publishing puts integrity, honor and respect at the forefront of our operations.

We strive for each book and outreach program that's launched to not only entertain and touch or comment on issues that affect our readers, but also to strengthen and support the Dark Fiction field and its authors.

Not only do we publish authors who are legends in the field and as hardworking as us, but we look for men and women who care about their readers and fellow human beings. We only publish the very best Dark Fiction, and look forward to launching many new careers.

We strive to know each and every one of our readers, while building personal relationships with our authors, reviewers, bloggers, pod-casters, bookstores and libraries.

Crystal Lake Publishing is and will always be a beacon of what passion and dedication, combined with overwhelming teamwork and respect, can accomplish: Unique fiction you can't find anywhere else.

We do not just publish books, we present you worlds within your world, doors within your mind, from talented authors who sacrifice so much for a moment of your time.

This is what we believe in. What we stand for. This will be our legacy.

Welcome to Crystal Lake Publishing—Tales from the Darkest Depths

Printed in February 2021
by Rotomail Italia S.p.A., Vignate (MI) - Italy